Oracle Application Express 5.1
Basics & Beyond

A practical guide to rapidly develop data-centric web
applications accessible from desktop, laptops,
tablets, and smartphones

Riaz Ahmed

Oracle Application Express 5.1 Basics & Beyond

Copyright © 2017 Riaz Ahmed

ISBN-13: 978-1-542-45254-0
ISBN-10: 1542452546

You will find stuff about workspace, application, page, and so on in every APEX book. But this book is unique because the information it contains is not available anywhere else! Unlike other books, it adopts a stimulating approach to reveal almost every feature necessary for the beginners of Oracle APEX and also takes them beyond the basics.

As a technology enthusiast I write on a variety of new technologies, but writing books on Oracle Application Express is my passion. The blood pumping comments I get from my readers on Amazon (and in my inbox) are the main forces that motivate me to write a book whenever a new version of Oracle APEX is launched. This is my fifth book on Oracle APEX (and the best so far) written after discovering the latest 5.1 version. As usual, I'm sharing my personal learning experience through this book to expose this unique rapid web application development platform.

In Oracle Application Express you can build robust web applications. The new version is launched with some more prolific tools to maximize developers' productivity. Once again, I've left out the boring bits and have adopted the same practical inspirational approach that has exposed the anatomy of Oracle Application Express to thousands of beginners in the past.

The most convincing way to explore a technology is to apply it to a real world problem. In this book, you'll develop a sales web application that not only reveals the anatomy of Oracle Application Express, but at the same time provides hands-on techniques that build a solid foundation for you to become a web developer.

Since there are lots of changes in the new version, all content has been revised to slot in these changes, including the features new to version 5.1. The short list below summarizes the features of Oracle APEX 5.1 covered in this book:

- Hands-on exposure to the new features, such as Interactive Grid, Oracle JET Charts, the new declarative Master-Detail-Detail capabilities, dozens of new properties, and new development procedures
- Teaches how to rapidly develop data-centric web application for desktops, laptops, tablets, and latest smartphones
- A complete chapter dedicated to reveal Oracle APEX's concepts
- Create comprehensive applications declaratively without writing tons of code
- Create application pages with the help of wizards
- Create custom application pages by adding components manually
- Format and tailor application pages using the Page Designer
- Use same interface and code to develop applications for a wide array of devices
- Present data using a variety of eye-catching charts (Pie, Column, Bar, Line with Area, and more)
- Produce highly formatted PDF reports, including invoices, grouped reports, and pivot tables (not covered in any other APEX book)
- Design and implement a comprehensive custom security module (unique to this book)

- Step-by-step instructions to create mobile version of the application using existing desktop application pages (not covered in any other beginner's guide)
- Elaboration of every property and aspect used in the project
- A comprehensive book index from where you can find a term to see its usage. For example, you can search for the *Display Extra Values* property to see what is the purpose of this property and the segments where it is used in the project

This is a concise yet a concrete book on Oracle Application Express, written for those who want to become web application developers. The sticky inspirational approach adopted in this book not only exposes the technology, but also draws you in and keeps your interest up till the last exercise. I'm grateful to all my readers whose helpful feedback enabled me to further polish my work in this edition.

Special offer! For those who are new to SQL or those who want to strengthen their SQL knowledge, I'm providing my e-book "SQL – The Shortest Route For beginners" with this book for FREE! Please send the purchase proof of this book to oratech@cyber.net.pk to get the free SQL e-book.

I Want to Hear from You!

Your precious comments act as the lifeblood for my publications. I value your opinion and am anxious to know how I could do better. Please e-mail me your comments at oratech@cyber.net.pk to let me know what you did or **didn't** like about this book.

URL to Download Book Code

http://www.creating-website.com/code51.rar

- Riaz Ahmed
Author
oratech@cyber.net.pk

ABOUT THE AUTHOR

Riaz Ahmed is an IT professional with more than 25 years of experience. He started his career in early 1990's as a programmer and has been employed in a wide variety of information technology positions, including analyst programmer, system analyst, project manager, data architect, database designer and senior database administrator. Currently he is working as the head of IT for a group of companies. His core areas of interest include web-based development technologies, business intelligence, and databases. Riaz possesses extensive experience in database design and development. Besides all versions of Oracle, he has worked intensively in almost all the major RDBMSs on the market today. During his career he designed and implemented numerous databases for a wide range of applications, including ERP. You can reach him via oratech@cyber.net.pk.

Books Authored by Riaz Ahmed

Create Rapid Web Applications Using Oracle Application Express – First Edition

A concise hands-on guide to learn Oracle APEX 4.0
ISBN-13: 978-1466350656

SQL – The Shortest Route For Beginners

A hands-on book that covers all top DBMS and teaches SQL in record time
ISBN-13: 978-1514130971

Implement Oracle Business Intelligence

Analyze the Past
Streamline the Present
Control the Future
ISBN-13: 978-1475122015

Oracle Application Express 5 For Beginners

Develop Web Apps for Desktop and Latest Mobile Devices using Oracle APEX 5.0
ISBN-13: 978-1512003307

**The Web Book -
Build Static and Dynamic Websites**

The ultimate resource to building static and dynamic websites
http://www.creating-website.com
ISBN-13: 978-1483929279

Cloud Computing Using Oracle Application Express

Rapidly develop internet facing business applications accessible anywhere and anytime
ISBN-13: 978-1484225011

Create Rapid Web Applications Using Oracle Application Express – Second Edition

A practical guide to rapidly develop professional web & mobile applications using Oracle APEX 4.2
ISBN-13: 978-1492314189

Beginning Windows 10 With Anniversary Update

A compact guide to explore the latest operating system
ISBN-13: 978-1532831065

CONTENTS

Chapter 1: The Essence of the Book   1

Chapter 2: Oracle Application Express Concepts   19

Chapter 3: Create Application Components   43

Chapter 4: Prepare Application Dashboard   63

Chapter 5: Managing Customers   83

Chapter 6: Set Up Products Catalog   111

Chapter 7: Taking Orders   127

Chapter 8: Present Data Graphically   199

Chapter 9: Produce Advance Reports   225

Chapter 10: Develop a Mobile Version for Smartphones   245

Chapter 11: Define Application Segments for Security   289

Chapter 12: Create Groups and Assign Application Privileges   301

Chapter 13: Create Users and Assign Groups   315

Chapter 14: Implement Application Security   329

Chapter 15: Deploy Oracle APEX Applications   337

Chapter 1

The Essence of the Book

1.1 What are you going to create?

Oracle Application Express (APEX) is a browser-based rapid application development (RAD) tool that helps you create rich interactive Oracle-based web applications very quickly and with relatively little programming effort. A web application is an application that is accessed by users over a network such as the Internet or an intranet. It is a software coded in a browser-supported programming language (such as JavaScript, combined with a browser-rendered markup language like HTML) and dependent on a common web browser to render the application. The popularity of web applications is due to the ubiquity of web browsers, which is the only requirement to access such applications. Another major reason behind the popularity of web applications is the ability to update and maintain these applications without distributing and installing software on potentially thousands of client devices.

Developing web applications can be a real challenge because it's a multidisciplinary process. You have to be proficient in all the core technologies involved such as HTML, CSS, JavaScript (on the client side) and PHP or any other scripting language to interact with the database on the server side. Also, you've to take into account the type-less nature of the web environment and above all, the need to put it all together in a manner that will allow the end users to execute their jobs efficiently and in a simplified manner.

Oracle Application Express is a hosted declarative development environment for developing and deploying database-centric web applications. Oracle Application Express accelerates the application development process. Thanks to its built-in features such as user interface themes, navigational controls, form handlers, and flexible reports that off-loads the extra burden of proficiency acquisition in the core technologies.

The format of this book is to introduce you to the art of building desktop and mobile web applications by iteratively developing the sample sales application (provided with Oracle Application Express) from scratch. This application has been chosen as an example because you can learn most of the techniques from it for your own future work. The primary purpose of this book is to teach you how to use Oracle Application Express to realize your own development goals. Each chapter in this book explores a basic area of functionality and delivers the development techniques to achieve that functionality. By the time you reach the end of the examples in this book, you will have a clear understanding of Oracle Application Express and will be able to extend the application in almost any direction. There are a number of features that provide APEX a clear edge over other available RAD development tools. APEX uses SQL and PL/SQL as core languages for development and because of this ability people who have been working with Oracle database can easily tread the path. Following are some of the major benefits of developing web applications in Oracle APEX:

- **Declarative Development:** Declarative development is the most significant feature, which makes Oracle APEX a good choice for rapid application development. Most of the tasks are performed with the help of built-in wizards that help you create different types of application pages. Each wizard walks you through the process of defining what you are expecting to achieve. After getting the input, the wizard data is stored as metadata in Oracle database tables. Later on, you can call page definition to modify or enhance the metadata to give your page the desired look. You can even add more functionality by putting your own custom SQL and PL/SQL code. Once you're comfortable with Oracle APEX, you can ignore the wizards and generate your applications directly. The Application Express engine renders applications in real time using the metadata. When you create or extend an application, Oracle Application Express creates or modifies metadata stored in database tables. When the application is run, the Application Express engine reads the metadata and then displays the application.

- **Mobile Applications:** Another significant feature provided in Oracle APEX is the ability to create applications for mobile devices. Content to these devices are delivered through jQuery Mobile that is incorporated in APEX. jQuery Mobile supports mobile device-specific events, such as orientation change and touch events. You easily change the look and feel of jQuery Mobile-based applications by modifying the CSS using tools such as ThemeRoller. Being the future, mobile application development is the need of the hour. This platform will definitely aid the over-burdened business professionals, who are facing increasing time constraints, to enhance their productivity by enabling them to work from anywhere at any time. These applications will make the busy community more effective because the features they carry allow people of high cadre to stay informed and take correct in-time decisions even sitting away from their desks.

1.2 Understanding the Application

The application you will be creating in this book features an easy-to-use interface for adding, updating, deleting and viewing order and related products and customers information. Users can navigate among the pages using a new desktop navigation menu. In addition to the desktop version, you'll be guided to create a mobile version of the same application so that it could be accessed from a variety of mobile devices including latest smartphones and tablets. Before we dig into details of the application, let's first have a quick look at some of the major areas of our sample Sales Web Application to know what we're going to create.

1.2.1 Chapter 4 - Prepare Application Dashboard

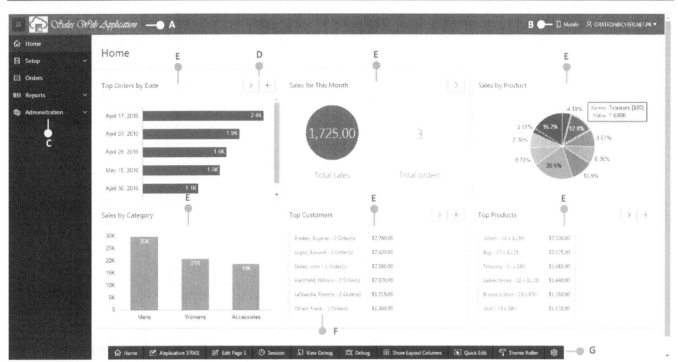

Figure 1-1 – Application Dashboard

In Chapter 4, you'll create the home page of the application. It is a dashboard that users see when they successfully access the application after providing valid credentials. Let's first take a look at the tagged areas to acquaint ourselves with different sections of this page:

A. Application name or logo
B. Navigation Bar
C. Main Navigation Menu
D. Buttons
E. Regions
F. Text Links
G. Developers Toolbar

The Home page contains six regions to display different summarized information. It uses a 12 columns layout to place these regions accordingly. Besides application name or logo (A) (whichever you prefer), the page carries a main navigation menu (C), which is used to move to other application segments. The navigation bar (B) to the right side allows you to switch to the application's mobile version. It also displays the currently logged-in user, along with a Sign Out link. The data from different perspectives is displayed in multiple regions (E). Some regions have buttons (D) that allow you to drill into further details. In addition to buttons, the page also contains text links (F) to dig details of the summarized information. Using the options provided in the Developers Toolbar (G), you can switch to the Page Designer instantly and perform various other development tasks. You will use Oracle JET Charts (a new feature introduced in version 5.1) on the Home page to present data graphically using different types of charts.

What You'll Learn

- How to create dashboards in web applications
- Adding multiple regions to a page to segregate content
- Use of 12 columns grid layout to arrange multiple regions on a page
- Create links to drill-down into details
- Badge List, Pie Chart, and Column Chart to display data in different graphical formats
- Summarized text information
- Use of buttons to navigate to other application pages

1.2.2 Chapter 5 – Customers Profiling

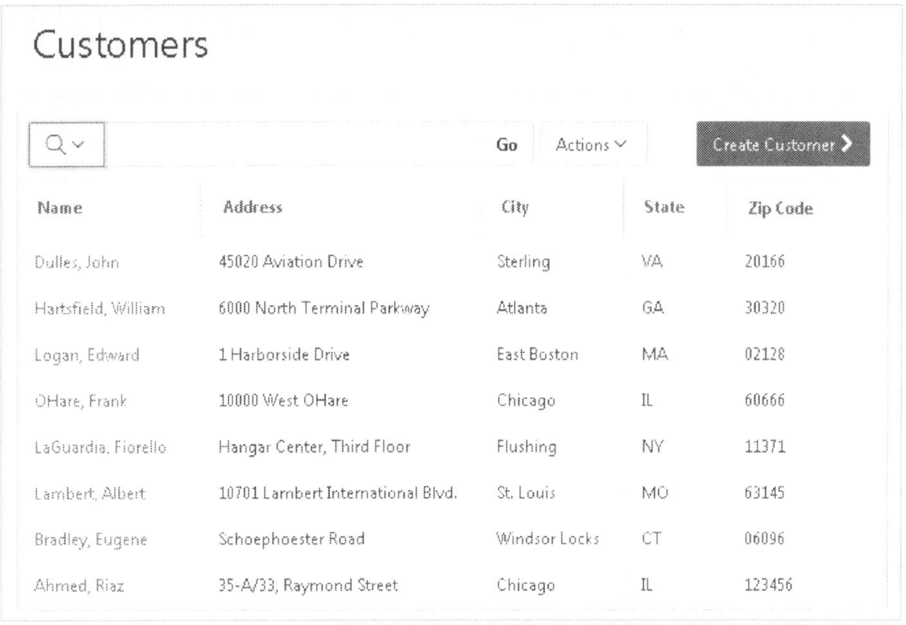
Customers
Go
Actions
Create Customer
Name
Address
City
State
Zip Code
Dulles, John
45020 Aviation Drive
Sterling
VA
20166
Hartsfield, William
6000 North Terminal Parkway
Atlanta
GA
30320
Logan, Edward
1 Harborside Drive
East Boston
MA
02128
OHare, Frank
10000 West OHare
Chicago
IL
60666
LaGuardia, Fiorello
Hangar Center, Third Floor
Flushing
NY
11371
Lambert, Albert
10701 Lambert International Blvd.
St. Louis
MO
63145
Bradley, Eugene
Schoephoester Road
Windsor Locks
CT
06096
Ahmed, Riaz
35-A/33, Raymond Street
Chicago
IL
123456

Figure 1-2
Customers Interactive Grid Report

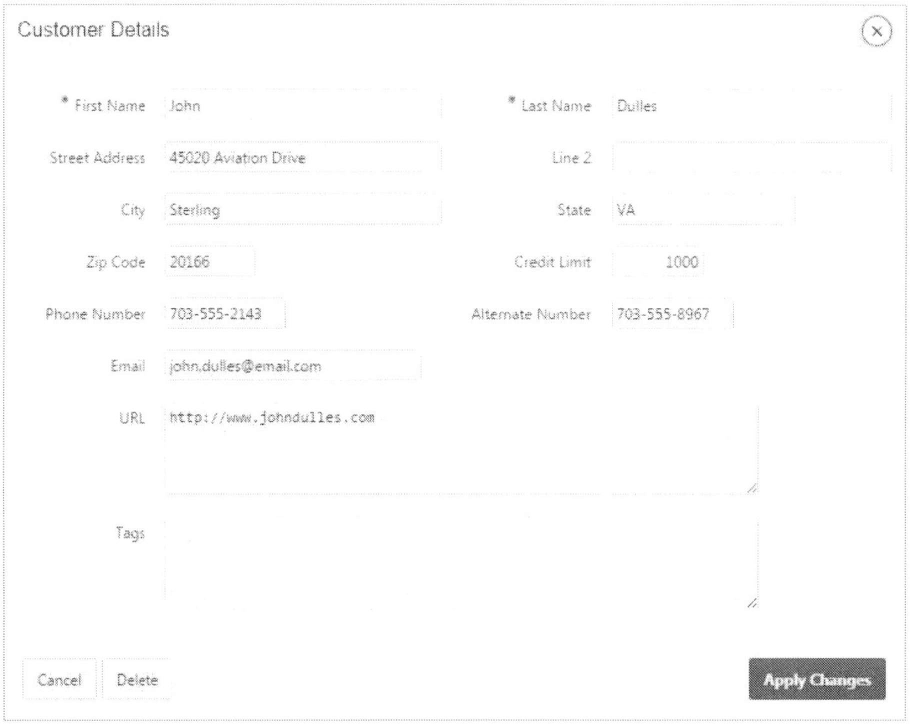
Customer Details
* First Name
John
* Last Name
Dulles
Street Address
45020 Aviation Drive
Line 2
City
Sterling
State
VA
Zip Code
20166
Credit Limit
1000
Phone Number
703-555-2143
Alternate Number
703-555-8967
Email
john.dulles@email.com
URL
http://www.johndulles.com
Tags
Cancel
Delete
Apply Changes

Figure 1-3
Customer Details Page

The sales application to be created in this book comprises several setups, including this one. Using this module, you will create customers profiles. Each customer will be provided a unique ID that will be generated automatically through a database object called a Sequence. After creating customers' profiles, you will use this information in Chapter 6 (Taking Orders), where you will select these customers to process orders. The setup consists of two pages. The first page (Figure 1-2) is a report (based on the new Interactive Grid feature) that lists all customers. The page carries links to the details page (Figure 1-3), which is a form where you can create, modify, or delete customer's records individually.

What You'll Learn

- Create application pages using wizards
- Interactive Grid (a new feature in version 5.1)
- Web input form
- Use of Modal Page
- Customizing wizard-generated pages to make them more professional
- Creating custom links to switch between the two module pages
- Positioning form input elements using 12 columns layout
- Marking mandatory fields
- Enforce data validation
- Get to know how APEX transparently manages DML operations without writing a single line of code

1.2.3 Chapter 6 – Set Up Products Catalog

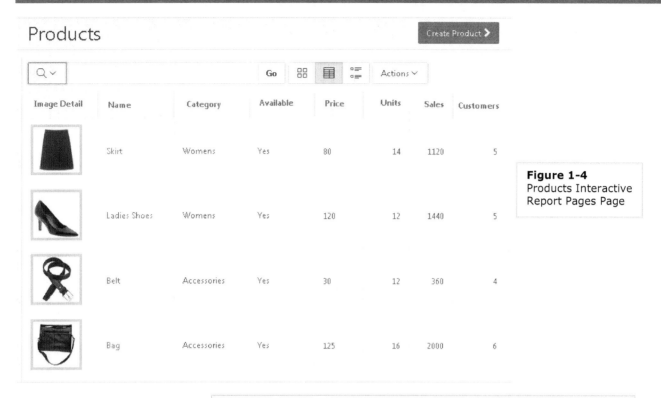

Figure 1-4
Products Interactive
Report Pages Page

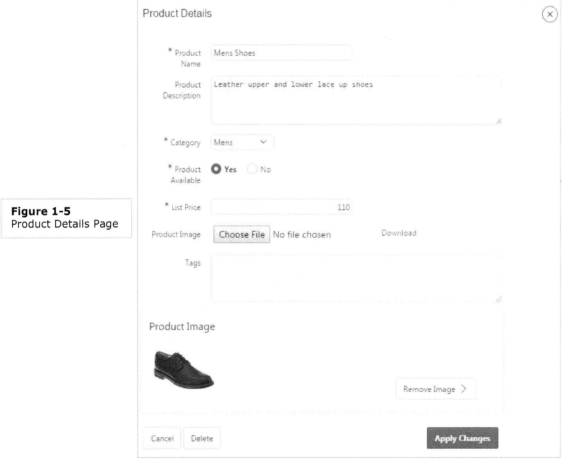

Figure 1-5
Product Details Page

Since sales applications are developed to handle sales of products, a properly designed product setup is an integral part of this application. To fulfill this requirement, you will create a comprehensive products setup for the sales application to manage products information along with respective images. The products you set up here will be selected in customers' orders. Just like the Customers setup, this segment also comprises two pages. The initial page, which is an interactive report, will be customized to create three different views to browse product information. The second page of this module is an input form where you can add, modify, or delete a product.

What You'll Learn

- Interactive Report
- Image handling (upload, download, save, retrieve, and delete from database)
- Customize interactive report to get different views of data
- Use of Cascading Style Sheet (CSS) to add custom styles to a page
- Change item type and attach LOVs
- Hiding report columns
- Replacing wizard-generated links with customized links
- Displaying data in an HTML table element
- Styling HTML table element
- Saving a primary report
- Set dimensions of a modal page
- Making and marking page items as mandatory

1.2.4 Chapter 7 – Taking Orders

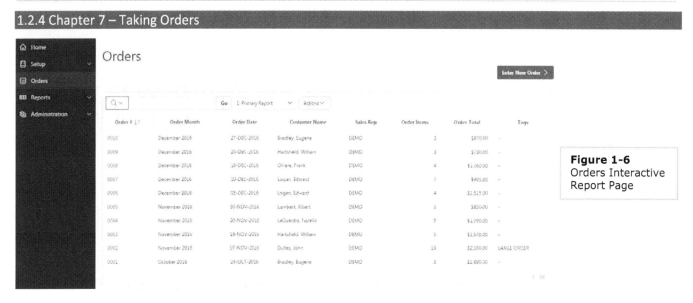

Figure 1-6
Orders Interactive Report Page

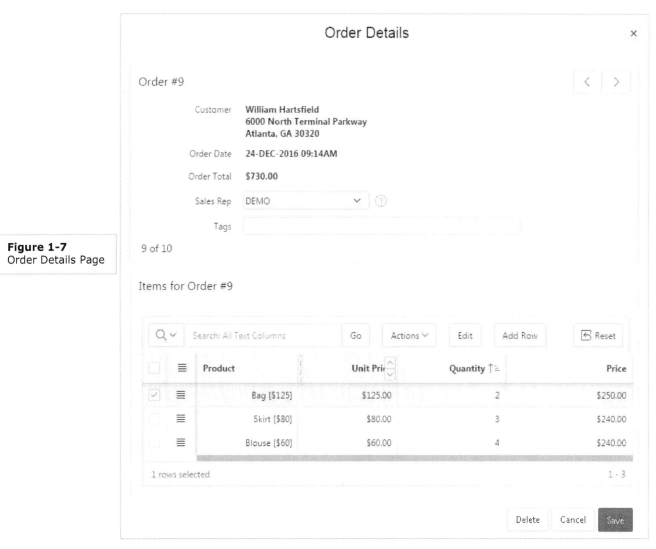

Figure 1-7
Order Details Page

This is the most comprehensive chapter of the book. It will teach you lots of techniques. In this chapter, you will create a module to take orders from customers. Initially, you'll create this segment with the help of wizards and later you will customize it to record orders through a sequence of wizard steps.

What You'll Learn

- Implement master/detail forms
- Sorting Interactive Report
- Add Control Breaks to interactive report to group related data
- Apply highlight rules to mark specific records
- Using Aggregate functions
- Using Chart and Group By views in an interactive report
- Creating Primary, Public, and Alternative versions of interactive report
- Utilizing Copy Page utility
- APEX Collection
- Adding custom processes and dynamic actions
- Using HTML in PL/SQL code
- Using CSS in APEX pages

1.2.5 Chapter 8 – Present Data Graphically

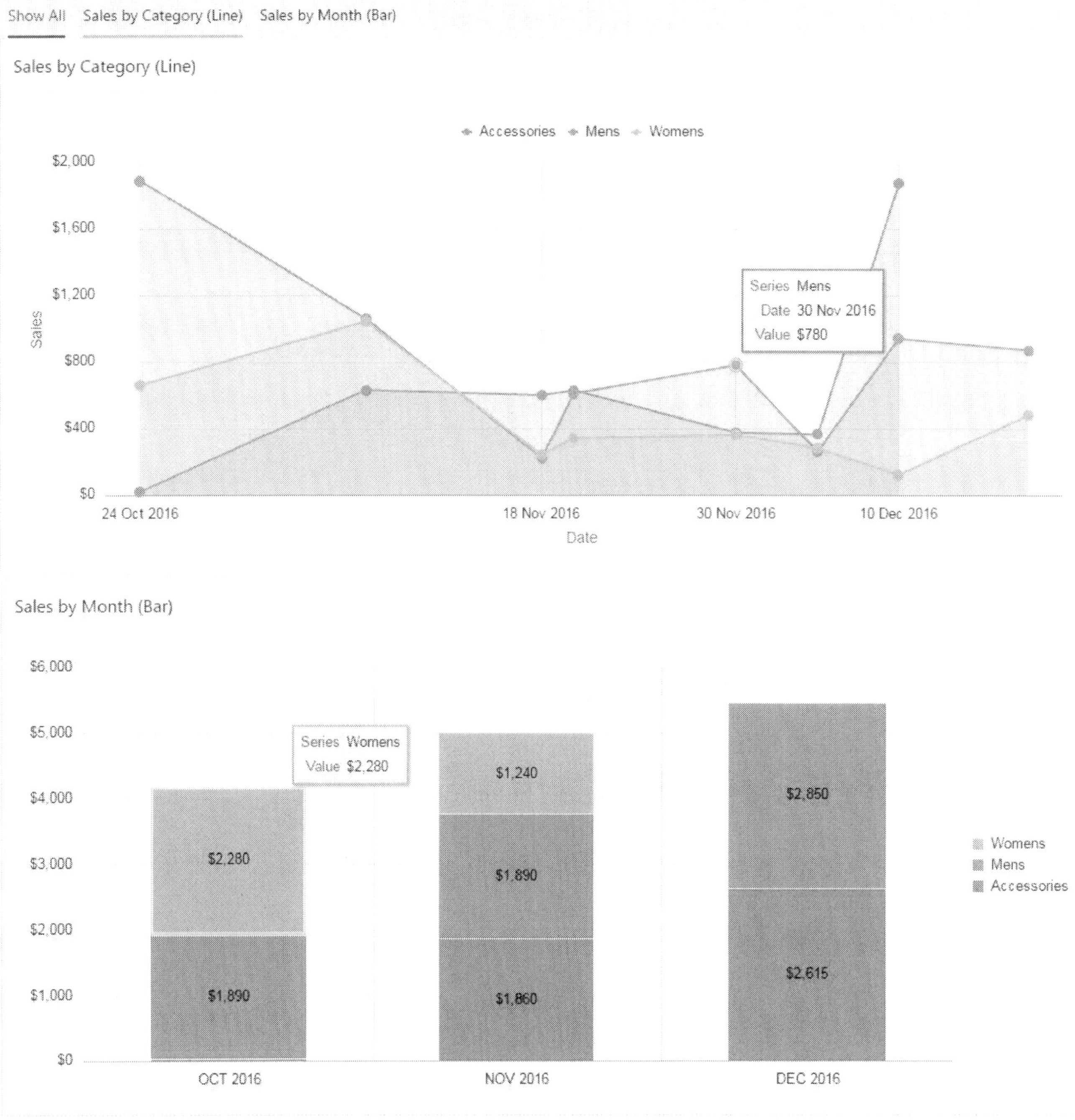

Show All   Sales by Category (Line)   Sales by Month (Bar)

Sales by Category (Line)

Sales by Month (Bar)

Figure 1-8 – Graphical Report in Oracle APEX

After getting thorough knowledge of data manipulation techniques, you move on to present graphical output of the sales data. In this chapter, you will be taught the use of different types of charts, maps, tree, and calendar to present data from different perspectives.

What You'll Learn

- Stacked Bar chart
- 3d Pie, Bar, and Column Charts
- Display customer orders in a calendar
- Show number of customers in different states using a map
- Hierarchical presentation of data using a tree component
- Drill-down to details from charts

1.2.6 Chapter 9 – Produce Advance Reports

ABC CORPORATION
35-A/3, ABC House, Raymond Street off Mansfield Street,
Chicago-IL, 6350, USA.

Orders Monthly Review Report

Figure 1: Monthly Order Chart

Order Month: December 2016

Order#	Order Date	Customer	State	Sales Rep	Order Items	Order Total
10	27-DEC-2016 09:14AM	Bradley, Eugene	CT	DEMO	3	870.00
6	05-DEC-2016 09:14AM	Logan, Edward	MA	DEMO	4	1,515.00
7	10-DEC-2016 09:14AM	Logan, Edward	MA	DEMO	7	905.00
8	18-DEC-2016 09:14AM	OHare, Frank	IL	DEMO	4	1,060.00
9	24-DEC-2016 09:14AM	Hartsfield, William	GA	DEMO	3	2,355.00
						Average Order: 1,341.00

Figure 1-9
PDF Reports in
Oracle APEX

Order Month: November 2016

Order#	Order Date	Customer	State	Sales Rep	Order Items	Order Total
2	07-NOV-2016 09:14AM	Dulles, John	VA	DEMO	10	2,350.00
3	18-NOV-2016 09:14AM	Hartsfield, William	GA	DEMO	5	1,640.00
4	20-NOV-2016 09:14AM	LaGuardia, Fiorello	NY	DEMO	5	1,090.00
5	30-NOV-2016 09:14AM	Lambert, Albert	MO	DEMO	5	950.00
						Average Order: 1,507.50

Order Month: October 2016

Order#	Order Date	Customer	State	Sales Rep	Order Items	Order Total
1	24-OCT-2016 09:14AM	Bradley, Eugene	CT	DEMO	4	1,910.00
						Average Order: 1,910.00

ABC CORPORATION
35-A/3, ABC House, Raymond Street off Mansfield Street,
Chicago-IL, 6350, USA.

Table 1: Revenue By States

State	Customer	December 2016	November 2016	October 2016	Total
CT		870.00	0.00	1,910.00	2,780.00
	Bradley, Eugene	870.00	0.00	1,910.00	2,780.00
GA		2,355.00	1,640.00	0.00	3,995.00
	Hartsfield, William	2,355.00	1,640.00	0.00	3,995.00
IL		1,060.00	0.00	0.00	1,060.00
	OHare, Frank	1,060.00	0.00	0.00	1,060.00
MA		2,420.00	0.00	0.00	2,420.00
	Logan, Edward	2,420.00	0.00	0.00	2,420.00
MO		0.00	950.00	0.00	950.00
	Lambert, Albert	0.00	950.00	0.00	950.00
NY		0.00	1,090.00	0.00	1,090.00
	LaGuardia, Fiorello	0.00	1,090.00	0.00	1,090.00
VA		0.00	2,350.00	0.00	2,350.00
	Dulles, John	0.00	2,350.00	0.00	2,350.00
TOTAL		**6,705.00**	**6,030.00**	**1,910.00**	**14,645.00**

14

By default, APEX has the ability to produce simple generic matrix reports comprising rows and columns. This chapter will show you how to produce advance report in APEX. Here, you will be provided with step-by-step instructions to generate:

- A highly formatted MIS report
- Commercial Invoice
- Pivot Table

- Create Report Query
- Design report layout in Microsoft Word using XML data
- Data grouping and sorting
- Formatting reports using standard Microsoft Word tools
- Add conditional formatting to display data differently in the same report
- Add calculations
- Create parameterized report
- Offline report testing
- Upload RTF layout to APEX
- Attach custom report layout to the default report query
- Add link in the application to run advance reports

1.2.7 Chapter 10 – Develop Mobile Version for Smartphones

Figure 1-10
Mobile App in
Oracle APEX

Because of an eruption in the market for smartphones and mobile devices, there is a huge demand of applications for this platform. Things that used to be done traditionally by people on their laptops are now being done increasingly on mobile devices. Feeling the heat, APEX incorporates a significant feature to build applications specifically for latest smartphones and tablets. In this chapter, you will explore the mobile platform by developing a mobile version of the desktop sales web application.

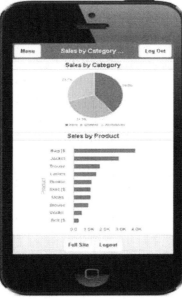

Figure 1-11
Mobile Graphical
Report

What You'll Learn

- Create mobile interface
- Add styles to mobile pages
- Mobile menus
- Present data on mobile pages
- Mobile input forms
- Product catalog including images
- Taking orders
- Graphical reports

1.2.8 Application Security (Chapters 11-14)

Figure 1-12
Application Security Module

In this book, you will learn how to create a comprehensive security module for your application. The first step in developing this module is to define all the application segments where you want to apply security. These segments include: menus, pages, and page items. After defining all application segments in Chapter 11, you will create user groups in Chapter 12 where you will assign access privileges to each group on the application segments specified in Chapter 11. Next, you will create a setup in Chapter 13 to create application users. Each user is created and assigned a group. This way, all the privileges granted to a group are automatically inherited to its enrolled users. In the same chapter, you will allow users to set and reset their passwords. Finally in Chapter 14, you will create some authorization schemes and will modify all application segments to incorporate these schemes.

What You'll Learn

- Create a hierarchy of application segments
- Present application segments hierarchically in a tree view
- Create groups with different application privileges
- Allow and revoke access right on individual application segments
- Implement custom authentication scheme
- Add custom validations, processes and dynamic actions

1.2.9 Deploy APEX Application (Chapters 15)

In this chapter, you will be guided to export an application from your development PC to a production environment. For this purpose, you will utilize APEX's Export and Import utilities. To keep things simple, you will deploy the application in the same workspace to understand the deployment concept. First, you will export the application to a script file and then, using the Import utility, the same script file will be imported to create the application in the same workspace with a new ID. The same technique is applicable to the production environment.

Summary

This chapter provided an overview about the essence of the book: a web-based data-centric application. You'll create this application in two flavors (desktop and mobile) using the browser-based declarative development environment to get hands-on exposure to the features provided by Oracle APEX. The next chapter is aimed at providing some core concepts about Oracle APEX. Read the chapter thoroughly because the terms used in that chapter are referenced throughout the book.

Chapter 2

Oracle Application Express Concepts

2.1 Introduction to Oracle Application Express

If you are interested in developing professional web applications, then you have chosen the right track. Oracle Application Express (Oracle APEX) is a rapid application development (RAD) tool that runs inside an Oracle database instance and comes as a free option with Oracle database. Using this unique tool you can develop and deploy fast and secure professional web applications. The only requirements are a web browser and a little SQL and PL/SQL experience.

Oracle Application Express provides a declarative programming environment, which means that no code is generated or compiled during development. You just interact through wizards and property editor to build web applications on existing database schemas. Reports and charts are defined with simple SQL queries, so some knowledge of SQL is very helpful. If you want to create more robust applications, then you can add procedural logic by writing PL/SQL code. Oracle Application Express is a declarative tool and has a vast collection of pre-defined wizards, HTML objects, database handling utilities, page rendering and submission processes, navigation and branching options, and more. You can use all these options to build your database-centric web applications comprising web pages carrying forms, reports, charts, and so on with their layouts and business logic. The APEX engine translates it all into an HTML code for the client side and SQL and PL/SQL code for the server side. If you do not get a solution from built-in options, you are allowed by Oracle APEX to create your own SQL and PL/SQL code for the server side and HTML, CSS, and JavaScript code for the client side.

2.2 Why Use Oracle APEX

Velocity in the demand for new applications and functionality rises as businesses grow. As a developer, you are expected to rapidly respond to these needs. Over the years, desktop database and spreadsheet tools have enormously contributed to data management due to the ease and user friendliness these applications extend to their users. Besides benefits, these applications have scalability and functionality limitations that not only results in dozens of different applications and data sources but also adds extra overhead in their maintenance. Because of these issues, organizations are unable to continue their standard practices, leaving mission-critical data at risk. These fragmented systems may also cause loss of business opportunities. Finally, significant amount of time and resource is required to put these data blocks together to get the desired information. The following list provides some advantages of using Oracle APEX:

Oracle APEX Advantages

- Central management of data and applications
- No installation of software is required on client machines
- The only requirement is a supported browser
- Shared development and application access
- Being central, data and applications become a part of regular backup procedure
- Data and application access control, empowered by audit trail

2.3 Oracle APEX Structure

I know you are curious to start the proceedings, but first you need to understand some basic concepts before you dive into Oracle APEX's pool. This chapter will introduce some basic structures of Oracle APEX you must be aware of prior to executing the exercises. As depicted in Figure 2-1, Oracle APEX is an integral part of an Oracle database. It is a free rapid application development tool that runs inside an Oracle database instance. In Oracle APEX, you can create multiple *workspaces* to host different types of applications. Each workspace can also hold multiple applications. Database applications created in Oracle APEX comprise two or more *pages*. Each page can carry multiple *regions* to display or receive data. The data is fed and displayed using *page items* such as Text field, Select List, Radio Group, and so on. Just like desktop applications, you use *buttons* in Oracle APEX to manipulate your data and submit various requests. The following sub-sections provide further details on these structural elements.

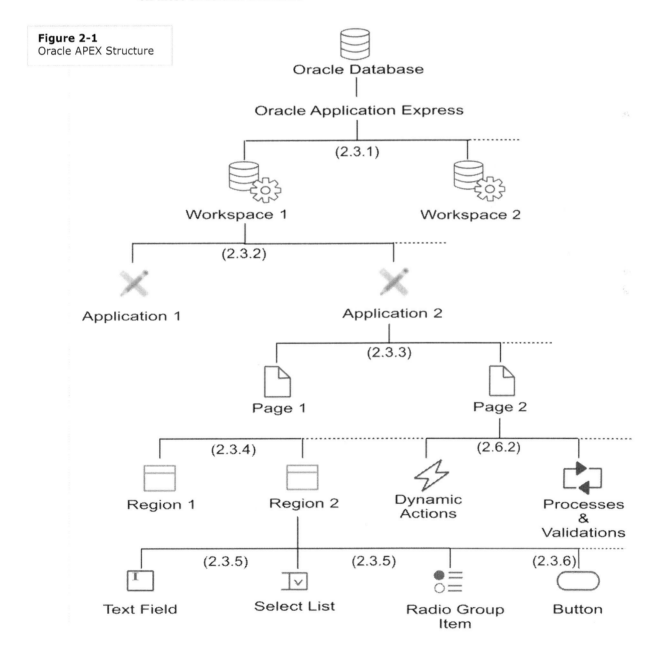

Figure 2-1
Oracle APEX Structure

21

2.3.1 Workspace

To access Oracle Application Express development environment, users sign in to a shared work area called a *Workspace*. A workspace is a virtual private container allowing multiple users to work within the same Oracle Application Express installation while keeping their objects, data and applications private. You have to create a workspace before you create an application. It is necessary because you have to specify which workspace you want to connect to when you log in. Without this piece of information, you are not allowed to enter Oracle Application Express.

To use the exercises presented in this book, you have to select a development option from the following:

- Download and install Oracle APEX on your own PC or within your private cloud.

- Get your own free workspace from Oracle to execute the exercises online on their servers. This is the most convenient way for beginners. So, execute the following steps to request a free workspace that will be provided to you in minutes.

Requesting a Free Workspace

Go to https://apex.oracle.com/en/, click the **Get Started** button, and then click the *Free Workspace* option. Follow the instructions mentioned below to get your free workspace:

1. On the *Type* page, select **Application Development** and click **Next**.
2. On the *Identification* page, enter your first and last names, e-mail address, and the name of the workspace you intend to create–for example, MYWORKSPACE.
3. On the next wizard page, enter a *Schema Name*–for example, MYSCHEMA. Also, select 25MB from the *Space Allocation* list and click **Next**. A schema is a set of metadata (data dictionary) used by the database, typically generated using DDL statement. You should consider a schema to be the user account and collection of all objects therein. Oracle APEX will create the schema you specify here with some default objects including data tables carrying some dummy data for evaluation.
4. Fill out the short survey questionnaire and move on by clicking **Next**.
5. Accept the terms and click **Next**.
6. On the final wizard page, click the **Submit Request** button. Please note down your credentials from this page because you'll need this information to access Oracle APEX's development environment. After submitting the request, you'll get the message "*Your workspace (workspace name) has been successfully requested.*" Once this request is approved, your login credentials will be e-mailed to your e-mail address.
7. Soon after submitting the request, you'll get an e-mail from Oracle. Click the **Create Workspace** button in the email to complete the approval process. The link will take you to Oracle APEX's website, and after a little while, your request will be approved with the message "*Workspace Successfully Created.*"
8. Click the **Continue to Sign In Screen** button.
9. A screen appears requesting to change password. Enter and confirm your password and click the **Apply Changes** button. Write down the workspace name, e-mail address (you provided in step 2), and the password you entered here. You need this information whenever you attempt to access your online Oracle APEX account–see Section 2.9 in this chapter.
10. Here you go! Your Workspace Home Page comes up resembling Figure 2-2.
11. To leave the Oracle APEX environment, click your name (appearing at top-right) and select **Sign out**.

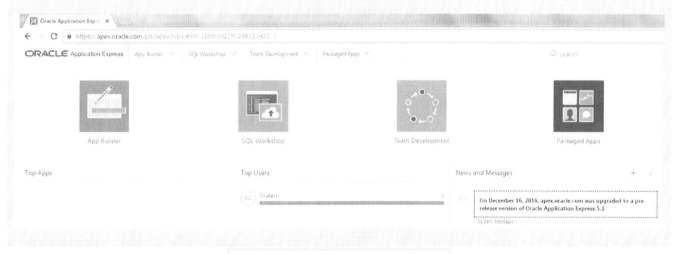

Figure 2-2 – Workspace Home Page

2.3.2 Application

Applications in Oracle APEX are created via App Builder and each application consists of one or more pages that are linked together using navigation menu, buttons, or hypertext links. Usually, each page carries items, buttons, and application logic. You can show forms, reports, charts, and calendars on these pages and can perform different types of calculations and validations. You can also control movement within an application using conditional navigation. You do all this declaratively using built-in wizards or through custom PL/SQL code.

Figure 2-3
ThemeRoller

At this stage, it is necessary to introduce you to two significant features in Oracle APEX: *Universal Theme* and *ThemeRoller*. The Universal Theme is a new application user interface that does away with excessive templates and supports effortless customizations with ThemeRoller, Template Options, and Theme Styles. The Universal Theme empowers developers to build modern, responsive, sophisticated, accessible applications without requiring expert knowledge of HTML, CSS, and JavaScript.

ThemeRoller displays in the runtime Developer Toolbar. It is a live CSS editor that enables developers to quickly change the colors, rounded corners and other properties of their applications without touching a line of code. To change all the colors of the theme style at once, drag the circle in the color palette. Adjust a number of style properties and see changes applied to your application in real time. Once you are satisfied with the result, you can save your changes as a Theme Style directly to your application.

The three types of applications you can create using the App Builder are: Desktop, Mobile, and Websheet. The *Create Application* wizard helps you to create these applications. While desktop and mobile applications are geared toward application developers, Websheet applications are designed for end users with no development experience.

Desktop Applications: These applications interact with a backend database to store and retrieve data. It is a collection of pages linked together using menus, buttons, or hypertext links. Pages are created declaratively through wizards. Each page can have multiple containers called regions. Each region can contain text, reports, charts, maps, web service content, calendars, or forms. Web forms hold items such as text fields, radio groups, checkboxes, date pickers, list of values, and more. In addition to these built-in types, you can create your own item types using plug-ins. When you build a database application, you can include different types of navigation controls, such as navigation menu, navigation bar entries, lists, breadcrumbs, and trees. Most of these navigation controls are shared components, which mean you create them at the application level and use them in any page within your database application. All pages in a database application share a common session state that is transparently managed by Oracle APEX.

Mobile Applications: Mobile database applications are designed to run specifically on smartphone devices.

Websheet Applications: Besides professional developers, Oracle APEX also cares for those who are not expert in the development field. It offers Websheet applications to such users to manage structured and unstructured data. Websheet applications are interactive web pages that combine text with data. These applications are highly dynamic and defined by their users. Websheet applications include navigation controls, search capabilities, and the ability to add annotations such as files, notes, and tags. Websheet applications can be secured using access control lists and several built-in authentication models. Pages can contain sections, reports, and data grids and everything can be linked together using navigation. All information is searchable and completely controlled by the end-user.

2.3.3 Page

A page is the basic unit of an application. When you build an application using App Builder, you create pages containing user interface elements, such as regions, items, navigation menu, lists, buttons, and more. Each page is identified by a unique number. By default, page creation wizards automatically add controls to a page based on your selections. You can add more controls to a page after its creation by using the Page Designer interface. Usually, the Create Page wizard is used to add components such as report, chart, form, calendar, or tree to a page. In addition to creating application pages through wizards, you have the option to create a blank page and add components to it according to your own specific needs. The Application Express engine dynamically renders and processes pages based on data stored in Oracle database tables. To view a rendered version of your application, you request it from the Application Express engine with a URL. When you run an application, the Application Express engine relies on two processes:

Show Page is the page rendering process. It assembles all the page attributes (including regions, items, and buttons) into a viewable HTML page.

Accept Page performs page processing. It performs any computations, validations, processes, and branching.

When you request a page using a URL, the engine is running Show Page. When you submit a page, the Application Express engine is running Accept Page or performing page processing during which it saves the submitted values in the session cache and then performs any computations, validations, or processes.

You can create the following types of pages for your application:

Blank Page: Creates a page without any built-in functionality.

Form: The following list provides different types of form pages you can create in Oracle APEX.

Form on a Table. Creates a form interface with which users can update a single row or multiple rows within a table. You can choose a table on which to build a form.

Form Editable Interactive Grid. An interactive grid presents users a set of data in a searchable, customizable report. In an editable interactive grid, users can also add, modify, and refresh the data set directly on the page. Functionally, an interactive grid includes most customization capabilities available in interactive reports plus the ability to rearrange the report interactively using the mouse. You choose a table on which to build the interactive grid.

Report with Form on Table. Creates two pages. One page displays as an interactive grid. Each row provides a link to the second page to enable users to update each record. You can select the table on which to build the report and form.

Single Page Master Detail Form. Creates single page master detail with editable interactive grids. With this page, users can query, insert, update, and delete values from two related tables or views. You choose the tables on which to build the master and detail regions.

Two Page Master Detail Form. A two page master detail features two related interactive grids. On the first page, users can query, insert, update, and delete values from two related tables or views. You choose the tables on which to build the master and detail regions.

Report: Used to present a SQL query in a formatted style, a report has the following options:

Interactive Grid. An interactive grid presents users a set of data in a searchable, customizable report. Functionally, an interactive grid includes most customization capabilities available in interactive reports plus the ability to rearrange the report interactively using the mouse. Users can lock, hide, filter, freeze, highlight, and sort individual columns with the Actions menu. Advanced users can also define breaks, aggregations, and computations against columns. Users can also directly customize the appearance of an interactive grid. Users can use the mouse to resize the width of a column and drag and drop columns into different places in the grid.

Interactive Report. Creates an interactive report based on a custom SQL SELECT statement you provide. Users can alter the layout of report data by selecting specific columns, applying filters, highlighting, and sorting. They can also define breaks, aggregations, different charts, and their own computations. Note that Interactive reports are not supported by jQuery Mobile Smartphone.

Classic Report. Creates a report based on a custom SQL SELECT statement or a PL/SQL function.

Plug-ins: Creates a new page based on a region type plug-in. Plug-ins enable developers to declaratively extend, share, and reuse the built-in types available with Oracle Application Express.

Chart: Enables you to create graphical charts.

Map: Creates a Flash map based on the AnyChart AnyMap Interactive Maps Component.

Tree: Creates a tree to graphically communicate hierarchical or multiple level data.

Calendar: Generates a calendar with monthly, weekly, and daily views.

Feedback Page: Adds a feedback page. Feedback is the process of gathering real-time comments, enhancement requests, and bugs from your application users.

Login Page: Creates a login page.

Access Control: Creates a page containing an access control list, enabling developers to control access to an application, individual pages, or page components.

Data Loading: Creates a new data loading wizard allowing the end user to manage the loading of data into a table to all schemas for which the user has privileges.

Global Page: A Global Page functions as a master page in your application. You can define separate Global Page, Login Page, and Home Page for desktop and mobile interfaces. This facilitates different pages being shown to end users when they access the application from a mobile device as opposed to a desktop system. The Application Express engine renders all components you add to a Global page on every page within your application. You can further control whether the Application Express engine renders a component or runs a computation, validation, or process by defining conditions.

2.3.4 Region

You can add one or more regions to a single page in an Oracle APEX application. It is an area on a page that serves as a container for content. You control the appearance of a region through a specific region template. The region template controls the look of the region, its size, determines whether there is a border or a background color, and what type of fonts to display. A region template also determines the standard placement for any buttons placed in region positions. You can use regions to group page elements (such as items or buttons). Oracle APEX supports many different region types including Static Content, Classic Report, Interactive Report, Interactive Grid, Chart , and more.

2.3.5 Items

After creating a region on a page, you add items to it. An item can be a Text Field, Textarea, Password, Select List, Checkbox, and so on. Each item has its own specific properties that affect the display of items on a page. For example, these properties can impact where a label displays, how large an item is, and if the item displays next to or below the previous item. The name of a page item is preceded by the letter P followed by the page number–for example, P7_CUSTOMER_ID represents customer ID item on page 7.

2.3.6 Buttons

Just like desktop applications where you place buttons on your form to perform some actions, in web applications too, you can create buttons to *submit* a page or to take users to another page (*redirect*) within the same site or to a different site. In the former case where a user *submits* a page, the Oracle APEX engine executes some processes associated with a particular button and uploads the page's item values to the server. In case of a *redirect*, nothing is uploaded to the server. If you change some items' values on a page and press a button created with a redirect action, those changes will be lost. You have three button options that you can add to a web page, these are: Icon, Text, and Text with Icon. You can place buttons either in predefined region positions or with other items in a form.

Being an important component to control the flow of database applications, buttons are created by right-clicking a region in which you want to place the button and selecting *Create Button* from the context menu. By placing buttons (such as Create, Delete, Cancel, Next, Previous , and more) on your web page, you can post or process the provided information or you can direct user to another page in the application or to another URL. Buttons are used to:

- Submit a page. For example, to save user input in a database table. When a button on a page is clicked, the page is submitted with a REQUEST value that carries the button name. You can reference the value of REQUEST from within PL/SQL using the bind variable :REQUEST. By using this bind variable, you can conditionally process, validate, or branch based on which button the user clicks. You can create processes that execute when the user clicks a button. And you can use a more complex condition as demonstrated in the following examples:

    If :REQUEST in ('EDIT','DELETE') then ...
    If :REQUEST != 'DELETE' then ...

These examples assume the existence of buttons named EDIT and DELETE. You can also use this syntax in PL/SQL Expression conditions. Be aware, however, that the button name capitalization (case) is preserved. In other words, if you name a button *LOGIN*, then a request looking for the name *Login* fails.

- Take user to another page within the same application with optional additional properties for resetting pagination, setting the request value, clearing cache, and setting item values on the target page.

- Redirect to another URL.

- Do nothing–for example, if the button's behavior is defined in a Dynamic Action.

- Download Printable Report Query. This creates a Submit Page button and also a corresponding branch. When the button is clicked, the output is downloaded from the Report Query.

2.4 Oracle APEX Development Environment

Oracle APEX has the web-based application development environment to build web applications. You are not required to install any client software to develop, deploy, or run Oracle APEX applications. Following are the primary tools provided by Oracle APEX:

App Builder – to create dynamic database driven web applications. This is the place where you create and modify your applications and pages. It comprises the following:

- **Create:** Using this option in the App Builder, you can create four types of applications: Desktop, Mobile, Websheet and Packaged applications.
- **Import:** Used to import an entire Oracle APEX application developed somewhere else, along with related files.
- **Dashboard:** Presents different metrics about applications in your workspace including: Developer Activity, Page Events, Page Count by Application, and Most Active Pages.
- **Workspace Utilities:** It contains various workspace utilities. The most significant one is Export. Using this utility, you can export application and component metadata to SQL script file format that you can import on the same or another compatible instance of Application Express.

SQL Workshop – to browse your database objects and to run ad-hoc SQL queries, SQL Workshop is designed to allow Application Developers to maintain database objects such as tables, packages, functions, views, and so on. It is beneficial in hosted environments like apex.oracle.com where direct access to underlying schemas is not provided. It has five basic components:

- **Object Browser:** to review and maintain database objects (tables, views, functions, triggers, and so on).
- **SQL Commands:** to run SQL queries.
- **SQL Scripts:** to upload and execute script files.
- **Utilities:** includes Query Builder, Data Workshop, Generate DDL, Schema Comparison , and more.
- **RESTful Services:** to define Web Services using SQL and PL/SQL against the database.

Team Development – Team Development allows development teams to better manage their Oracle APEX projects by defining milestones, features, to-dos, and bugs. Features, to-dos, and bugs can be associated with specific applications and pages as necessary. Developers can readily configure feedback to allow their end-users to provide comments on applications. The feedback also captures relevant session state details and can be readily converted to a feature, to-do or bug.

Packaged Apps – Packaged applications are a suite of business productivity applications, easily installed with only a few clicks. These solutions can be readily used as production applications to improve business processes and are fully supported by Oracle.

The Oracle APEX environment has two broad categories:

Development Environment: Here you have complete control to build and test your applications, as mentioned in this book.

Runtime Environment: After completing the development and testing phase, you implement your applications in a production environment where users can only run these applications and do not have the right to modify them.

2.5 About Browser Requirements

Because Oracle Application Express relies upon standards-compliant HTML5, CSS3, and JavaScript, Oracle recommends that you use the latest web browser software available for the best experience.

2.6 The Page Designer

The Page Designer is the main development interface where you manipulate page components. You use the Page Designer to view, create, and edit the controls and application logic that define a page. It was a feature incorporated in Oracle APEX 5, which greatly improves developer's productivity and quickly enhances and maintains pages within Oracle Application Express. It allows you to undo and redo changes as necessary before saving the page. In the Layout tab, it visually presents how your regions and items appear on the page. Moreover, you can drag new components from component Gallery and move or copy existing components within a page. Similarly, you can drag to move multiple components at once in the Tree pane. It also has a new code editor with new functionalities, such as: SQL and PL/SQL validation with inline errors, auto completion, syntax highlighting, search and replace, and undo/redo support.

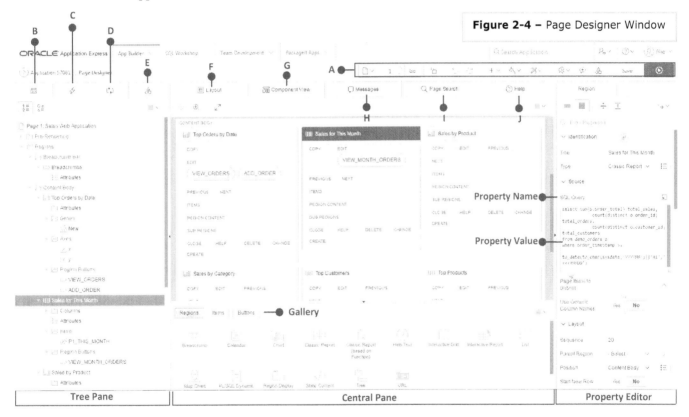

Figure 2-4 – Page Designer Window

2.6.1 Toolbar

The Page Designer toolbar (A) appears at the top of the page. It comprises various tools to find a page, lock/unlock a page, undo/redo actions, save and run page, and so on. When you pass your cursor over an active button and menu, a tooltip indicates what that particular toolbar option does. The *Utilities* menu has an option that lets you delete the page being displayed in your browser. A lock icon indicates whether a page is currently locked. If a page is unlocked, the icon appears as an open padlock. If the page is locked, the icon appears as a locked padlock. A lock icon appears on the Application home page and on the page–as illustrated in Figure 2-5. You can prevent conflicts during application development by locking pages in your application. By locking a page, you prevent other developers from editing it.

Figure 2-5
Page Lock
Indicator

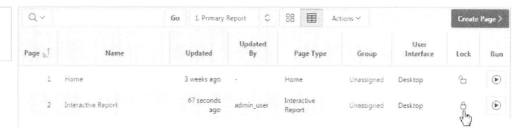

2.6.2 Tree Pane

The Tree pane is displayed on the left side in the Page Designer. It contains regions, items, buttons, application logic (such as computations, processes, and validations), dynamic actions, branches, and shared components as nodes on a tree. It comprises four tabs:

- **Rendering (B)** - Displays regions, page items, page buttons, and application logic as nodes in a tree. The components defined in this section appear when a page is rendered. These components can be viewed as a tree, organized either by processing order (the default) or by component type. The first two buttons to the right of the Rendering label can be used to toggle between the rendering trees. Rendering is divided in three stages. In the *Pre-Rendering* stage preliminary computations are performed. The main rendering stage comprises regions and its components, while the *Post-Rendering* stage also carries computations that occur after rendering a page.

- **Dynamic Actions (C)** - Displays dynamic actions defined on this page. By creating a dynamic action, you can define complex client-side behavior declaratively without the need for JavaScript. Refer to Dynamic Actions entry in the book's index to see its utilization in the project application.

- **Processing (D)** - Use this tab to specify application logic such as computations, validations, processes, and branches. *Computations* are Oracle APEX's declarative way of setting an item's values on the page. These are units of logic used to assign session state to items and are executed at the time the page is processed. *Validation* is a server-side mechanism designed to check and validate the quality, accuracy, and consistency of the page submitted data, prior to saving it into the database. If a validation fails, further processing is aborted by the server and the existing page is redisplayed with all inline validation errors. *Processes* are logic controls used to execute Data Manipulation Language (DML) or PL/SQL. Processes are executed after the page is submitted. A page is typically submitted when a user clicks a button. *Branches* enable you to create logic controls that determine how the user navigates through the application. The left iconic button to the right of the *Processing* label displays the components under this tab according to the server's processing order. The middle button organizes these components according to their type, while the third one provides a menu to create a new component in the selected folder.

- **Page Shared Components (E)** - Displays shared components associated with this page. The list on this tab get populated automatically when you use shared components on a page.

2.6.3 Central Pane

The central pane in the Page Designer has two sections. The upper section contains five tabs: Layout, Component View, Messages, Page Search, and Help. The lower pane is called Gallery and it is associated with the Layout tab.

- **Layout (F)** - Layout is a visual representation of the regions, items, and buttons that define a page. You can add new regions, items and buttons to a page by selecting them from the Gallery at the bottom of the page.

- **Component View (G)** - It is the traditional user interface for accessing page components. Unlike Layout, Component View does not offer a visual representation of a page or support the dragging and dropping of page components.

- **Messages (H)** - When you create components or edit properties in the Page Designer, Messages notifies you of errors and warnings you need to address.

- **Page Search (I)** - Use Page Search to search all page metadata including regions, items, buttons, dynamic actions, columns, and so on.

- **Help (J)** – The Help displays help text for Property Editor properties. Click a property in the Property Editor and then click the Help tab (in the Central pane) to see the purpose of the selected property. As you move from one property to the next in the property editor, the Help tab displays the help text for the currently selected property.

2.6.4 Property Editor

The Property Editor appears in the right pane and displays all the properties and vales for the current component. As you select different components in either Tree View or Layout tab, the Property Editor automatically updates to reflect the current selection. Properties are organized into functional groups (Identification, Source, Layout, Appearance, and more) that describe their purpose. When you modify or add a value to a property, a blue triangle appears in the same place. The four buttons provided at the top of this sections determine which properties are displayed. To only see the commonly used properties, click the leftmost button. The button to its right is used to display all properties. Use the last two buttons to collapse/expand the displayed properties.

2.7 Understanding Oracle APEX URL Syntax

A URL in Oracle APEX consists of the f?p= string followed by a colon delimited string of values. Each application has its own unique ID and is referenced by this ID in URL. Similarly, you create pages in an application with respective numbers that uniquely identify each page. The Application Express engine assigns a session ID, which is used as a key to the user's session state when an application is run. Here is the URL syntax example:

http://apex.abc.com/pls/apex/f?p=101:1:440323506685863558

This example indicates:

- *apex.abc.com* is the URL of the server
- *pls* is the indicator to use the mod_plsql cartridge
- *apex* is the database access descriptor (DAD) name. The DAD describes how HTTP server connects to the database server so that it can fulfill an HTTP request. The default value is *apex*.
- *f?p=* is a prefix used by Oracle Application Express
- *101* is the application being called
- *1* is the page within the application to be displayed
- *440323506685863558* is the session number to keep track of user's session state

It is important to understand how f?p syntax works. App Builder includes many wizards that automatically create these references for you. However, you may have to create the syntax yourself in some situations. For instance, in section 6.3.1 (Chapter 6) you will create a manual link in a SQL statement using this syntax, and in section 4.3.2, a link will be created on a column using the *Target* property of that column.

2.7.1 Using f?p Syntax to Link Pages

Here is the syntax you can use to create links between pages in your application.

f?p=App:Page:Session:Request:Debug:ClearCache:itemNames:itemValues:PrinterFr iendly

The following are the arguments you can pass when using f?p syntax:

App: Indicates an application ID or alphanumeric alias.

Page: Indicates a page number or alphanumeric alias.

Session: Identifies a session ID. Web applications use HTTP by which browsers talk to Web servers. Since HTTP doesn't maintain state, it is known as a stateless protocol. Here, your Web server reacts independently to each individual request it receives and has no way to link requests together even if it is logging requests. For example, a client browser requests a page from a web server. After rendering the page, the server closes the connection. When a subsequent request is forwarded from the same client, the web server doesn't know how to associate the current request with the previous one. To access values entered on one page on a subsequent page, the values must be stored as session state. It is very crucial to access and manage session state while designing an interactive, data-driven web application. Fortunately, Oracle Application Express transparently manages session state behind the scenes for every page and provides developers with the ability to get and set session state values from any page in the application. When a user requests a page, the Application Express engine uses session ID to get session state information from the database. You can reference the session ID either using *&SESSION.* substitution string or by using *:APP_SESSION* bind variable. See substitution string and bind variables in section 2.8. Whenever you run an Oracle APEX application page during development phase, you see a horizontal bar at the bottom of the page. This is a *Developer Toolbar*. Among other tools for developers it contains a *Session* option, which shows you the current session state. Clicking it opens a window (called *Session Page, shown in Figure 2-6*) carrying all items and their current session values. It is useful for developers to debug pages. When you change some item value on a page and submit it, the value in the session window for that item changes to reflect the current state. Use the *Page, Find*, and *View* parameters to view session state for the page. The drop-down *View* menu comprises *Page Items, Application Items, Session State, Collections*, and *All* options. Select an option from this list and click the *Set* button to refresh the Session State report.

Figure 2-6
Session Page

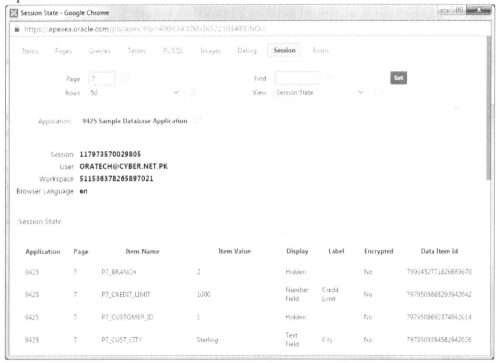

Request: Here you place an HTML request. Each application button sets the value of REQUEST to the name of the button, which enables the called process to reference the name of the button when a user clicks it. You can assess requests using the *:REQUEST* bind variable.

Debug: Displays application processing details. Valid values for the DEBUG flag include: Yes or No. Setting this flag to YES you get details about application processing. You can reference the Debug flag using *&DEBUG.* substitution string.

ClearCache: You use Clear Cache to make item values null. To do so, you provide a page number to clear items on that page. You can also clear cached items on multiple pages by adding a list of page numbers separated by comma. For example, typing 4,5,8 in the Clear Cache position in the URL will clear the session state for all items on pages 4, 5, and 8.

itemNames: Comma-delimited list of *item names* used to set session state with a URL.

itemValues: List of *item values* used to set session state within a URL. See Chapter 4 Section 4.3.2 for the utilization of itemNames and itemValues syntax parameters.

PrinterFriendly: Determines if the page is being rendered in printer friendly mode. If PrinterFriendly is set to Yes, then the page is rendered in printer friendly mode. The value of PrinterFriendly can be used in rendering conditions to remove elements such as regions from the page to optimize printed output.

2.8 Substitution Strings and Bind Variables

To make your application more portable, Application Express provides many features. On top of the list are the Substitution Strings that help you avoid hard-coded references in your application. As mentioned earlier, every application in Oracle APEX has its own unique ID and which is used to identify the application and the corresponding metadata within the Application Express repository. When you move these applications from your development environment to the production environment, and if you've hard-coded application references, you might be placed in an awkward situation. For example, you hard-coded the application ID (101) like this: f?p=101:1:&APP_SESSION.. If you take this application to the production environment that already has an application with the same ID, you'll be forced to use a different ID, which will point all your links within the application to the wrong ID.

To avoid such situations, you should always use substitution strings. You can avoid hard-coding the application ID by using the APP_ID substitution string, which identifies the ID of the currently executing application. With the substitution string, the URL looks like: f?p=&APP_ID.:1:&APP_SESSION.. This approach makes your application more portable.

The following table describes the supported syntax for referencing APP_ID.

Reference Type	Syntax
Bind variable	:APP_ID
Substitution string	&APP_ID.

You need to know how to get a page to access the value of a session state variable. There are two ways. If you want to reference the variable from within SQL or PL/SQL code, use bind variable , in other words, precede the item name with a colon. If you want to reference an item from within an HTML expression, then make use of substitution string. In substitution string you prefix an ampersand to the item name and append a period at its end. For example, consider an item named P7_CUSTOMER_ID on a page. To refer to it as a substitution string, write "&P7_CUSTOMER_ID.". To refer to it as a bind variable, write ":P7_CUSTOMER_ID".

About Using Substitution Strings

You can use substitution strings in the following ways:

- Include a substitution string within a template to reference component values
- Reference page or application items using &ITEM. syntax
- Use built-in substitution strings

Substitution Strings within Templates

Special substitution strings available within a template are denoted by the number symbol (#). For example: #PRODUCT_ID# - see Chapter 4 Section 4.3.2, 4.3.5, and 4.3.6.

Substitution Strings for Page or Application Items

To reference page or application items using substitution variables:

1. Reference the page or application item in all capital letters.
2. Precede the item name with an ampersand (&).
3. Append a period (.) to the item name.

For example, you would refer to a page item named P7_CUSTOMER_ID in a region, a region title, an item label, or in any of numerous other contexts in which static text is used, like this: &CUSTOMER_ID..

Notice the required trailing period. When the page is rendered, Application Express engine replaces the value of the substitution string with the value of item P7_CUSTOMER_ID.

Using Built-in Substitution Strings

Oracle APEX supports many built-in substitution strings. You can reference these substitution strings to achieve specific types of functionality. APP_ID, APP_IMAGES, APP_PAGE_ID, APP_SESSION, APP_USER, LOGIN_URL, and LOGOUT_URL are some of the built-in substitution strings you will use in this book.

2.9 Start Building the Application

Now that you have gone through all the basic concepts about Oracle APEX, let's start the thrill! Follow the instructions mentioned in this section to create the barebones of your application.

1. If you have logged out, sign back in to Oracle APEX development environment by typing the URL **https://apex.oracle.com/pls/apex** in your browser's address bar.

2. Enter the credential comprising your Workspace, Username (your e-mail address), and Password (you provided in Chapter 2 Section 2.3.1) in the Sign In form.

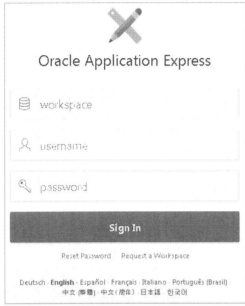

3. Click the **App Builder** icon.

4. On the App Builder page, click the **Create** icon or button to create a new application.

5. Select the first **Desktop** option for the type of application. You will create a mobile application in Chapter 10.

6. Enter **Sales Web Application** in the *Name* box. In the *Name* attribute you provide a short descriptive name for the application to distinguish it from other applications in your development environment. Match other attribute values with those set in the following figure, except schema and Application ID that would be different in your scenario. The *Theme* attribute defaults to the new *Universal Theme*. The Universal Theme is an application user interface that does away with excessive templates and supports effortless customizations with ThemeRoller, Template Options, and Theme Styles. The Universal Theme empowers developers to build modern, responsive, sophisticated, accessible applications without requiring expert knowledge of HTML, CSS, or JavaScript. Oracle APEX provides you with some default theme styles. A theme style defines a CSS style sheet that is added to the base CSS to alter the look and feel of an application. Theme styles are used to customize themes, to switch to a different color scheme, apply a flat look, or make a theme responsive. A theme can have multiple theme styles with one style set as active. You can modify a theme style CSS file using ThemeRoller. The Theme Style defaults to *Vita (Accessibility Tested)* that you can change by accessing *Shared Components > User Interface Attributes > Desktop* interface. Accept the default values appearing for these two properties, and click **Next**.

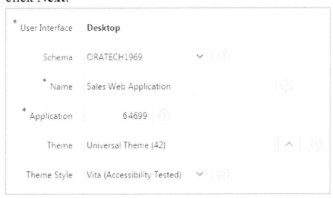

7. Accepting the default values on the "*Pages*" screen, click **Next** to move on. By default, the App Builder wizard creates a blank Home page along with a login page. This step shows the Home page information.

8. In *Shared Components* screen, select **No** for *Copy Shared Components from Another Application* and click **Next**. We will create our application's shared components in the next chapter.

9. In the *Attributes* screen, set date and time formats using the adjacent LOV buttons. Accept default values for *Authentication Scheme* and other properties, shown in the

figure below. Oracle APEX provides a number of predefined authentication mechanisms, including a built-in authentication framework and an extensible custom framework. In the selected default scheme (*Application Express Accounts*) users are managed and maintained in the Oracle APEX workspace. Note that in Chapter 13 you will replace this default scheme with a custom authentication scheme to control user access to this application. For the time being, click **Next** to proceed.

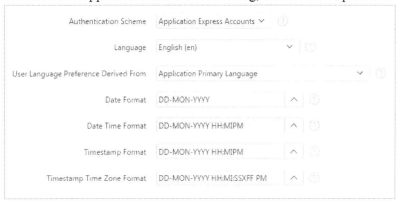

10. Click the **Create Application** button on the *Confirm* screen to finish the wizard. Your screen should resemble Figure 2-7. Note that Oracle APEX created the application with two pages: Page 1 (Home) and Page 101 (Login Page). Using the two buttons (*Icon View* and *Report View*), you can get different views of this interface. The screen shot illustrated below presents the iconic view. You can see the ID and name of your application (A) in this interface. At this stage, if you want to modify properties of your application (for example, application name), then click the *Edit Application Properties* button (B). In the *Edit Application Definition* interface you will see a small question mark icon for each property to display help text for its corresponding property. Click this icon when a property is unfamiliar and you want to learn about it. To delete an application click the *Delete this Application* link (C) in the *Tasks* bar, or make a copy of your current application using the *Copy this Application* link (D). It makes an exact copy of the application with a different ID. You will use the *Create Page* button (E) in subsequent chapters to create new application pages.

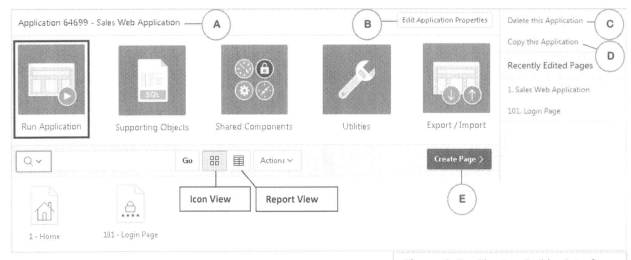

Figure 2-7 – The App Builder Interface

11. Click **Run Application**. The application login form, created by the App Builder, will come up. Type the same username (your e-mail ID) and the password you entered earlier to access the development environment and click the **Login** button. A new browser window will open with the Home page of your application, also created by the App Builder. At the bottom of this page, you will see a row of buttons–see Figure 1-1 in Chapter 1. This row is called the Developer Toolbar and it appears whenever you run a page during the development phase. The *Edit Page* button in this toolbar takes you to the Page Designer for the current page so that you can edit the page. The *Application* button takes you to the home page for the current application so that you can work on a different page. And the *Session* button brings up a window that displays the current state of the application so that you can verify its behavior. Right now, click the **Logout** link to exit the application.

Figure 2-8
Desktop
Application
Home Page

2.10 The Underlying Database Objects

While creating the workspace (in Chapter 2 section 2.3.1), you provided a schema name to hold database objects for your application. The following table lists some default objects created by Oracle APEX. These are the objects you'll use in this book to build the sales application. The *Table* objects come with sample data, while the *Sequence* database objects are added to provide unique auto-generated IDs to each record in respective tables. For example, the Sequence DEMO_CUST_SEQ provides a unique ID to each customer in DEMO_CUSTOMERS table. A *trigger* is a special kind of stored procedure that automatically executes when an event occurs in the database server. DML triggers execute when a user tries to modify data through a data manipulation language (DML) event. The common DML events are INSERT, UPDATE, and DELETE statements that are executed to manipulate data in a table or view. You can view these objects using the *Object Browser* utility in *SQL Workshop*. In addition to the following objects, you will create some more tables in the final chapters of this book to set up a custom security module.

Tables	Sequences	Triggers
DEMO_CUSTOMERS	DEMO_CUST_SEQ	DEMO_CUSTOMERS_BIU
DEMO_ORDERS	DEMO_ORD_SEQ	DEMO_ORDERS_BIU
DEMO_ORDER_ITEMS	DEMO_ORDER_ITEMS_SEQ	DEMO_ORDER_ITEMS_BI
DEMO_PRODUCT_INFO	DEMO_PROD_SEQ	DEMO_PRODUCT_INFO_BIU
DEMO_STATES	-	-
DEMO_TAGS	-	DEMO_TAGS_BIU

Summary

This chapter introduced you to some of the important basic concepts of Oracle Application Express. Besides the theoretical stuff, you were guided to request a free workspace. You also created the basic structure of your application with two default pages (you will work in detail on the Home pages in Chapter 4 to convert it into a dashboard) and went through the underlying database objects that Oracle APEX created for you.

In the next chapter, you will create the building blocks (shared components) for your application. The Shared Components wizards allow us to define a variety of components we can use and re-use throughout our application. In the coming chapters, our main focus will be on the practical aspect of this robust technology. Once you get familiar with Oracle Application Express, you can explore other areas on your own to become a master. The rest of the book will guide you to build professional looking web-based data-centric desktop and mobile applications, which will provide you the techniques in building your own.

Chapter 3

Create Application Components

3.1 The Shared Components

Shared components are application structures used in application pages. These structures are called shared components because you create them once and utilize them across all the pages in the application. For example, in this chapter you will create a list comprising application menu options that will appear on every application page. If you click *Component View* in the Page Designer, you will see *Shared Components* section containing a list of common elements applied to that particular page. Note that shared components are only displayed in this section after you add them to a page. The following sub-sections introduce you to shared component elements.

3.1.1 Application Definition Attributes

This link (which appears under *Application Logic*) will take you to the *Edit Application Definition* page where you can modify your application attributes, including its name, versions, build option, and more.

3.1.2 Application Processes

Application Processes run PL/SQL logic at specific points for each page in an application. You can apply conditions to control when the process executes.

3.1.3 Authentication Schemes

The significance of security cannot be ignored when building web applications, as it enables us to prevent unauthorized access and activity in our applications. Not all applications require security; a public website doesn't, for example. However, for many applications, we need to be able to control who can run and gain access to them. Once users are logged into our application, we also need to further control what functionality they have permission to access. In Application Express, these security features are implemented through the use of *Authentication* and *Authorization Schemes*. These schemes enable us to declaratively define the security for our applications quickly and easily. Authentication is the process of establishing the identity of every user of your application. The most common type of authentication process requires a user to provide some type of credentials such as a username and password. These credentials are then evaluated either through the built-in *Application Express Authentication* scheme or using a custom scheme with more control. Authentication could involve the use of digital certificates or a secure key, too. If the credentials pass, the user is allowed to access the application. Otherwise, access is denied. Once a user has been identified, the Application Express engine keeps track of each user by setting the value of the built-in substitution string APP_USER.

As you create your application, you must determine whether to include authentication. You can:

- **Choose to not require authentication.** Oracle Application Express does not check any user credentials. All pages of your application are accessible to all users. A public informational application website is a good candidate, which doesn't require authentication.

- **Select a built-in authentication scheme**. Create an authentication method based on available preconfigured authentication schemes. Here are the preconfigured authentication schemes available in Oracle Application Express. Each scheme follows a standard behavior for authentication and session management.

  - *Application Express Accounts*. These are user accounts created within and managed in the Oracle Application Express user repository. When you use this method, your application is authenticated against these accounts.

  - *Database Account Credentials*. It utilizes database schema accounts. This authentication scheme requires that a database user (schema) exist in the local database. When using this method, the username and password of the database account is used to authenticate the user. Choose *Database Account Credentials* if having one database account for each named user of your application is feasible and account maintenance using database tools meets your needs.

  - *HTTP Header Variable*. It supports the use of header variables to identify a user and to create an Application Express user session. Use this authentication scheme if your company employs a centralized web authentication solution like Oracle Access Manager, which provides single sign-on across applications and technologies.

  - *LDAP Directory Verification*. You can configure any authentication scheme that uses a login page to use Lightweight Directory Access Protocol (LDAP) to verify the username and password submitted on the login page. App Builder includes wizards and pages that explain how to configure this option. These wizards assume that an LDAP directory accessible to your application for this purpose already exists and that it can respond to a SIMPLE_BIND_S call for credentials verification.

  - *Application Server Single Sign-On Server*. This one delegates authentication to the Oracle AS Single Sign-On (SSO) Server. To use this authentication scheme, your site must have been registered as a partner application with the SSO server.

- **Create custom authentication scheme**. Using this method, you can have complete control over the authentication interface. To implement this approach, you must provide a PL/SQL function the Application Express engine executes before processing each page request. The Boolean return value of this function determines whether the Application Express engine processes the page normally or displays a failure page. You will use this authentication scheme in Chapter 13 to protect your application. This is the best approach for applications when any of the following is true:

- Database authentication or other methods are not adequate
- You want to develop your own login form and associated methods
- You want to control security aspects of session management
- You want to record or audit activity at the user or session level
- You want to enforce session activity or expiry limits
- Your application consists of multiple applications that operate seamlessly (for example, more than one application ID)

3.1.4 Authorization Schemes

By defining authorization schemes, you control users' access to specific components of your application. It is an important security measure implemented to augment the application's authentication scheme. An authorization scheme can be specified for an entire application, page, or specific page components such as a region, button, or item. For instance, you can apply an authorization scheme to determine which menu options a user can see, or whether he is allowed to create a new order (using the Create button).

3.1.5 List of Values

List of values (abbreviated as LOVs) are defined by running the LOV wizard. Once created, LOVs are stored in the List of Values repository and are utilized by page items. You can create two types of LOVs: static and dynamic. A static LOV displays and returns predefined values such as Yes and No, while a dynamic list is populated using a SQL query that fetches values from database tables. After creating an LOV you associate it to page items such as select list, radio group, checkbox, and so on. By creating a list of values at the application-level, you have the advantage to add it to any page within an application, and since all LOV definitions are stored in one location, it makes them easy to locate and update.

3.1.6 Plug-Ins

With the increase in Application Express usage the demand for specific features also surfaced. To meet these demands, the plug-ins framework was introduced in Oracle APEX 4.0, which allows developers to create their own plug-ins to add additional functionality in a supported and declarative way.

Usually, a tool like Ajax is used to add custom functionality. The con of this approach is to place the code in different locations such as within the database, in external JavaScript files, and so on. On the other hand, turning that code into a plug-in is more convenient to use and manage because the code resides in one object. With the help of open source jQuery components you can create plug-ins without generating huge amount of code manually.

Plug-ins are shared component objects that allow you to extend the functionality of item types, region types, dynamic actions, and process types. The plug-in architecture includes a declarative development environment that lets you create custom versions of these built-in objects. For example, you can create your own star rating item that allows your user to provide feedback using a one-to-five star graphic. This new item type can then be used across all your applications. The main part of a plug-in consists of PL/SQL code and can be supplemented with JavaScript and CSS code. A plug-in consists of one or more PL/SQL functions. These functions can either reside in the database (in a package or a set of functions) or be included within the plug-in.

The Plug-in OTN page (http://www.oracle.com/technetwork/developer-tools/apex/application-express/apex-plug-ins-182042.html) has several different plug-ins developed by the APEX development team.

3.1.7 Shortcuts

By using shortcuts you can avoid repetitive coding of HTML or PL/SQL functions. You can use a shortcut to define a page control such as a button, HTML text, or a PL/SQL procedure. Once defined, you can invoke a shortcut using specific syntax unique to the location in which the shortcut is used. Shortcuts can be referenced many times, thus reducing code redundancy.

When you create a shortcut, you must specify the type of shortcut you want to create. Oracle Application Express supports the following shortcut types:

- PL/SQL Function Body
- HTML Text
- HTML Text with Escaped Special Characters
- Image
- Text with JavaScript Escaped Single Quotes
- Message
- Message with JavaScript Escaped Special Quotes

3.1.8 Lists

A list is a collection of links. For each list entry, you specify display text, a target URL, and other attributes to control when and how the list entry displays. Once created, you can add a list to any number of pages within an application by creating a region and specifying the region type as *List*. You control the display of the list and the appearance of all list entries by linking the list to a template. Lists are of two types:

Static Lists

When you create a static list you define a list entry label and a target (either a page or a URL). You can add list entries when you create the list (from scratch), by copying existing entries or by adding the list entries. You can control when list entries display by defining display conditions.

Dynamic Lists

Dynamic lists are based on a SQL query or a PL/SQL function executed at runtime.

3.1.9 Navigation Menu

You might have seen a horizontal bar at the top of a website. The options provided on this bar help you navigate to different pages within that site. Application Express provides you with a similar component called Navigation Menu. It is an effective way to navigate users between pages of an application. You can create different navigation menu for different interfaces. For example, you can create two separate navigation menus one each for your desktop and mobile apps. Note that navigation menus are only supported in applications using the Universal Theme - 42.

3.1.10 Breadcrumb

A breadcrumb is a hierarchical list of links rendered using a template. For example, you can display breadcrumbs as a list of links or as a breadcrumb path. A breadcrumb trail indicates where you are within the application from a hierarchical perspective. In addition, you can click a specific breadcrumb link to instantly view the page. For example, in the screen shot below you can access the Shared Components page by clicking its breadcrumb entry. You use breadcrumbs as a second level of navigation at the top of each page, complementing other navigation options such as Navigation Menu and Navigation Bar.

Figure 3-1
Breadcrumb

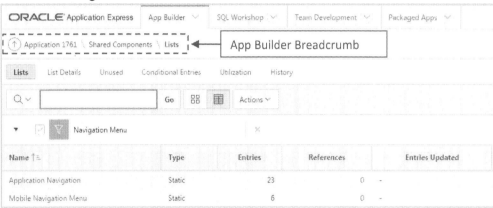

3.1.11 Navigation Bar List

Just like menus, lists, and breadcrumb, a navigation bar is also created to link users to various pages within an application. Typically, a navigation bar carries links such as login, logout, feedback, help, and so on. It appears on every application page according to the selected page template. While creating a navigation bar, you can specify an image name, text, display sequence, and target location. A navigation bar entry can be an image, text, or an image with text beneath it. Navigation bars are different from other shared components in that you do not need to reference them on a page-by-page basis. If your page template includes the #NAVIGATION_BAR# substitution string, the Application Express engine automatically includes any defined navigation bars when it renders the page.

3.1.12 User Interface Attributes

When you create a database application you select a user interface. The application user interface (such as Desktop or Mobile) determines default characteristics of the application and optimizes the display for the target environment. This is the place where you define your application's logo, too.

48

3.1.13 Themes and Templates

Instead of telling the App Builder how to design and style your pages using HTML, CSS, and JavaScript code, which you may not be aware of, you only apply theme and templates you want to use and the Oracle APEX engine does the rest of the job for you.

A theme is a named collection of templates that defines the look and feel of application user interface. Each theme contains templates for every type of application component and page control, including individual pages, regions, reports, lists, labels, menus, buttons, and list of values.

Templates control the look and feel of the pages in your application using snippets of HTML, CSS, JavaScript and image icons. As you create your application, you specify templates for pages, regions, reports, lists, labels, menus, buttons, and pop-up lists of values. Groups of templates are organized into named collections called themes.

The App Builder also allows you to access the themes and template mechanism so you can create new ones according to your own requirements or amend existing ones. Oracle Application Express ships with an extensive theme repository. Administrators can add themes to the theme repository, as follows:

- Workspace administrators can create themes that are available to all developers within the workspace. Such themes are called *workspace themes*.

- Instance administrators can create *public themes* by adding them to the Oracle Application Express Administration Services. Once added, these public themes are available to all developers across all workspaces in an instance.

- Newer themes, such as Universal Theme - 42 and Mobile - 51, include *theme styles*. A *theme style* is a CSS style sheet added to the base CSS. Developers can change the appearance of an application by altering the theme style using the ThemeRoller utility.

3.1.14 Static Application/Workspace Files

Use these two links to upload, edit, and delete static files including style sheets (CSS), images, and JavaScript files. An application file can be referenced from a specific application only, whereas a workspace file can be accessed by any application in the workspace. In this book, you will use the *Static Application Files* link to upload your application's logo.

3.1.15 Data Load Definition

Applications with data loading capability enable end users to dynamically import data into a table within any schema to which the user has access. To import the data, end users run the Data Load Wizard to upload the data from a file or copy and paste the data directly into the wizard. An application developer creates a Data Load Wizard by creating a Data Load page with the Create Page Wizard. During the creation process, developers can specify the upload table and its unique columns, table lookups, and data transformation rules. The Create Page Wizard creates a Data Load table that defines the Data Load Wizard.

3.1.16 Web Service References

Web services enable applications to interact with one another over the web in a platform-neutral, language independent environment. In a typical web services scenario, a business application sends a request to a service at a given URL by using the protocol over HTTP. The service receives the request, processes it, and returns a response. You can incorporate calls with external web services in applications developed in App Builder.

Web services are typically based on Simple Object Access Protocol (SOAP) or Representational State Transfer (REST) architectures. SOAP is a World Wide Web Consortium (W3C) standard protocol for sending and receiving requests and responses across the Internet. SOAP messages can be sent back and forth between a service provider and a service user in SOAP envelopes. RESTful Web services are resource oriented. The scope of the web service is found in the URI and the service process is described by the HTTP method that is used such as GET, POST, PUT, HEAD, and DELETE.

SOAP offers two primary advantages:
- SOAP is based on XML, and therefore easy to use.
- SOAP messages are not blocked by firewalls because this protocol uses simple transport protocols, such as HTTP.

REST offers similar advantages:
- REST messages are also not blocked by firewalls because this protocol uses the HTTP protocol.
- REST requests do not require the overhead of XML and SOAP envelopes and inputs are typically provided in the URI.

3.1.17 Report Queries

A report query is a printable document, which can be integrated with an application using buttons, list items, branches, or any other navigational components that allow for using URLs as targets. A report query is based on a standard SQL query. It can be downloaded as a PDF document, a Word document (RTF based), an Excel Spreadsheet (HTML based), or as an HTML file. The layout of a report query is customizable using RTF templates.

3.1.18 Report Layouts

Use Report Layouts in conjunction with a report region or report query to render data in a printer-friendly format, such as PDF, Word, or Excel. A report layout can be designed using the Template Builder Word plug-in and uploaded as a file of type RTF or XSL-FO. Report regions use a generic XSL-FO layout, which is customizable.

3.1.19 Globalization Attributes

If you want to develop applications that can run concurrently in different languages, then Application Express is the right platform for this. In the Globalization interface, you can specify options such as the application Primary Language, Date/Time format, and some other options related to application globalization.

3.1.20 Translate Application

A single Oracle database and Oracle Application Express instance can support an application in multiple languages. Translating an application involves multiple steps. To translate an application developed in App Builder, you must map the primary and target language, seed and export text to a translation file, translate the text, apply the translation file, and publish the translated application.

Having gone through the conceptual sections, the following are some of the Shared Components you will create for the Sales Web Application:

- Lists
- List of Values (LOV)
- Application Logo

If you are logged off, log back in to the application development environment to create some shared components. Execute the following three steps to access the Shared Components page.

1. Click the **App Builder** icon.

2. Click the **Edit** icon for Sales Web Application.

3. Click the **Shared Components** icon.

3.2 Create Lists

First, we are going to play with the *Lists* shared component. A list is a collection of links rendered using a template. For each list entry, you specify display text, a target URL, and other properties to control when and how the list entry displays. You control the display of the list and the appearance of all list entries by linking the list to a template.

3.2.1 Modify Desktop Navigation Menu List

Figure 3-2
Desktop
Application
Menu

Oracle APEX used tabs that acted as application's main menu up to version 4.2. Now, a default navigation list named *Desktop Navigation Menu* is created with each new application as a shared component. Note that navigation menus are only supported in applications using the Universal Theme. It is a hierarchical list of navigation, which incorporates additional features like pull-down menus and submenus. It is displayed as a responsive sidebar. Based on the available space, the navigation bar either displays a full menu or collapses to a narrow icon bar. The default menu list (*Desktop Navigation Menu*) carries just one item, which is labeled Home. In this exercise, you'll modify this list to add more application menu entries.

1. In Shared Components, click the **Lists** option in the *Navigation* section.

2. On the Lists page, click the **Desktop Navigation Menu** option, which carries one entry (Home) created by the App Builder wizard to call the default Home page. Modify this entry by clicking its name (Home) under the *Name* column. On the *Create/Edit* page, which lists properties for this menu item, click the pop-up LOV icon representing *Image/Class* attribute. From the *Show* list, select **Font APEX**, and from *Category*, select **Web Application**. Click the **Go** button to refresh the view. Scroll down to the middle of the icons list and select **fa-home** icon. This image will be displayed for the Home menu at run time. Note that you can select any image from the list or input its name directly in the *Image/Class* attribute if you do not want to bother selecting it from the image list. Hit the **Apply Changes** button to save your work.

3. On the main *List Details* page, click the **Create Entry** button to create a new menu item. Enter the following values against the specified properties. Do not select anything in the first attribute (*Parent List Entry*), because initially you will create level one entries that do not have parent entries. The target is either a page in the current application or any valid URL. Since the *Setup* menu entry itself is not associated to any application page, its *Target Type* is set to *No Target*.

Property	Value
Parent List Entry	No Parent List Item
Image/Class	fa-database
List Entry Label	Setup
Target Type	No Target

4. Using the button **Create and Create Another**, create three more level-1 entries as follows. After adding the last entry (Administration), click the *Create List Entry* button. The *Target Type* and *Page* properties inform Oracle APEX where to land when a menu item is clicked.

Parent List Entry	Image/Class	List Entry Label	Target Type	Page
No Parent List Item	fa-list-alt	Orders	Page in this Application	4
No Parent List Item	fa-table	Reports	Page in this Application	26
No Parent List Item	fa-cogs	Administration	No Target	-

These three entries along with the Setup entry (created in step 3) will form the main menu of our application and because of this reason we set *No Parent List Item* for all four entries. Note that *Setup* and *Administration* entries have no target, because these two entries are not directly linked to application pages. In the next step, you will create submenus under these two main entries to call respective pages.

5. Using the same process you executed in the previous step, create the following level-2 menu entries:

Parent List Entry	Image/Class	List Entry Label	Target Type	Page
Setup	fa-users	Manage Customers	Page in this Application	2
Setup	fa-shopping-cart	Manage Products	Page in this Application	3
Setup	fa-ellipsis-h	Reset Password	Page in this Application	65
Reports	fa-bar-chart	Graphical Reports	Page in this Application	26
Reports	fa-file-pdf-o	Advance Reports	Page in this Application	26
Administration	fa-sitemap	Application Segments	Page in this Application	60
Administration	fa-group	User Groups	Page in this Application	62
Administration	fa-male	Users	Page in this Application	63

The first three entries will come under the main *Setup* menu item. The *Reports* menu will contain two child entries (Graphical Reports and Advance Reports), while *Administration* will have 3 entries.

6. Now create level 3 entries. Note that the *Page* attribute for *Monthly Review Report* entry is set to zero, because it will be invoked through a print request you will configure in Chapter 9.

Parent List Entry	List Entry Label	Target Type	Page
Graphical Reports	Customer Orders	Page in this Application	17
Graphical Reports	Sales By Category/Products	Page in this Application	16
Graphical Reports	Sales by Category/Month	Page in this Application	5
Graphical Reports	Order Calendar	Page in this Application	10
Graphical Reports	Customer Map	Page in this Application	15
Graphical Reports	Product Order Tree	Page in this Application	19
Advance Reports	Monthly Review Report	Page in this Application	0
Advance Reports	Customer Invoice	Page in this Application	50

After creating the menu items list, you will see the first twenty entries on the *List Details* page. Use the pagination icon (provided at the bottom) to see the rest.

The first six entries will appear as submenu choices under *Graphical Reports* menu. Similarly, *Monthly Review Report* and *Customer Invoice* will be placed under *Advance Reports*. All the previous settings will setup a hierarchical navigation for your application, as shown in Figure 3-2.

3.2.2 Desktop App Reports List

The *Reports* list contains six links that lead to different graphical reports in your desktop application. You will utilize this list in Chapter 8 section 8.2

1. Go to *Shared Components | Navigation | Lists*. Click the **Create** button to create a new list.

2. Select **From Scratch** on the *Source* wizard screen and click **Next**. On the next screen, enter **Reports List** for *Name*, select **Static** as the list *Type*, and click **Next**.

3. Enter the following values in *Query or Static Values* screen. Initially, the wizard allows you to create five entries. The remaining entries and *Image/Class* properties are created and set after saving the first five.

List Entry Label	Target Page ID	Image/Class
Customer Orders	17	fa-bar-chart-o
Sales by Category and Product	16	fa-pie-chart
Sales by Category / Month	5	fa-line-chart
Order Calendar	10	fa-calendar
Customer Map	15	fa-globe
Product Order Tree	19	fa-sitemap
Monthly Review Report	0	fa-bar-chart-o
Customer Invoice	50	fa-print

4. Click **Next**, accept the default values in the next screen, and click the **Create List** button. You will be taken back to the Lists page, where you will see this new list.

5. Modify the list by clicking the **Reports List** name.

6. Click the **Create Entry** button to add the sixth entry. Enter **Product Order Tree** in *List Entry Label*. Set *Target Type* to **Page in this Application** and enter **19** in the *Page* attribute. Click the **Create and Create Another** button to add the final two entries, as shown in the table.

7. Modify each entry by clicking its name in the *List Details* interface and add image references, as shown in the table. Click the **Apply Changes** button after adding the image reference.

3.2.3 Order Wizard List

This is another utilization of lists. Rather than associating list items to pages in the application, you'll use it for visual representation. It will be used while creating orders in Chapter 7. In our application, we will create an order using a set of wizard steps in the following sequence:

- a) Identify Customer
- b) Select Items
- c) Order Summary

1. Go to *Shared Components | Navigation | Lists* and click the **Create** button.

2. Select the first option **From Scratch** and click **Next**.

3. Type **Order Wizard** in the *Name* box, set *Type* to **Static**, and click **Next**.

4. On the *Query or Static Values* screen, enter the following values and click **Next**.

	List Entry Label	Target Page ID or custom URL	
1	Identify Customer		∧
2	Select Items		∧
3	Order Summary		∧

5. Click the **Create List** button on the *Confirm* screen.

6. Click the newly created **Order Wizard** list in the *Lists* interface.

7. Edit each list item and set *Target Type* attribute to **No Target** for all three list items. The *No Target* value is set because this list is intended to display the current order wizard step the user is on, and not to call a page in the application. In the *Current List Entry* section, set *List Entry Current for Pages Type* to **Comma Delimited Page List** for the three list items, and set the *List Entry Current for Condition* attribute individually, as shown in the following table. Click the **Apply Changes** button to save the modifications.

Property	Identify Customer	Select Items	Order Summary
List Entry Current for Condition	11	12	14

Current List Entry

List Entry Current for Pages Type	Comma Delimited Page List ∨
List Entry Current for Condition	11

The *List Entry Current for Pages Type* attribute specifies when this list entry should be current. Based on the value of this attribute, you define a condition to evaluate. When this condition is true then the list item becomes current. The template associated with list item gives users a visual indication about the active list item. The following figure illustrates the use of Order Wizard list. Being the first step in the order wizard, the *Identify Customer* list item is marked as current (when Page 11 is called to enter a new order), while the remaining two are displayed as non-current. After selecting a customer, when you move on to the next step to select ordered items, the *Select Items* entry becomes current and the first and last entries become inactive.

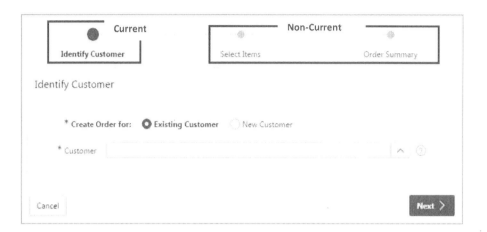

3.3 Desktop Navigation Bar

A navigation bar is used to link various pages within an application. Typically, a navigation bar is used to access Help pages and also carries a *Sign Out* link. The location of a navigation bar depends upon the associated page template. When you

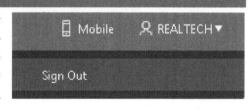

create a navigation bar, you specify an image name, label, display sequence, and target location (a URL or a page).

The navigation bar used in our application will have *Mobile* and *Sign Out* links. In addition, it will show the currently logged-in user associated to the *Sign Out* link. In this exercise, we are going to create just the mobile link, because the *Sign Out* entry was created automatically when we initially created the application in the previous chapter.

3.3.1 Mobile Entry

This navigation bar entry will take users to the home page of the mobile application. To create this entry, go to **Shared Components**, select the **Lists** option, and click **Desktop Navigation Bar**. This will bring up the default navigation bar carrying the sole logout entry. Click the **Create Entry** button to add some more entries using the following table. The page ID (in my case it is 30) defined for the mobile entry will be generated by App Builder wizard in Chapter 10, where you will create a mobile interface. After creating the mobile interface in that chapter, replace this ID with that of yours. By defining a parent entry (see the third column), the *Sign Out* entry appears as a submenu item. APP_USER and LOGOUT_URL are built-in substitution strings. The APP_USER substitution string holds the ID of the current user running the application, while LOGOUT_URL is an application-level attribute used to identify the logout URL. This is a URL that navigates the user to a logout page or optionally directly logs out a user. To use these substitution variables in your application properties, you have to prefix them with an & and postfix with a period.

Property	New Entry 1	New Entry 2	Modify Log Out Entry
Parent List Entry	No Parent List Item	No Parent List Item	&APP_USER.
Image/Class	fa-mobile	fa-user	-
List Entry Label	Mobile	&APP_USER.	Sign Out
Target Type	Page in this Application	No Target	URL
Page	30 *(in my scenario)*	-	-
URL Target	-	-	&LOGOUT_URL.

3.4 List of Values (LOV)

List of values is used to control the values displayed and limits the user's selection. You can define two types of lists: Static and Dynamic. A static list of values is based on predefined display and return values. A dynamic list of values is based on a SQL query, executed at runtime. In the following exercise, you will create both types of LOVs.

3.4.1 CATEGORIES LOV

In our application we have two integrated setups: Categories and Products. The application uses three categories. Each product in the application falls under one of these categories. This LOV is created with the intention to provide three static values to the user (while creating a product record) to choose a category to which the product belongs. This LOV is utilized in Chapter 6 section 6.4.2, and Chapter 10 section 10.8.1.

1. In Shared Components, click **Lists of Values** under the *Other Components* section.

2. Click the **Create** button.

3. Select the **From Scratch** option and click **Next**.

4. Enter **Categories** in the *Name* box, select the default **Static** type, and click **Next**.

5. Fill in the values as shown in the following figure and click the **Create List of Values** button.

Sequence	Display Value	Return Value
1	Mens	Mens
2	Womens	Womens
3	Accessories	Accessories

In the last step, you entered a pair of static *Display* and *Return* values. These entries will display in the order entered. *Return Value* does not display, but is the value that is returned as a user selection to the Application Express engine.

3.4.2 PRODUCTS WITH PRICE LOV

Similar to the categories list of value, this one also limits user's selection by displaying product names with prices during order creation. Here you'll generate the list dynamically with the help of a SQL statement. You will utilize this LOV in Chapter 7 section 7.4.2.

1. Once again, click the **Create** button in *Lists of Values*.

2. Select **From Scratch** and click **Next**.

3. Enter **Products with Price** in the *Name* box. This time, select the **Dynamic** *Type* and click **Next**.

4. In the *Query* box, enter the following query, which is also available in BookCode\Chapter3 folder. If you are new to SQL, then read Chapter 3 - *Retrieve Data From Database* in my free SQL ebook.

```
select apex_escape.html(product_name) || ' [$' || list_price || ']' d,
    product_id r
from demo_product_info
where product_avail = 'Y'
order by 1
```

5. Click **Create List of Values** button to finish the wizard.

APEX_ESCAPE.HTML

The function APEX_ESCAPE.HTML is used to protect against XSS (Cross Site Scripting) attacks. It replaces characters that have special meaning in HTML with their escape sequence.

It converts occurrence of & to &amp
It converts occurrence of " to &quot
It converts occurrence of < to &lt
It converts occurrence of > to &gt

3.4.3 STATES LOV

This is a dynamic LOV and is based on a SQL SELECT query to fetch State names from DEMO_STATES table. The query fetches both columns from the table. This LOV is used in Chapter 5 section 5.4.2 and Chapter 10 section 10.6.1, where it is attached to an item in an input form.

1. In *Lists of Values*, click the **Create** button.

2. Select the **From Scratch** option and click **Next**.

3. Enter **States** in the *Name* box, select **Dynamic** for its type, and click **Next**.

4. In the *Query* box type:
   **select initcap(state_name) display_value, st return_value
   from demo_states order by 1**

5. Click the **Create List of Values** button.

3.4.4 Y or N LOV

This LOV will be used in the Product setup module (Chapter 6 section 6.4.3) to specify whether the product is available.

1. In *Lists of Values*, click **Create**.

2. Select **From Scratch** and click **Next**.

3. Enter **Y or N** in the *Name* box, select **Static** as its *Type*, and click **Next**.

4. Fill in the values as shown in the following figure and click **Create List of Values**.

Sequence	Display Value	Return Value
1	Yes	Y
2	No	N

3.4.5 NEW OR EXISTING CUSTOMER LOV

This static list will be incorporated in the initial Order Wizard step (Chapter 7 Section 7.5.4) to select an existing customer or to create a new one.

1. In *Lists of Values*, click **Create**.

2. Select **From Scratch** and click **Next**.

3. Enter **NEW OR EXISTING CUSTOMER** in the *Name* box, select **Static** as its *Type*, and click **Next**.

4. Fill in the values as shown in the following figure and click the **Create List of Values** button.

Sequence	Display Value	Return Value
1	Existing Customer	EXISTING
2	New Customer	NEW

3.5 Images

You can reference images within your application by uploading them to the Images Repository. When you upload an image, you can specify whether it is available to all applications or a specific application. Images uploaded as shared components can be referenced throughout an application. They may include images for application menus or buttons or may represent icons that, when clicked, allow users to modify or delete data. One important point to remember here is that the images uploaded to the images repository should not be directly related to the application's data such as images of products and employees. Such images must be stored in the application's schema alongside the data to which the image is related. You'll follow this approach in Chapter 6 to save each product's image along with other information in a database table.

Application Express images are divided into two categories:
- **Workspace images** are available to all applications for a given workspace
- **Application images** are available for only one application

In the following set of steps, you'll add your application's logo to the images repository. The logo appears at the top of every page in the application.

1. In Shared Components, click **Static Application Files** under the *Files* section.

2. Click the **Upload File** button.

3. Click the **Choose Files** button and select *logo.png* file, which is available in the book code.

4. Click the **upload** button. After uploading the image, you need to tell Oracle APEX to use this file as your application logo. To pass this information, execute the following steps.

5. In Shared Components click **User Interface Attributes** under the *User Interface* section.

6. For *Logo Type*, select **Image**.

7. Enter **#APP_IMAGES#logo.png** in the *Logo* box. Note that you must use the correct case for the image file name and extension, else the logo will not be displayed at runtime. Click the **Apply Changes** button. The built-in substitution string (APP_IMAGES) is used to reference uploaded images, JavaScript, and cascading style sheets that are specific to a given application and are not shared over many applications. You must use this substitution string if you upload a file and make it specific to an application.

Summary

In this chapter, you created all the components required by the application with relevant references. These shared components were created declaratively with the help of Oracle APEX wizards to demonstrate yet another great feature of this technology to tackle redundancy. From the next chapter, you will create all the pages of your web application (starting with the Home page) and will see all these shared components in action. After creating an application page, you can see a list of all Shared Components utilized on that page by accessing its Shared Components tab ⬡ in the Page Designer.

Chapter 4

Prepare Application Dashboard

4.1 About the Home Page

Figure 4-1 – The Home Page

Every website on the Internet has a home page. Technically referred to as the default page, it is the page that comes up when you call a website without mentioning a specific page. For example, if you call Oracle's official website using the URL www.oracle.com, the first page you see is the default or home page of the website. It is the page that represents the objective of a website. Similar to a website, a web application also carries this page. By default, Oracle APEX creates this page along with a login page, for both desktop and mobile interfaces. The desktop login page, which you used to access the application in a previous chapter, doesn't require any modification or enhancement. It comes with out-of-the-box functionalities and utilizes current authentication scheme to process the login request. The Home page, on the other hand, is created as a blank slate and needs to be populate with content relevant to your application's theme. For instance, the Home page of your Sales Web Application (illustrated in Figure 4-1) will show stuff related to sales.

Let's experience the Oracle APEX declarative development environment by completing this page of our web application, which is a dashboard and holds six regions to present different views of sales data.

4.2 Modify the Home Page

Before you start the proceedings, I recommend to first take a look at Chapter 2 section 2.6 to acquaint yourself with the Page Designer interface. Once you're comfortable with that, execute the following steps to modify properties of the Home page.

1. Sign in to your workspace. Click **App Builder**, and then click the **Edit** icon ✎ under *Sales Web Application.*

2. Click the **Home** icon (if you're browsing the page in Icon view). This will bring up the Page Designer.

4.2.1 Modify Page Attributes

Modify *Name* and *Title* properties of the Home page with meaningful labels. The *Name* property gives the page a meaningful name for recognition, while the Application Express engine uses the title you specify here in place of the #TITLE# substitution string used in the page template. This title is inserted between the HTML tags <TITLE> and </TITLE>.

On the *Rendering* ▦ tab to your left, click the root node ▢ Page 1: Home to refresh the Property Editor (on the right side) with the main page properties. Set the properties mentioned in the following table and click the **Save** button (at the top-right corner). These are the properties that are usually enough to set for the main page. However, there are some more you must be curious to know about. Click a property in the *Property Editor* and then click the *Help* tab (in the Central pane) to see the purpose of that attribute. Each page in an application is recognized by a unique number, which is used for internal processing–for example, in a URL. By providing a unique name, you *visually* differentiate it from other application pages.

Property	Value
Name	Sales Web Application
Title	Sales Web Application

4.3 Create Regions

You put items (Text Field, Select List, Radio Group, and so on) on a page under a specific region. A region is an area on a page that serves as a container for content. You can create multiple regions to visually segregate different sections on a page and to group page elements. A region may carry a SQL report, static HTML content, items, buttons, and some other types you will utilize in this book. Each region can have its own template applied, which controls its appearance. The following sub-sections demonstrate how you can create multiple regions to present different information on a single page. Some of these regions will use Oracle JET Charts—a new feature incorporated in version 5.1. Charts in Oracle APEX have been completely revamped. Now Oracle APEX has integrated charting based on Oracle JavaScript Extension Toolkit (JET) charting library. Oracle JET Charts is a component of the Oracle JavaScript Extension Toolkit (JET), an open source toolkit based on modern JavaScript, CSS3, and HTML5 design and development principles. These charts are fully HTML5 capable and work on any modern browser regardless of platform, screen size, or features. Up to version 5, Oracle APEX used AnyChart charts that can be migrated using the Upgrade Application wizard.

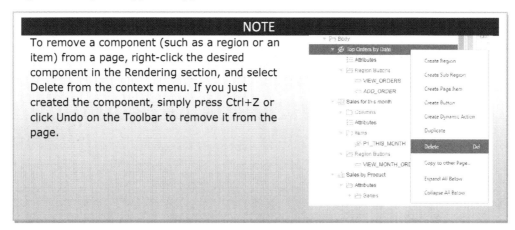

NOTE

To remove a component (such as a region or an item) from a page, right-click the desired component in the Rendering section, and select Delete from the context menu. If you just created the component, simply press Ctrl+Z or click Undo on the Toolbar to remove it from the page.

4.3.1 Top Orders by Date → (R-1)

Let's create the first region on the Home page. This region will display top five orders by date from the database using a bar chart. The chart is populated using a SQL SELECT statement, which fetches summarized sales figures for each date from the Orders table.

On the *Rendering* tab, right-click **Regions** Regions, and select **Create Region** from the context menu to create a new region. This will create a new folder named *Content Body* and will place a new region </> **New** under it. The region will also have a child node (named *Attributes*) of its own. The *New* region contains the properties common to all regions, whereas the *Attributes* component contains the properties specific to the region's type. For example, the properties of a *Static Content* type region are different from a Chart region. Click the </> **New** node and set the following properties in the Property Editor on the right side. After setting the second attribute (*Type*), you will be informed through the Messages tab that there are some errors on the page. Ignore them! These messages relate to some mandatory properties you will set accordingly in subsequent sections.

	Property	Value
1	Title	Top Orders by Date
2	Type	Chart
3	SQL Query	select to_char(o.order_timestamp,'Mon DD, YYYY') order_day, SUM(o.order_total) sales from demo_orders o group by to_char(o.order_timestamp,'Mon DD, YYYY'), order_timestamp order by 2 desc nulls last fetch first 5 rows only
4	Start New Row	Yes *(default)*
5	Column	Automatic *(default)*
6	Column Span	4
7	Body Height *(under Template Options)*	240px
Click the Attributes folder under the new region and set the following properties:		
8	Type	Bar
9	Orientation	Horizontal
Click the New sub-node under *Series* and set the following properties:		
10	Type *(under Source)*	Region Source
11	Label	ORDER_DAY
12	Value	SALES
13	Type *(under Link)*	Redirect to Page in this application
Click No Link Defined under *Target* and set the following properties in the Link Builder dialog box:		
14	Type	Page in this application
15	Page	4

The first property provides a meaningful title to the region–see Figure 4-1. It is good practice to always provide a unique title to every region on a page. The title not only describes the purpose of a region, but also distinguishes it from others in the Page Designer. If you are familiar with HTML and CSS, then you can also style this property by adding some HTML & CSS elements, like this:

```
<span style="color:blue"><i><b>Top Orders by Date</b></i></span>
```

In the second attribute, we set the *Type* of this region to *Chart*, because we want to display sales data graphically. By default, a new region is assigned the type *Static Content* with an empty source text, which is often used to explain the purpose of a page or a page component. For example, the *About* section on the right side of the App Builder interface is a static content region whose source is the displayed text. The third attribute is a SQL SELECT statement, which fetches summarized sales data from the DEMO_ORDERS table. The database applications created in Oracle APEX use a layout (comprising 12 columns) to position page elements. The fourth attribute (*Start New Row*) used in this region is set to *Yes* (which is the default) to put the region on a new row. Compare this value with the next region (*Sales for This Month*), where it is set to *No* to place that region adjacent to this one. The value *Automatic* in the *Column* attribute (5) automatically finds a column position for the region. Since there exists no elements on the current row, column number 1 will be used as the starting place to position this region. As you can see in Figure 4-2, there are three regions on a single row. Equally divided in a 12 columns layout, each region spans 4 columns and this is the value we will set for all the six regions on the Home page. The first region will span from column number 1 to 4, the second one from 5 to 8, and the third one from 9 to 12–see Figure 4-2. We also defined the height of this region in attribute 7, which you can set by clicking the *Template Options*. Then, in the *Attributes* folder (8 and 9) you set the *Type* of this chart to horizontal bar. When you set the region type to *Chart* (2), a *Series* folder is placed under *Attributes* with a *New* sub-node under it. In this node you specify *Type* (10) for the *Series*, which defaults to *SQL Query*. Since an SQL Query has already been defined, we set it to *Region Source*, which points to the region's SQL Query defined in the third attribute. By default, a chart is created with one series (named *New*), but you can add more (see Chapter 8 section 8.3 steps 5 and 6). The chart's *Label* attribute (11) is set to *ORDER_DAY* column to display values from this column as labels and its *Value* (12) is set to *SALES* to show sales figures. You can also define links on charts (as done in properties 13-15) that let you call another application page for browsing details. When you click *No Link Defined* under *Target*, a small window titled *Link Builder* comes up, where you specify details of the target page. Once you set the link type to "*Redirect to Page in this Application*", a property named *Target* appears, where you provide the ID of the target application page you want to link with the chart (properties 14 and 15). The *Template* property (not indicated in the previous table) is set to *Standard* by default, which forms a border around the region and displays the region's title across the top.

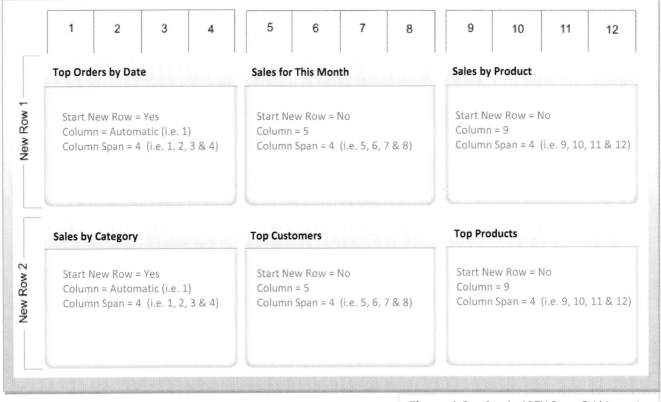

Figure 4-2 – Oracle APEX Page Grid Layout

Oracle APEX enables you to test your work from time to time. For example, after completing this region you can save and run the page (by clicking the *Save and Run Page* button appearing at the top-right corner) to check how the region appears on it. At this stage, your Home page will be carrying just one region (*Top Orders by Date*) containing a bar chart. If you click any bar in the chart, the application tries to open Page 4 and throws an error, because the page doesn't exist. After completing Page 4 (Orders) in Chapter 7, when you run the Home page and click any of these links, the orders interactive report (Page 4) will appear.

4.3.2 Sales For This Month ➜ (R-2)

As the name implies, this region will present sales figures in graphical format (using a Badge List) along with number of orders placed for the current month. The list is dynamically rendered based on a SQL Statement each time the page is viewed.

On the *Rendering* tab to your left, right-click **Regions**, and select **Create Region** from the context menu. Again, a new region will be created under the previous one. Set the following properties for this region in the *Property Editor*.

	Property	Value
1	Title	Sales for This Month
2	Type	Classic Report

3	SQL Query	select sum(o.order_total) total_sales,
		    count(distinct o.order_id) total_orders,
		    count(distinct o.customer_id) total_customers
		from demo_orders o
		where order_timestamp >=
		    to_date(to_char(sysdate,'YYYYMM')||'01','YYYYMMDD')

4	Start New Row	No
5	Column	5
6	Column Span	4
7	Body Height (*under Template Options*)	240px

A *Classic Report* is a simple Oracle APEX report, which is based on a custom SQL SELECT statement or a PL/SQL function. In this exercise, we used it to fetch the desired data set. Later on, we will transform it to present the fetched data in graphical format. When you specify a SQL Query for a region, all columns you define in the query appear in a separate folder (*Columns*) under that region.

Next, create a hidden page item by right-clicking the *Sales for this Month* region and selecting **Create Page Item** from the context menu. A new folder named *Items* Items will be created with a new item P1_NEW. Select the new item and set the following properties:

Property	Value
Name	P1_THIS_MONTH
Type	Hidden
Value Protected	Yes *(default)*
Type *(under Source)*	PL/SQL Expression
PL/SQL Expression	to_char(sysdate ,'MM')||'01'||to_char(sysdate ,'YYYY')

The page item *P1_THIS_MONTH* is a hidden item and is used in the next section. It is added to store first day of the current month. You create hidden items on a page to store some values for behind-the-scene processing. This one evaluates current month using the *sysdate* function. Hidden items can be seen in the Page Designer, but they do not appear on the page at run time. Note that whenever you refer to a page item in links, you present it as a substitution string, which is preceded with an & and terminated with a period–see the *Value* property in serial 6 below. The *Value Protected* property specifies whether the item is protected. The *Yes* value prevents the value stored in the item from being manipulated when the page is posted. Note that if the Order Date column on Page 4 is rendered as 09-JAN-2017, then you will have to change the PL/SQL Expression like this:

'01-'\|\|to_char(sysdate ,'MON')\|\|'-'\|\|to_char(sysdate ,'YYYY')

In the *Rendering* section, expand the **Columns** folder under *Sales for This Month* region, and click the **TOTAL_SALES** column. This will refresh the *Properties* pane to show properties of the currently selected column. Set the following properties for TOTAL_SALES to transform it into a link.

	Property	Value
1	Type	Link
2	Format Mask	5,234.10
Click No Link Defined under *Target* and set the following properties:		
3	Type	Page in this application
4	Page	4
5	Name	IRGTE_ORDER_DATE
6	Value	&P1_THIS_MONTH. *(do not forget to add the trailing period)*
7	Clear Cache	RIR,4
8	Reset Pagination	Yes (default)
Click OK to close the **Link Builder - Target** dialog box		
9	Link Text	#TOTAL_SALES# *(select this value using the Quick Pick button ☰)*

In the first attribute (*Type*), you specify that the column is to be displayed as a link. The *Format Mask* property (2) is actually a list of values that shows some common currency and date/time formats when you click the up-arrow. When you select a format from this list, its mask appears in the property's text box. In the current scenario, you selected 5,234.10 as the format mask for TOTAL_SALES column, which produces the mask 999G999G999G999G990D00. In this mask, 9 denotes an optional digit, 0 a required digit, G stands for thousand separator, and D is for decimal point. Here, the sales value will be displayed with thousand separators and two decimal places. The remaining properties actually define the link. First, you specify that the link should call a page in the current application (property # 3) followed by the target page number (property # 4). To call another application page, it is suffice to transform a column into a link by setting these three values (*Link, Page in this application*, and *Page Number*). Recall that in the previous region you formed a similar kind of link. The *Name* (5) and *Value* (6) properties form a filter argument to display current month's order on the target page (Page 4 – Orders, to be created in Chapter 7). In the current scenario, we used just one name/value pair to filter the interactive report on the target page. However, this section allows you to set as many filters as you want. Each time you provide a value, another row is appended, thus allowing you to enter another pair of name/value. You can use this section to also specify target page's items in the *Name* column and can set their values using the *Value* box. For example, to set a customer's credit limit item's value on the target page, enter the name of that item (P7_CREDIT_LIMIT) in the *Name* box and type the corresponding value (5000) in the *Value* box. This way, when you call the target page, the value (5000) appears in the credit limit item. The *Clear Cache* attribute (7) resets the interactive report on Page 4. The eighth attribute resets pagination of the target page. The *Link Text* attribute (9) is set to Total Sales, which specifies the column to be displayed as a link. Note that column names are enclosed in # symbol when you specify them in *Link Text* attribute. This is a mandatory attribute whose value is selected using the *Quick Pick* button appearing next to it.

At run-time the link is formed like this:
Syntax: f?p=&APP_ID.:Page:Sessionid::NO:RP,RIR,4:IRGTE_(itemname):itemvalue (held in &P1_THIS_MONTH item)
Formed Link: f?p=64699:4:8824748217892::NO:RP,RIR,4:IRGTE_ORDER_DATE:01012017

The following table defines the parameters used in the above URL:

Argument	Explanation
&APP_ID.	The first argument in the URL is reserved for application ID (2444). The expression used here is called a substitution string that holds the application ID. Instead of hard-coding application IDs, Oracle APEX uses this substitution string to make an application more portable. Note that substitution strings are always preceded with an "&" and end with a period.
:	The colon special character is used in the APEX URL as an argument separator. Since the URL contains no REQUEST argument, the position of this argument is left empty–see the additional colon before the debug argument (NO).
4	This is the target page (Page 4 – Orders) we are calling in the URL.
Sessionid	The number (113289530924899) appearing in the URL is the session ID of our application and is used to create links between application pages by maintaining the same session state among them.
NO	References the debug flag, which is used to display application processing details. The value NO says do not enter the debug mode.
RP,RIR,4	Placed in the URL's ClearCache position, this argument resets pagination for the interactive report on Page 4. *RP* stands for *Reset Pagination* and *RIR* for *Reset Interactive Report*. Pagination provides the end user with information about the number of rows and the current position within the result set. You control how pagination displays by making selections from *Pagination Type* attribute in the Property Editor. The clear cache section can have RIR or CIR or RP to reset, clear, or reset the pagination of the primary default reports of all interactive report regions on the target page.
IRGTE_ORDER_DATE	This argument is used in the *itemNames* position. The IR (Interactive Report) string is used along with the *greater than and equal to* operator (GTE), followed by an item name (ORDER_DATE - an item on Page 4). This argument acts as a filter and is used in conjunction with the *itemValue* (&P1_THIS_MONTH. mentioned underneath) to only display current month's orders. In simple words it says: *The order date of the interactive report is greater than or equal to.*

&P1_THIS_MONTH.	Used in the *itemValue* position, the value stored in this hidden item is forwarded to the target page. To create a filter on an interactive report in a link, use the string *IR<operator>_<target column alias>* in the *ItemNames* section of the URL and pass the filter value in the corresponding location in the *ItemValues* section of the URL. See section 2.7 in Chapter 2 for further details on Oracle APEX f?p syntax. Other operators you can use to filter an interactive report include:
	• EQ = Equals (the default operator)
• LT = Less than
• GT = Greater than
• LTE = Less than or equal to
• GTE = Greater than or equal to
• LIKE = SQL LIKE operator
• N = Null
	To apply the filter, you must use correct date format mask in the SQL query for order_timestamp column. For example, if the Order Date column on Page 4 appears as 01-JAN-2017, then you must use 'DD/MON/YYYY' format mask.

Select the **TOTAL_CUSTOMERS** column and set the *Type* attribute of this column to **Hidden Column**. By setting a column's *Type* property to *Hidden*, you make it invisible at run-time. Click the **Attributes** folder under *Sales for This Month* region. Switch its *Template* from *Standard* to **Badge List**, click the *Template Options* and set *Badge Size* to **128px**, *Layout* to **Span Horizontally**, and click **OK**. By setting these region properties, the derived one row summarized report will be presented as a badge list, spanned horizontally. Also, set *Pagination Type* to **No Pagination (Show All Rows)**. Often only a certain number of rows of a report display on a page. To include additional rows, the application user needs to navigate to the next page of the report. Pagination provides the user with information about the number of rows and the current position within the result set. Pagination also defines the style of links or buttons used to navigate to the next or previous page.

Click **Save and Run Page** button to see this region with two badges on it displaying current month's sales and number of orders placed. The first badge acts as a link and leads you to Page 4 to display details of the summarized data. Since Page 4 will be created in Chapter 7, once again you will get *Page Not Found* message if you click this badge.

4.3.3 Sales by Product ➔ (R-3)

This region is intended to show sale figures for individual products using a pie chart. You see those figures when you move the mouse pointer over the pie slices. Create another region as mentioned in the previous exercises, and set the following properties.

If you are creating a multi-series chart, then you can use legend (9) to identify each series on the chart. Using the legend properties you can specify whether to display it, and if so, where it should be placed on the chart. You will use these properties in Chapter 8.

	Property	Value
1	Title	Sales by Product
2	Type	Chart
3	SQL Query	SELECT p.product_name||' [$'||p.list_price||']' product, SUM(oi.quantity * oi.unit_price) sales FROM demo_order_items oi, demo_product_info p WHERE oi.product_id = p.product_id GROUP BY p.product_id, p.product_name, p.list_price ORDER BY p.product_name desc
4	Start New Row	No
5	Column	9
6	Column Span	4
7	Body Height (under Template Options)	240px
Click the **Attributes** sub-node under the new region and set the following properties:		
8	Type	Pie
9	Show (under Legend)	No
Click the **New** sub-node under *Series* and set the following properties:		
10	Type (under Source)	Region Source
11	Label	PRODUCT
12	Value	SALES

4.3.4 Sales by Category ➔ (R-4)

This region will present sale figures for each product category. Note that there are three categories in the products table: Men, Women, and Accessories. Each product in the DEMO_PRODUCT_INFO table belongs to one of these categories. This time, we will add a region using the drag and drop feature provided in Oracle APEX. Following the figure illustrated below, drag the **Chart** icon from the *Regions* gallery and drop it just under the *Top Orders by Date* region. A chart region will appear with relevant properties. After placing the chart region at its proper location, set the properties presented in the table provided after the illustration.

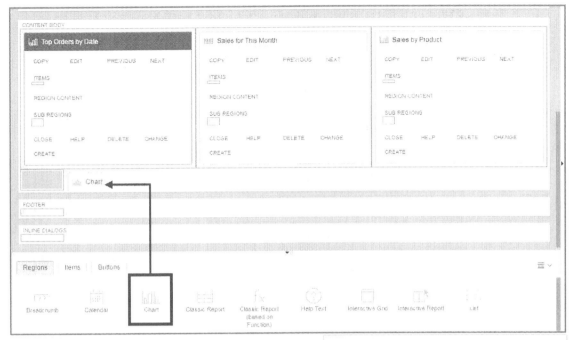

Figure 4-3 – Drag Item in Page Designer

Here are the modified region properties. Note that I changed the default chart color (13) using the Color Picker tool.

	Property	Value
1	Title	Sales by Category
2	Type	Chart *(this time it will be set by default)*

3	SQL Query	SELECT p.category Category, sum(o.order_total) Sales
		FROM demo_orders o, demo_order_items oi,
		          demo_product_info p
		WHERE o.order_id = oi.order_id AND
		          oi.product_id = p.product_id
		GROUP BY category
		ORDER BY 2 desc

4	Start New Row	Yes
5	Column	1
6	Column Span	4
7	Body Height *(under Template Options)*	240px
Click the Attributes sub-node under the new region and set the following properties:		
8	Type	Bar
9	Show *(under Legend)*	No
Click the New sub-node under *Series* and set the following properties:		
10	Type *(under Source)*	Region Source
11	Label	CATEGORY
12	Value	SALES
13	Color *(under Appearance)*	#18A0C2

4.3.5 Top Customers Region → (R-5)

This region will display top six customers with highest orders and will present the information in text format. Create a new region by dragging the **Classic Report** icon from the gallery and dropping it under the *Sales by Category* region. The source of a *Classic Report* is a SQL query. Each time the page is rendered, Oracle APEX evaluates the query and displays the result within the region. Once you specify row and column properties using the following table, the region will appear next to the *Sales by Category* region.

	Property	Value
1	Title	Top Customers
2	Type	Classic Report *(should be already set)*

3	SQL Query	SELECT b.cust_last_name || ', ' || b.cust_first_name
		     || ' - '|| count(a.order_id) ||' Order(s)' customer_name,
		     SUM(a.ORDER_TOTAL) order_total, b.customer_id **id**
		FROM demo_orders a, DEMO_CUSTOMERS b
		WHERE a.customer_id = b.customer_id
		GROUP BY b.customer_id, b.cust_last_name || ', '
		     || b.cust_first_name
		ORDER BY NVL(SUM(a.ORDER_TOTAL),0) DESC

4	Start New Row	No
5	Column	5
6	Column Span	4
7	Body Height *(under Template Options)*	240px

On the *Rendering* tab, expand the **Columns** folder under the *Top Customers* region, and click the **CUSTOMER_NAME** column. Set the following properties to transform this column into a link. The *#ID#* substitution string references the third column in the previous SELECT query. Just like you use substitution strings to reference a page item, the standard procedure in Oracle APEX to refer to a column value is to enclose it between the # symbols.

	Property	Value
8	Type	Link
Click No Link Defined under *Target* and set the following properties:		
9	Type	Page in this application
10	Page	7
11	Name	P7_CUSTOMER_ID
12	Value	#ID#
13	Clear Cache	7
Click OK to close the Link Builder - Target dialog box		
14	Link Text	#CUSTOMER_NAME# *(select this value using the Quick Pick button ≣)*

In this table, we specified properties about a link we want to create. The purpose of setting these properties is to place hyperlinks on customer name column to provide drill-down capability. We specified the CUSTOMER_NAME column in the *Link Text* attribute. When you run this page, each customer's name appears as a hyperlink, clicking which calls customer's profile page (Page 7). We set *Page* attribute to 7, which is the page we want to navigate to. We also forwarded the customer's ID (#ID#) to Page 7. The value P7_CUSTOMER_ID refers to an item on Page 7 that will be populated with the value held in #ID#. It is forwarded to Page 7 from the Home page to display profile of the selected customer.

Click the **ORDER_TOTAL** column and set *Format Mask* to **$5,234.10**. Select the **ID** column and set the *Type* property to **Hidden Column** to hide this column at run-time.

Click the **Attributes** node under this region to set the following properties:

Property	Value
Pagination Type	No Pagination *(Show All Rows)*
Maximum Row to Process *(under Performance)*	6
Type *(under Heading)*	None

Pagination is suppressed since we want to see only six records in the region. We also set *Heading Type* to *None* to suppress column headings.

Click **Save and Run Page** button to test the progress.

4.3.6 Top Products Region ➔ (R-6)

Add another classic report region just like the one you created above. This region is similar to *Top Customers* and displays six top selling products.

	Property	Value
1	Title	Top Products
2	Type	Classic Report
3	SQL Query	SELECT p.product_name||' - '||SUM(oi.quantity)||' x' ||to_char(p.list_price,'L999G99')||'' product, SUM(oi.quantity * oi.unit_price) sales, p.product_id FROM demo_order_items oi, demo_product_info p WHERE oi.product_id = p.product_id GROUP BY p.Product_id, p.product_name, p.list_price ORDER BY 2 desc
4	Start New Row	No
5	Column	9
6	Column Span	4
7	Body Height *(under Template Options)*	240px

Expand the *Columns* folder and click the **PRODUCT** column to set the following properties:

	Property	Value
8	Type	Link
Click No Link Defined under *Target* and set the following properties:		
9	Type	Page in this application
10	Page	6
11	Name	P6_PRODUCT_ID
12	Value	#PRODUCT_ID#
13	Clear Cache	6
Click OK to close the Link Builder - *Target* dialog box		
14	Link Text	#PRODUCT#

Click the **SALES** column and set its *Format Mask* to **$5,234.10**. Select the **PRODUCT_ID** column and set its *Type* property to **Hidden Column**.

Click the **Attributes** folder for this region to set the following properties:

Property	Value
Pagination Type	No Pagination (Show All Rows)
Maximum Row to Process (under *Performance*)	6
Type (under *Heading*)	None

Click the **Save and Run Page** button to see how all the six regions appear on the Home page.

4.4 Create Buttons

After creating all the regions, your next task is to create buttons on top of each region. These buttons provide drill-down functionality and take user to relevant pages to dig further details for the provided summarized information. Some of these regions will have a pair of buttons (add and view) to create a new record and to browse further details of the provided information. For instance, if you click the *Add Order* button in the *Top Order by Date* region, you will be redirected to Page 11 to add a new order.

4.4.1 View Orders Button ➔ (B-1)

This button is used to view a list carrying all orders. To create this button, right-click the **Top Orders by Date** region and select the **Create Button** option from the context menu. This way, the button will be created in the selected region. A new node *Region Buttons* will be added with a ⊝ New button. The *Button Position* property provides you with over a dozen values. The best way to understand the other options is to try each one to see its effect. Set the following properties for the new button.

78

Property	Value
Button Name	VIEW_ORDERS
Label	View Orders *(appears as a tooltip when you move over the button)*
Region	Top Orders by Date
Button Position	Edit *(try other options as well to observe different positions)*
Button Template	Icon *(the button will be displayed as an icon)*
Icon CSS Classes	fa-chevron-right *(the name of an icon residing in APEX's repository)*
Action	Redirect to Page in this Application
Target	Type = Page in this application Page = 4

4.4.2 Add Order Button ➔ (B-2)

This one calls Order Wizard (to be created in Chapter 7) to place a new order. Right-click **Region Buttons** under the *Top Orders by Date* region and select **Create Button** to add another button under this region. Set the following properties for this new button:

Property	Value
Button Name	ADD_ORDER
Label	Enter New Order
Region	Top Orders by Date
Button Position	Edit
Button Template	Icon
Icon CSS Classes	fa-plus
Action	Redirect to Page in this Application
Target	Type = Page in this application Page = 11 Clear Cache=11

4.4.3 View Orders For This Month Button ➔ (B-3)

This button will drill-down into current month's order details. As illustrated in the following figure, drag an icon button from the *Buttons* gallery and drop it in the **EDIT** position under the *Sales for this Month* region. A new button will be added to this region. Select it and set the properties mentioned just after the illustration. The link properties set here are similar to those set earlier in section 4.3.2.

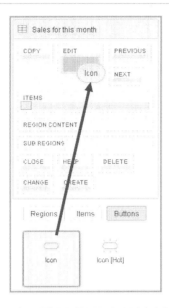

Property	Value
Button Name	VIEW_MONTH_ORDERS
Label	View Orders for This Month
Region	Sales for This Month
Button Position	Edit *(already set)*
Button Template	Icon *(already set)*
Icon CSS Classes	fa-chevron-right
Action	Redirect to Page in this Application
Target	Type = Page in this Application Page = 4 Name = IRGTE_ORDER_DATE Value = &P1_THIS_MONTH. Clear Cache = RIR,4

4.4.4 View Customers Button ➔ (B-4)

You'll place two buttons in the *Top Customers* region. Create these buttons using either of the two methods applied above and set respective properties as mentioned below. The first button will be used to view a list of customers on Page 2 of the application.

Property	Value
Button Name	VIEW_CUSTOMERS
Label	View Customers
Region	Top Customers
Button Position	Edit
Button Template	Icon
Icon CSS Classes	fa-chevron-right
Action	Redirect to Page in this Application
Target	Type = Page in this Application Page = 2

4.4.5 Add Customer Button ➔ (B-5)

This button is used to add a new customer record. When clicked, it will call Page 7 (Customers – to be created in the next chapter). The target page will appear on top of the Home page (as a modal dialog) carrying a blank form to enter new customer's credentials.

Property	Value
Button Name	ADD_CUSTOMER
Label	Add Customer
Region	Top Customers
Button Position	Edit
Button Template	Icon
Icon CSS Classes	fa-plus
Action	Redirect to Page in this Application
Target	Type = Page in this application Page = 7 Clear Cache = 7

4.4.6 View Products Button ➔ (B-6)

Create the following two buttons in the *Top Products* region. The first one leads you to the main products page to display a list of all products.

Property	Value
Button Name	VIEW_PRODUCTS
Label	View Products
Region	Top Products
Button Position	Edit
Button Template	Icon
Icon CSS Classes	fa-chevron-right
Action	Redirect to Page in this Application
Target	Type = Page in this Application Page = 3

4.4.7 Add Product Button ➜ (B-7)

This one calls Page 6 to add a new product.

Property	Value
Button Name	ADD_PRODUCT
Label	Add Product
Region	Top Products
Button Position	Edit
Button Template	Icon
Icon CSS Classes	fa-plus
Action	Redirect to Page in this Application
Target	Type = Page in this Application Page = 6 Clear Cache = 6

At this stage, all the seven buttons are placed at their proper locations with the expected functionalities and are ready for partial test. To remind you again, these buttons will be productive only after creating all relevant pages indicated in their respective *Target* properties.

Test Your Work

Click the **Save and Run Page** button to see the Home page, which should now look similar to the one illustrated in Figure 4-1 at the beginning of this chapter.

Summary

Congratulations! You've created your first professional looking page in Oracle APEX. In this chapter, you were provided with the flavor of declarative development where you added contents to a blank page using simple procedures. You also learned how to modify properties to customize the look and feel of this page. This is the uniqueness and beauty of Oracle Application Express that allows you to create pages rapidly without writing tons of code. The following list reminds you of Oracle APEX features you learned in this chapter:

- *Region* – You added six regions to the Home page to display different types of contents. You used different types of charts, badge list, and classic reports to populate these regions via simple SQL statements.
- *Grid Layout* – You learned how to arrange multiple regions on a page using Oracle APEX's 12 columns grid layout.
- *URL & Links* – Oracle APEX makes it fairly easy to link application pages together by setting a handful of properties. You also got an idea about how Oracle APEX formulates a URL and passes values to the target page using a handful of link properties.
- *Buttons* – A button can also be used to link application pages. You created a few buttons to access different application pages.

In the next chapter, you will learn about Interactive Grid (a new feature in Oracle APEX 5.1) and how to create web forms to take user input.

Chapter 5

Managing Customers

5.1 About Customer Management

Whenever you create a sales application you add a mandatory customer management module to it. In this setup, you maintain profiles of customers including their IDs, names, and addresses. This information is then used in several reports–for example, customer invoices. Every new customer is provided with a unique ID, either manually or automatically, by a built-in process. In this book these IDs will be generated automatically through a database object called a *Sequence*. Using the information from this module you can analyze a business from the perspective of customers. For example, you can evaluate how much business you have done with your customers either by location or by product, as you did in the previous chapter where you created the *Top Customers* region. In this chapter, you will create a setup to manage customers' profiles that will allow you to:

- Browse and search customer records
- Modify customers profile
- Add record of a new customer to the database
- Remove a customer from the database

This module is based on a table named DEMO_CUSTOMERS, which was created by the App Builder with the packaged sales application. It contains some seed data for testing purpose. In this chapter, you'll create two pages with the help of Oracle APEX wizard to view and edit customers' information. The first one (Page 2 Figure 5-1) is an interactive grid, which displays a list of all customers from the aforementioned database table using a SQL SELECT query. The second one (Page 7 Figure 5-3) is an input form to receive details of a new customer, modify the record of an existing customer, and delete one from the database. To keep data integrity, those customers who have some existing orders cannot be removed from the database. Each customer's name appears as a link in the interactive grid. When you click the name of a customer, the form page appears with complete profile of the selected customer. Let's get our hands dirty with some practical work to learn some more about the exciting declarative development environment offered by Oracle Application Express.

INTERACTIVE GRID

Up to version 5.0 APEX used the Interactive Report feature to present data in a tabular form. Now in version 5.1, you are provided with a new feature called an Interactive Grid, which is similar to the Interactive Report but allows you to manipulate data simply by clicking on a cell and editing its value. This functionality is the major difference between the two. The Interactive Grid includes every feature that the IR used to deliver. It introduces fixed headers, frozen columns, scroll pagination, multiple filters, sorting, aggregates, computations, and more. It is designed to support all item types and item type plug-ins. One more important thing about the Interactive Grid is that you can create mater-detail relationships to any number of levels deep and across. See section 5.6 in this chapter for further details.

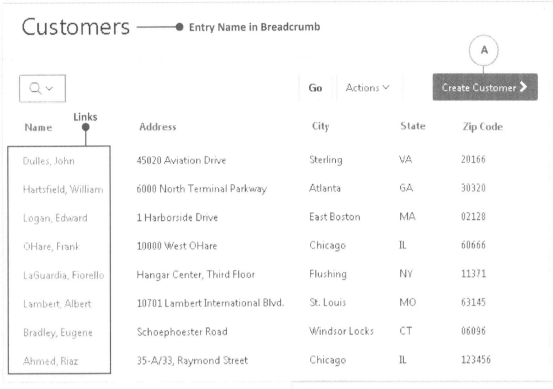

Figure 5-1 – Customers Interactive Grid Page

5.2 Create Pages to Manage Customers

The Home page of our application was created by the App Builder wizard at the time when the application was created. The rest of the pages in this application will be created manually with the help of wizards and copy utility. In this chapter, you will make use of Oracle APEX wizard to create pages for this setup by answering simple questions on different wizard screens. You can always move back to a previous wizard step by clicking the *Previous* button provided at the bottom of each screen. The following instructions step you through to create application pages via wizard.

1. In the main App Builder interface, click the Sales Web Application's **Edit** icon, and then click the **Create Page** button. You'll use this button throughout this book to create new application pages. If you want to delete an application page, open it in the Page Designer by clicking its name. Then, select *Delete* from the *Utilities* menu , which appear at the top-right.

2. Click the **Report** option . The initial wizard screen allows you to select a single option from a collection of multiple choices. We selected the *Report* option because the first page of this module will display a report of customers in an interactive grid.

3. On the next wizard screen, click **Interactive Grid** . This screen presents sub-categories of reports and requires a single selection the report will base on. The option you selected here means an interactive grid will act as a report to display all customers from the database.

85

4. In the next wizard step, set the following properties for the interactive grid page and click **Next**.

Property	Value
Page Number	2
Page Name	Customers
Page Mode	Normal
Breadcrumb	Breadcrumb
Parent Entry	No Parent Entry
Entry Name	Customers

In Application Express each page is identified with a unique number. The main page of this module (carrying an interactive grid) will be recognized by number 2, whereas the form page (to be created next) will have number 7. Just like numbers, a page is provided with a unique *name* for visual recognition. You can recognize a page by its name in the App Builder interface. The *Page Mode* property specifies how you want to see a page. It has three options: *Normal*, *Modal Dialog*, and *Non-Modal Dialog*. New pages created in Oracle APEX default to *Normal*. When you call a normal page, it simply replaces an existing page appearing in your browser. A non-modal page opens in a new browser window. To see an example of a non-modal page, click the *SQL Workshop* menu appearing at the top of your browser and select *SQL Commands* from the drop-down menu. In *SQL Commands*, click the *Find Tables* button. The page that pops up is called a non-modal page. A modal dialog page, on the other hand, is a stand-alone page, which appears on top of its calling page and doesn't allow users to do anything else unless it is closed. A modal page can be displayed only on top of another page. A breadcrumb shared component was created by the App Builder when you created this application earlier (see *Shared Components > Navigation > Breadcrumbs*). In this step, you selected the same breadcrumb component (fourth property value in the above table) and added an entry name (Customers) to it. Take a look at Figure 5-1 and see where the provided entry name appears in the breadcrumb region. A breadcrumb is a hierarchical list of links. It indicates where the user is within the application from a hierarchical perspective. Users can click a specific breadcrumb link to instantly view a page. You use breadcrumbs as a second level of navigation at the top of each page. If you want to create a hierarchy, select the Setup menu entry as the Parent Entry.

5. On the *Navigation Menu* wizard screen, set *Navigation Preference* to **Identify an existing navigation menu entry for this page**, set *Existing Navigation Menu Entry* to **Setup**, and click **Next**. This step will highlight the *Setup* entry in the main navigation menu (created in Chapter 3, section 3.2.1) when this page is accessed.

6. On the *Report Source* screen, set the following properties and click **Next**.

Property	Value
Editing Enabled	No
Source Type	Table
Table/View Owner	*accept the displayed value*
Table/View Name	DEMO_CUSTOMERS (table)

We disabled the most significant editing feature of the interactive grid because we will use a separate form to modify customers' records. You will see an example of editing records in an interactive grid later in this chapter. In the *Source Type* attribute we specified to use a database table data to populate this interactive grid. Next, you selected the default value appearing in *Table/View Owner* attribute. This is usually the database schema to which you are connected. Once you select a schema, all tables within that schema are populated in the *Table/View Name* drop-down list from where you select a table–DEMO_CUSTOMERS in the current scenario whose data will be displayed in the interactive grid. Note that in the current scenario you can select only one table from the provided list. When you choose a table, all the columns from that table are selected (moved to the right pane). For this exercise, leave the following columns in the right pane and exclude others by moving them to the left pane using Ctrl+click and the left arrow ⟨ icon. Here are the columns we want to *show* in the interactive grid.

Cust_First_Name, Cust_Last_Name, Cust_Street_Address1,
Cust_Street_Address2, Cust_City, Cust_State, and **Cust_Postal_Code**

7. Click the **Create** button to finish the report page creation process.

The page is created and its structure is presented in the Page Designer. The only significant aspect of this page is the *Customers* Interactive Grid region under the *Rendering > Regions > Content Body* folder to your left. The wizard created this region with all the columns you specified in step 6–see the *SQL Query* box in the Page Designer. All these columns appear under the *Columns* folder. The properties in the Interactive grid's *Attributes* folder control how an interactive grid works. For example, developers use these properties to determine if end-users can edit the underlying data, configure report pagination, create error messages, configure the toolbar and use download options, control if and how users can save an interactive grid, and add Icon and Detail Views to the toolbar. You will go through these properties later in this chapter. For now, walk around the Page Designer to observe page components and relevant properties.

Click the **Application 64699** breadcrumb at top-left to leave the Page Designer interface. Note that the ID of my application is 64699, so I will use it throughout this book to reference my application. In the next set of steps you will create a new page. This page will carry a form to add, modify, and delete customers and will be called from Page 2 – *Customers*. It will be created as a modal dialog. A modal dialog page is a stand-alone page, which appears on top of the calling page. An Oracle APEX page can be created as a dialog, which supports for all the functionality of a normal page, including computations, validations, processes, and branches.

87

1. Click the **Create Page** button. This time select the **Form** option 🖾 followed by the **Form on a Table** 🖽 option. As the name implies, the second option creates a form page based on a database table. After selecting the initial options, set the following properties on the next wizard screen.

Property	Value
Page Number	7
Page Name	Customer Details
Page Mode	Modal Dialog

2. On the *Navigation Menu* screen, set *Navigation Preference* to **Identify an existing navigation menu entry for this page**, set *Existing Navigation Menu Entry* to **Setup**, and click **Next**.

3. On the *Source* screen, set the following properties and click **Next**. This time, select all the columns from the DEMO_CUSTOMERS table to display all of them in the input form on Page 7 to populate the backend database table.

Property	Value
Table/View Owner	*accept the displayed value*
Table/View Name	DEMO_CUSTOMERS

4. For *Primary Key Type*, select the second option **Select Primary Key Column(s)**. Then, set the first *Primary Key Column* attribute to **CUSTOMER_ID**. For *Primary Key Source Type*, select *Existing sequence*, set *Sequence* to **DEMO_CUST_SEQ**, and click the **Create** button to complete the wizard. In this step, you specified the primary key column and the database sequence object the primary key will generate from. A primary key is a column or set of columns that uniquely identify a record in a table. A sequence is a database object that automatically generates primary key values for every new customer record. Forms perform insert, update, and delete operations on table rows in the database. The rows are identified using either a primary key defined on the table, or the ROWID pseudo column, which uniquely identifies a row in a table. Forms support up to two columns in the primary key. For tables using primary keys with more than two columns, the ROWID option should be used. See Chapter 2 section 2.10 – *Underlying Database Objects*.

5. Access the main App Builder interface by clicking the application ID breadcrumb to see the two new pages (*Customers* and *Customer Details*) with their respective page numbers.

5.3 Modify Customers Page - Page 2

The main page of this module (Page 2) holds an interactive grid, which is generated by the wizard with some default values such as a SQL SELECT statement and corresponding column names. In the following steps, you will change these values to generate a more meaningful output.

1. In the App Builder interface, click the **Customers** page to open it in the *Page Designer* for modification.

2. Click the **Customers** region ▦ Customers under the *Content Body* folder. The standard method to modify properties of a page component is to click the corresponding node. This action refreshes the *Properties* section (located to your right) with the properties of the selected page component for alteration.

3. Enter the following SQL statement in *SQL Query* text area, replacing the existing one. Here, the auto-generated SELECT SQL statement is replaced with a custom statement that uses the concatenation operator ‖ to join columns. The new statement joins last and first name of customers into a single column. The new concatenated column is recognized by *customer_name*. Similarly, the two address columns are combined to form a single address.

   ```
   SELECT customer_id,
   cust_last_name || ', ' || cust_first_name customer_name,
   CUST_STREET_ADDRESS1 ||decode(CUST_STREET_ADDRESS2, null, null, ', ' ||
   CUST_STREET_ADDRESS2) customer_address,
   cust_city, cust_state, cust_postal_code
   FROM demo_customers
   ```

DECODE FUNCTION

In the SELECT statement we used a DECODE function, which has the functionality of an IF-THEN-ELSE statement. It compares expression to each search value one by one. If expression is equal to a search, Oracle Database returns the corresponding result. If no match is found, Oracle returns default. If default is omitted, Oracle returns null. In this statement, the Decode function assesses if the returned value of the second street address is null, it stores null to the result; otherwise, concatenates the second address to the first address. The following syntax and example of the Decode function elaborates this concept further.

Decode Syntax:
decode(expression , search , result [, search , result]... [, default])

Example of Decode Function:
Select customer_name, decode(customer_id, 1, 'A', 2, 'B', 3, 'C', 'D')
result
From customers;

The equivalent IF-THEN-ELSE statement for the previous Decode function would be:
```
IF customer_id = 1 THEN
   result := 'A';
ELSIF customer_id = 2 THEN
   result := 'B';
ELSIF customer_id = 3 THEN
   result := 'C';
ELSE
   result := 'D';
END IF;
```

4. Change the *Template* property (under *Appearance*) from *Standard* to **Interactive Report**. If you keep the region's template to *Standard*, you will see two Customers labels appearing on the page, which doesn't look professional. **Save** your work after making this amendment.

5. Run the page. Click the **Actions** menu [Actions ⌄]. From the *Action* menu's list, select **Columns**. In the *Columns* window, make sure all the columns are selected–that is, they all have a checkmark in the *Displayed* column. If you remove a checkmark from a column, it disappears from the interactive grid report. When you click a column in the left pane, the right pane shows its name and width. You can input a numeric value to change the width of a column. Using the arrow icons (labeled *move up* and *move down*), arrange the selected columns in the following order:
   Customer Name, Address, City, State, and **Postal Code**

6. Click the **Save** button in the *Columns* window to apply the changes.

7. Click the **Actions** menu again, and select **Save** from the *Report* option. After you modify an interactive grid save it using this option, otherwise you'll lose the applied settings when you subsequently access it.

8. Click **Edit Page2** in the Developer Toolbar at the bottom of your screen to access the Page Designer.

9. Expand the *Customers* region and then expand the *Columns* folder. Click a column (for example, **Customer_Name**) and change its heading (under the *Heading* section) to **Name**. Change the headings of other columns as follows:
   Address, City, State, and **Postal Code**

10. Set the value of *Type* property for the CUSTOMER_ID column to **Hidden** to hide the column at runtime. Primary Key columns are added to database tables to enforce data integrity and are not displayed in applications. This is why such columns' *Type* property is set to hidden to make them invisible at runtime.

11. Click the **CUSTOMER_NAME** column to set the following properties. In these properties, you transformed the customer name column into a link that leads to Page 7. When you click a customer's name in the interactive grid report, the ID of that customer is stored in a substitution string (&CUSTOMER_ID.) (C) and is forwarded to the corresponding page item (P7_CUSTOMER_ID) (B) on Page 7, which displays the profile of the selected customer using this ID. You created similar kind of link in Chapter 4 for a region named *Sales for this Month*. Scroll down to the *Link* section and click **No Link Defined** under *Target* to bring up the *Link Builder* dialog box. In the *Link Builder* dialog box, set the link properties as shown in Figure 5-2. Use LOVs (A) in the *Set Items* section to select the item name and the value.

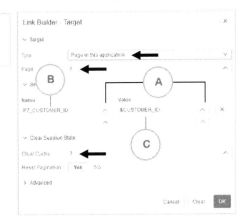

Figure 5-2
Link Builder
Dialog Box

12. After setting these properties, close the *Link Builder* dialog box using the **OK** button.

13. **Save and run** the page. The *Customer Name* column will appear as a link. Click any customer name to see the details on Page 7, which pops up on top of Page 2.

5.3.2 Create Button

In the previous section, you created a link on the customer name column that helped you browse, modify, or delete an existing customer's record. To create a new customer, you need to create a button to call Page 7 with a blank form. Execute the following steps to create this button on Page 2 - Customers.

1. On the *Rendering* tab to your left, right-click the **Breadcrumb** node under the *Breadcrumb Bar* folder, and select **Create Button** from the context menu. A button named *New* will be added. Set the following properties for the new button.

Property	Value
Label	Create Customer
Button Position	Create
Hot	Yes
Action (*under Behavior*)	Redirect to Page in this Application
Target	Type = Page in this Application Page = 7 Clear Cache =7

The *Label* of this button is set to *Create Customer* (A – Figure 5-1) and the button is placed in the *Create* position. The *Button Position* property provides you with over a dozen values. The best way to understand the other options is to try each one to see its effect. The *Hot* attribute renders the button in a dark color. The remaining properties create a link to call Page 7. The *Clear Cache* property makes all the items on the target page (Page 7) blank.

2. Save and run Page 2, which should look similar to Figure 5-1.

3. Click the **Create Customer** button. This will call the *Customer Details* page (Page 7) on top of the calling page as a modal dialog.

5.4 Modify Customer Details Page - Page 7

With Page 7 being displayed in your browser, click **Edit Page 7** in the Developer Toolbar at the bottom of your screen to call this page in the Page Designer for modifications.

5.4.1 Modify Item Properties

Click each item under the *Items* node and apply the following properties. Just like region placement in a 12 columns grid layout, which you performed for the six Home page regions, the page items can also be placed accordingly using Oracle APEX's gird layout, as follows. The *Width* property sets items' width on the page. In the following table, some values for the *Value Required* property are set to *Yes*. If *Value Required* is set to *Yes* and the page item is visible, Oracle Application Express automatically performs a NOT NULL validation when the page is submitted. If you set it to No, no validation is performed and a NULL value is accepted.

Item	Label	Layout	Width	Value Required
P7_CUST_FIRST_NAME	First Name	Start New Row=Yes Column=Automatic Column Span=Automatic Label Column Span=2	40	Yes
P7_CUST_LAST_NAME	Last Name	Start New Row=No Column=Automatic New Column=Yes Column Span=Automatic Label Column Span=2	40	Yes
P7_CUST_STREET_ADDRESS1	Street Address	Start New Row=Yes Column=Automatic Column Span=Automatic Label Column Span=2	48	No
P7_CUST_STREET_ADDRESS2	Line 2	Start New Row=No Column=Automatic New Column=Yes Column Span=Automatic Label Column Span=2	48	No
P7_CUST_CITY	City	Start New Row=Yes Column=Automatic Column Span=6 Label Column Span=2	40	No
P7_CUST_STATE	State	Start New Row=No Column=Automatic New Column=Yes Column Span=Automatic Label Column Span=2	-	Yes
P7_CUST_POSTAL_CODE	Zip Code	Start New Row=Yes Column=Automatic Column Span=6 Label Column Span=2	8	Yes

P7_CREDIT_LIMIT	Credit Limit	Start New Row=No Column=Automatic New Column=Yes Column Span=Automatic Label Column Span=2	8	Yes
P7_PHONE_NUMBER1	Phone Number	Start New Row=Yes Column=Automatic Column Span=Automatic Label Column Span=2	12	No
P7_PHONE_NUMBER2	Alternate No.	Start New Row=No Column=Automatic New Column=Yes Column Span=Automatic Label Column Span=2	12	No
P7_CUST_EMAIL	Email	Start New Row=Yes Column=Automatic Column Span=Automatic Label Column Span=2	30	No
P7_URL	URL	Start New Row=Yes Column=Automatic Column Span=Automatic Label Column Span=2	64	No
P7_TAGS	Tags	Start New Row=Yes Column=Automatic Column Span=Automatic Label Column Span=2	64	No

Save your changes and call this page by clicking any customer's name on Page 2. It should come up with the profile of the selected customer, as illustrated in Figure 5-3.

Figure 5-3
Customer
Details Page

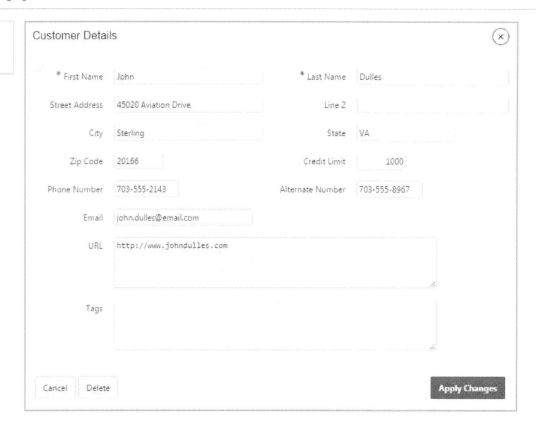

5.4.2 Change Item Type and Attach LOV

In the following set of steps, you'll work on the *State* column. First, you will alter its type from *Text Field* to a *Select List* and then you will attach a LOV to it. Oracle APEX allows you to change an item's type from its default state to another desirable type. For example, the P7_CUST_STATE item was generated as a text type by the wizard. Now, we want to change this item to a *Select List* to hold a predefined States list. To display this list, you'll attach the STATES LOV to this item. The LOV was created in Chapter 3 section 3.4.3 and will be tied to this field so that the user can save a valid State value for each customer.

1. Click the **P7_CUST_STATE** item.

2. Change its *Type* property from *Text Field* to **Select List**.

3. Set *Template* (under *Appearance*) to **Required**. This property will show an asterisk (*) along with the label to mark the column as a mandatory field. Note that this property was set automatically by the wizard for the first and last name columns. Set this property for postal code and credit limit columns as well to display them as mandatory fields.

4. Set *Value Required* to **Yes**. If set to *Yes* and the page item is visible, Application Express will automatically perform a NOT NULL validation when the page is submitted and will ask you to input a value for the field. This attribute usually works in conjunction with the previous one–*Template = Required*.

94

5. Set *Type* (under *List of Values*) to **Shared Components** and select **STATES** for *List of Values*. This step attaches the *States* LOV to the page item.

6. Set *Display Extra Values* to **No**. An item may have a session state value, which does not occur in its list of values definition. Select whether this list of values should display this extra session state value. If you choose not to display this extra session state value and there is no matching value in the list of values definition, the first value will be the selected value. For instance, while creating a new customer record you will see -*Choose a State*- as the first value in the list. This value is added to the list in the following steps.

7. Set *Display Null Value* to **Yes**, which is the default. The *Display Null Value* property makes it possible for a user to choose a null value instead of one of the list items. If you set this property to *Yes*, additional properties appear on the screen for you to specify the display value for this new entry. For example, - Choose State -.

8. Enter - **Choose State** - in *Null Display Value*. This step, along with the previous one, generates a placeholder that appears on top of the LOV asking for a selection whenever you call this page to create a new customer record.

9. Save your work.

5.4.3 Apply Input Mask to Items

Modify the two phone number items and set their *Value Placeholder* property (under *Appearance*) to **999-999-9999**. When a new customer record is added, this placeholder is shown in the two phone number items to receive input in the specified format. As you type in values, the placeholders will be replaced by the numbers entered.

5.4.4 Create Validation - Check Customer Credit Limit

Validations enable you to create logic controls to verify whether user input is valid. In this part, you'll create a validation to check customer's credit limit. The customer form contains a field named Credit Limit, which is used to assign a cap to each customer with a figure of $5,000. If you enter a value more than the assigned cap, you'll be prevented by presenting an appropriate message.

In the left pane, click the *Processing* tab ↩, right-click the *Validating* folder ☐ Validating, and select **Create Validation** from the context menu. This action will add a new validation. Set the following properties for this new validation. After providing a meaningful name to the validation, you set its *Type* to *PL/SQL Expression*. The selected type specifies an expression in valid PL/SQL syntax that evaluates to true or false. In the current scenario, if the value of the :P7_CREDIT_LIMIT page item is less than or equal to 5000, then the validation evaluates as true and the customer record is saved to the database. If the value of this item is more than 5000, then the validation evaluates as false and the message specified in the *Error Message* property is fired. Note that you use bind variables (the item name preceded with a colon) when you reference the value of a session state variable from within PL/SQL code.

Property	Value
Name	Check Credit Limit
Type	PL/SQL Expression
PL/SQL Expression	:P7_CREDIT_LIMIT <= 5000
Error Message	Customer's Credit Limit must be less than or equal to $5,000

5.4.5 Create Validation - Can't Delete Customer with Orders

This is the second validation to prevent the deletion of those customers who have placed orders. This check is performed to retain database integrity from the front-end. The validation is performed using a custom PL/SQL function, which returns either a true or false value. The return value is based on a SELECT query, which returns false if records exist for the selected customer. If the returned value is false, the error message is displayed and the record deletion process is aborted. The validation is associated to the DELETE button in the last attribute, which means that the validation will be performed only when the Delete button is pressed.

Once again, right-click the *Validating* node and select the **Create Validation** option to add a new validation under the previous one. Set the following properties for this new validation. You can control when and if a validation is performed by configuring *When Button Pressed* and *Condition Type* attributes of the validation. If you want a validation to execute only when the specified button is clicked, select a button from the list–see the last attribute in the following table. Setting a condition type involves selecting a condition from the list that must be met in order for a validation to be processed.

Property	Value
Name	Can't Delete Customer with Orders
Type	PL/SQL Function Body (Returning Boolean)

PL/SQL Function Body (Returning Boolean)	begin
	  for c1 in (select 'x' from demo_orders
	          where customer_id = :P7_CUSTOMER_ID) loop
	     RETURN FALSE;
	  end loop;
	     RETURN TRUE;
	end;

Error Message	Can't delete customer with existing orders
When Button Pressed	DELETE

Before running the customer module, let's take a look at the definitions of the *Customer Details* page–Page 7. If you see the definitions of this page, you'll observe some auto-generated buttons (Cancel, Delete, Save, and Create) with default functionalities. For example, when you fill in the form with a new customer's record and click the *Create* button, the record is added to the database table using a built-in process–discussed in a while. Just like buttons, Oracle APEX performs many other tasks transparently without us having to write a single line of code. For instance, expand the *Pre-Rendering* folder (under the root node - *Page 7: Customer Details*). You will see a process named *Fetch Row from DEMO_CUSTOMERS* under the *After Header > Processes* folder. The wizard created this *Automatic Row Fetch* (ARF) type process automatically. The purpose of this process is to fetch the record from the database using a specified key value, and put values of that record into relevant items on the page. For example, when you click a customer name in the Interactive Grid on Page 2, the ID of that customer is used by this process to fetch and display details on this page. The execution point of this process is set to *After Header*, which is the time when the server generates the page's HTML header information, but before it generates the page contents. The wizard also created individual input items (under the *Customer Details* region) for each column in the table. The *Source Type* property of these columns is set to *Database Column* and *Database Column* property is set to the column name in the table. For example, the two properties set for the P7_CUST_FIRST_NAME page item tells the ARF process to set the item with the value retrieved from the CUST_FIRST_NAME table column. Click the root node (*Page 7: Customer Details*) and scroll down to the *Function and Global Variable Declaration* section in the Property Editor, you'll see a global variable defined as *var htmldb_delete_message*. This variable was generated automatically along with a corresponding shortcut named DELETE CONFIRM MSG (in *Shared Components > Other Components > Shortcuts*) to control the record deletion process by presenting a confirmation dialog box before deleting a customer's record. Since this shortcut is created in Shared Components, other application pages will also utilize it to present the same confirmation. Note that the *Delete* button was created by the wizard with a SQL DELETE database action. Similarly, INSERT and UPDATE database actions were set automatically for *Create* and *Save* buttons, respectively–see the *Database Action* attribute under *Behavior*. When clicked, these buttons perform the selected SQL operations to trigger the specified database action within the built-in *Automatic Row Processing (DML)* type process, also created automatically by the wizard on the *Processing* tab. This process is named *Process Row of DEMO_CUSTOMERS* and is placed under the *Processing > Processes* folder and it is responsible to insert, update, or delete records into the backend database table. This process is used to process form items with a source of type Database Column. This process has three advantages. First, you are not required to provide any SQL coding. Second, Oracle Application Express performs DML processing for you. Third, this process automatically performs lost update detection. Lost update detection ensures data integrity in applications where data can be accessed concurrently. In addition, the wizard created a Dynamic Action (*Cancel Dialog*) to close this form when the *Cancel* button is clicked

These are some of the beauties of declarative development that not only generates basic functionalities of an application, but on the same time doesn't limit our abilities to manually enter specific and tailored code (demonstrated in subsequent chapters), both on the client and server sides to answer our specific needs.

Save and run the application. Access this module by clicking the *Manage Customers* menu item (under *Setup*). You'll see Page 2 – *Customers*, as shown in Figure 5-1, carrying an interactive grid. The grid has a search bar comprising a magnifying glass, a text area, and a *Go* button. The bar allows you to search a string in the report appearing underneath. The magnifying glass is a drop down list. You can use this list to limit your search to a specific column. Type **albert** in the text area and click the **Go** button. You'll see a row displaying record of Albert Lambert. Click the remove filter icon [×] to reinstate the grid to its previous state. Alternatively, you can click the *Reset* button appearing on the top-right of the gird. The *Actions* menu carries some more options that we'll explore in Chapter 7. Among other useful options, this menu has a couple of save options under *Report*. The first one (*Save*) is used when you customize the report by applying filters or moving columns. After modifying a report you must save it using this option, otherwise you'll lose the applied settings when you subsequently view the same report. Clicking the second option (*Save As*) presents a window with a *Type* drop-down list and a *Name* text box. Developers can save four types of reports: Primary, Alternative, Private, and Public. The initial interactive grid report rendered in your browser is called a *Primary* report. The default *Primary* report (you are looking at) is the initial report created by the application developer. It cannot be renamed or deleted. An *Alternative* report enables developers to create multiple report layouts. Only developers can save, rename, or delete an Alternative Report. An alternative report is based on the default primary report and is rendered in a different layout (see Section 7.3.3 in Chapter 7). A *Private* report is a report that can be viewed, saved, renamed, or deleted by the user who created it. In contrast, when you save a report as public, all users can view it. By default, end-users cannot save *Public* reports. To enable support for *Public* reports, developers edit the report attribute and enables users to save it as public report–see step 8 Section 7.3.1 in Chapter 7. After saving, all these reports display on the *Saved Reports* list on the toolbar. The Primary report is displayed under the heading, *Default*.

The *Create Customer* button calls the second page of this module (Page 7), where you enter profile of a new customer. As you can see, the customer name column appears as a link. If you want to modify a specific record, click the corresponding link. Again, the same form page comes up where all the fields are populated with relevant information from the database. Click the name of any customer to see the information, as presented in Figure 5-2.

You are free to test your work. Try by adding, modifying, and deleting a new customer. Try to delete *Eugene Bradley's* record. You won't be able to do that because there are some orders placed by this customer and the validation you created in section 5.4.5 will prevent the deletion process. Also, check the credit limit validation by entering a value more than 5000 in the *Credit Limit* box.

5.5 Add Dynamic Action

After adding a new customer record or editing an existing one, you might observe that the interactive grid on the Customers page doesn't reflect those changes. This is because the page doesn't get refreshed to show what you have added or amended. One way to see these modifications is to manually refresh your browser window, which in turn, retrieves fresh data from the database. But, a more professional approach would be to refresh the page automatically using a dynamic action. In this section, you will create a dynamic action to refresh the interactive grid region (Customers) when the modal dialog page (Page 7) is closed.

1. Access the Page Designer interface of Page 2 (Customers) and click the **Dynamic Actions** tab ⚡ appearing in the left pane.

2. Right-click **Dialog Closed** (listed under *Events*) and select **Create Dynamic Action** from the context menu. Set the following properties for this dynamic action.

Property	Value
Name	Refresh Interactive Grid
Selection Type	Region
Region	Customers

3. Click the *Refresh* sub-node and set *Region* to **Customers**. *Refresh* is an action, which executes when the condition evaluates to true–in other words, when model dialog page is closed. All is set! Save the page and run it. Now you will see immediate reflection of your modifications in the interactive grid.

5.6 Interactive Grid Features

Oracle APEX 5.1 comes with a new feature called Interactive Grid to display data in row/column matrix. In appearance, it looks similar to an Interactive Report (used in the next chapter) and delivers all features of an Interactive Report, but it also allows you to manipulate data simply by clicking on a cell and editing its value, which is not available in Interactive Reports. In many ways this grid looks and acts like an Interactive Report. Here are some new features and differences:

- Rows are fixed height and columns have a specific width that can be adjusted by dragging the border between column headers (G) or with Ctrl+Left/Right keys when the column header has keyboard focus.

- Columns can be reordered with drag and drop (dragging the handle (E) at the start of a column heading) or with Shift+Left/Right keys when the column header has keyboard focus.

- Columns can be sorted using the buttons (F) in the column heading or by using Alt+Up/Down key combination. Use the Shift key to add additional sort columns.

- Columns can be frozen using the Freeze button (D) in the column heading pop-up menu. For example, to freeze the customers' name column (on Page 2), click the *Name* column heading. A pop-up menu will appear with four options: Hide (A), Control Break (B), Aggregate (C), and Freeze (D). Select *Freeze*. Drag the border between the *Name* and *Address* columns (F) toward right to expand the *Name* column.

- By default the toolbar and column headings stick to the top of the page and the footer sticks to the bottom when scrolling.

- By default pagination uses a "Load More" button.

- The grid is keyboard navigable with a focused cell and current selected row (single selection by default).

- The toolbar includes a Reset button by default, which restores all the report settings to their defaults.

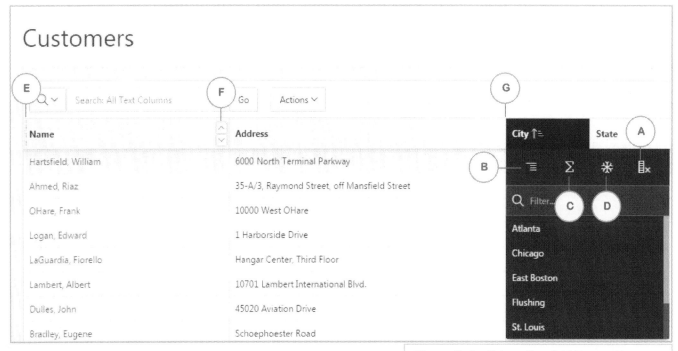

Figure 5-4 – Interactive Grid Pop-up Menu

Let's put off the development process of our Sales Web Application till the next chapter and explore the features of the new Interactive Grid. To get hands-on exposure, you need a couple of tables that come with a sample application. Execute the following steps to install the sample application and consequently the required tables.

1. Select **Sample Apps** from the *Packaged Apps* menu appearing at the top of your browser.

2. Click the icon representing **Sample Interactive Grids** application.

3. On the *Packaged App Details* page, click the **Install Packaged App** button.

4. On the *Install Packaged App* wizard screen, accept the default *Authentication* scheme (*Application Express Accounts*) and click **Next**.

5. On the next wizard screen, click the **Install Packaged App** button. After a while, you will see the message *Application installed.*

6. Click the **Object Browser** option in the **SQL Workshop** main menu and see the two required tables (EBA_DEMO_IG_EMP and EBA_DEMO_IG_PEOPLE) in the left pane under the *Tables* category.

5.6.1 Column Groups

Figure 5-5
Column Grouping in Interactive Grid

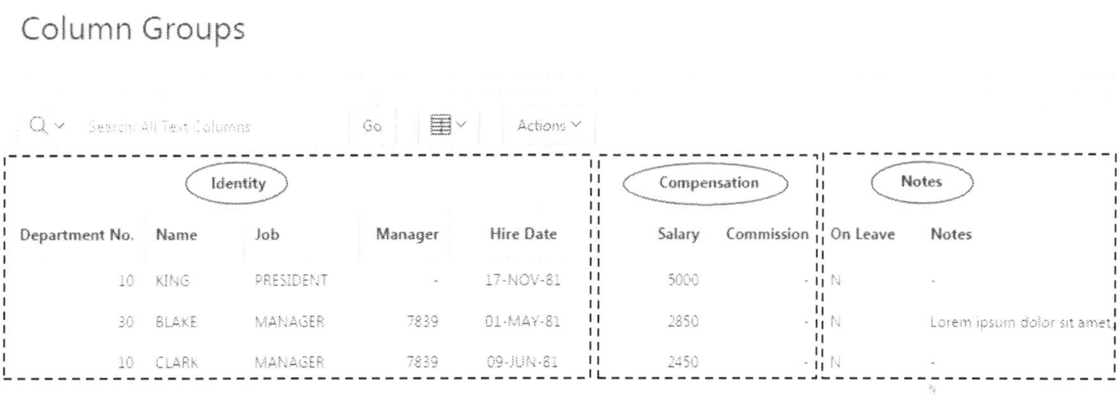

Groups are used to associate columns together in the grid and Single Row View. Groups are added by expanding the *Attributes* node within the *Rendering* tree, and right-clicking on *Column Groups*. Let's try this feature by executing the following steps:

1. Create a new page by clicking the **Create Page** button. Select the **Report** option in the first wizard screen, followed by the **Interactive Grid** option on the next screen.

2. Set *Page Number* to **100**, *Page Name* to **Column Groups**, *Page Mode* to **Normal**, *Breadcrumb* to **Breadcrumb**, *Parent Entry* to **No Parent Entry**, *Entry Name* to **Column Groups**, and click **Next**.

3. Set *Navigation Preference* to **Do not associate this page with a navigation menu entry**, because this page is not associated with our sales application. Click **Next**.

4. On the *Report Source* screen, set *Editing Enabled* to **No**, set *Source Type* to **SQL Query**, and enter the following SQL Statement in *Enter a SQL SELECT Statement* text area.

SELECT
empno,ename,job,mgr,hiredate,sal,comm,deptno,onleave,notes,flex4 as tags
FROM EBA_DEMO_IG_EMP

5. Click the **Create** button to finish the page creation process.

6. In the Page Designer, under the *Column Groups* region (in the *Rendering* tree), right-click the *Attributes* folder, and select **Create Column Group** from the context menu. In the *Properties* pane, set the *Heading* attribute for this new group to **Identity**.

7. Repeat step 6 to create two more groups. Enter **Compensation** and **Notes** for their headings.

8. Under the *Columns Group* region, expand the *Columns* folder. Click the **EMPNO** column and set its *Type* to **Hidden**.

9. Set the appropriate column headings, as shown in Figure 5-5.

10. Use the following table to associate each column with a group defined in steps 6 & 7. To establish this association, click any column (ENAME, for example), scroll down to the *Layout* section, and set the *Group* property as follows:

Column	Group Property
ENAME	Identity
JOB	Identity
MGR	Identity
HIREDATE	Identity
SAL	Compensation
COMM	Compensation
DEPTNO	Identity
ONLEAVE	Notes
NOTES	Notes

11. Save your work and run the page. Column group headings can be used to reorder columns just like column headings. Play around with column reordering (using drag and drop) to see how the group headings are split and joined.

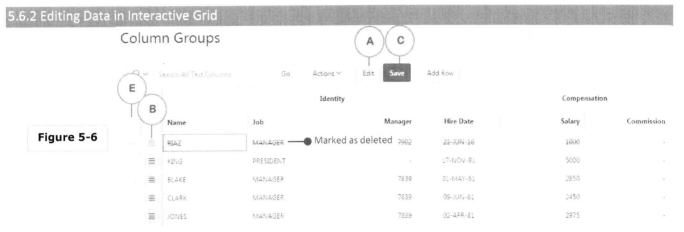

Figure 5-6

Interactive Grid allows you to manipulate data simply by clicking on a cell. When you add an Interactive Grid to a page, you specify (on *Report Source* wizard screen) whether it is editable–see step 4 in the previous section. If you initially set this attribute to *No*, you can reverse it to make the Interactive Grid editable. Here are some points to know about editing:

- Normally the grid is in navigation mode where arrow keys move from cell to cell. To enter edit mode, press the *Edit* button (A). Alternatively, double-click a cell or press either the Enter key or F2 key in a cell.
- To exit edit mode, press the *Edit* button (A) again or press the Escape key in a cell.
- Use the Delete key on your keyboard to delete the selected rows. Use the Insert key to add a row.
- The second column (B) is an actions menu. It allows you to perform actions on the selected row such as Delete or Duplicate. Use the *Revert Changes* option from this menu to revert a record marked for deletion.
- Editing is also supported in Single Row View.
- All edits are stored locally until you press the *Save* button (C). If you try to leave the page while there are unsaved changes you will be warned.
- Any action that causes refreshing the data such as changing a filter or sorting will warn if there are unsaved changes. Pagination does not affect changes.

Execute the following steps to enable editing in the Interactive Grid you added to Page 100 in the previous section.

1. Click the *Attributes* folder under the *Column Group* region and set the *Enabled* attribute (under *Edit*) to **Yes**. Make sure all three operations (Add Row, Update Row, and Delete Row) are enabled.

2. Scroll down to the *Toolbar* section. Ensure the *Show* property is set to **Yes** and the two toolbar buttons (*Reset* and *Save*) are enabled. *Reset* removes any customizations, such as filters, column width, ordering, and so forth, and reloads the report definition from the server. *Save* will only save changes made to this interactive grid, without needing to save the whole page. The save button will be

displayed only when the interactive grid is editable and the end user has the authorization to add, update, or delete records.

3. After making these changes, save and run the page. Notice that the row selector (E) and the actions menu (B) columns (in Figure 5-6) are added automatically. A process named *Save Interactive Grid Data* is also added on the *Processing* tab with an *Interactive Grid - Automatic Row Processing (DML)* type process to perform DML processing for you without writing any SQL code. This process is added by default when an Interactive Grid is made editable. Play around with the interactive grid by adding, modifying, and deleting rows.

5.6.3 Changing Column Type

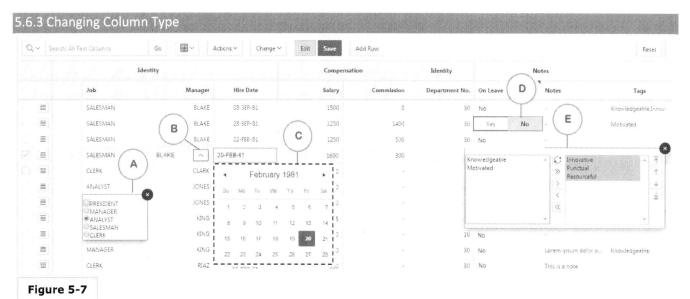

Figure 5-7

By default, the type of a column in an Interactive Grid is inherited from the base table. For example, the names of employees are displayed in a Text Field column type, while their salaries are shown in Number Field column type. In this exercise, you will change the default types of some columns to some other types, as follows:

A. The *Job* column will be presented as a *Radio Group* to select one from a list of distinct jobs
B. The value for the *Manager* column will be selected from a *pop-up LOV*
C. The *Hire Date* will use a *Date Picker* that opens on focus
D. Display *Yes*/No in *On Leave* column
E. The *Tags* column will use a *Shuttle* type to select multiple values

1. With Page 100 being displayed in the Page Designer, expand the *Columns* folder and click the *JOB* column. Set its *Type* attribute to **Radio Group**. When you select the radio group type, you are asked to associate a list of values to populate the item. For the *List of Values Type* attribute, select **SQL Query** and enter **SELECT DISTINCT job a, job b FROM EBA_DEMO_IG_EMP** in *SQL Query* box. Also, set *Display Extra Values* and *Display Null Values* to **No**–see section 5.4.2 for details. The SQL Query fetches distinct job IDs from the table and shows them in the *JOB* column using the radio group type.

2. Next, click the *MGR* column and change its *Type* to **Popup LOV**. If you want to display the query result in a drop-down list instead, set *Type* to *Select List*. Then, select *SQL Query* for *List of Values Type* and enter the following statement in *SQL Query* box.
   SELECT ENAME as d, EMPNO as r
   FROM EBA_DEMO_IG_EMP
   WHERE JOB = 'MANAGER' or JOB = 'PRESIDENT' order by 1

3. Click the *HIREDATE* column. The *Type* attribute of this column is already set to *Date Picker* and this is what we want. The only attribute of this column that needs to be changed is *Show* (under *Settings*). Change it from *on icon click* to **On focus** to display the date picker when the focus is on this column.

4. Click the *ONLEAVE* column and set its *Type* to **Switch**. This will display two values *Yes* and *No* for this column.

5. Finally, click the *TAGS* column. Change its *Type* from *Textarea* to **Shuttle**– you can also use *Checkbox* type for this purpose. Set *List of Values Type* to **Static Values** and enter **STATIC:Punctual,Innovative,Motivated,Resourceful,Knowledgeable** in the *Static Values* box. This is another way to define static values for a LOV. Recall that you created a Static LOV through Shared Components interface in Chapter 3 - Section 3.4.1. There you specified a pair of static *Display* and *Return* values. Here, you didn't use the *Return* value, because the *Return* value is optional. If a *Return* value is not included, the return value equals the display value.

6. Save and run the page. Click different cells under the *JOB* column and press F2 to see values in a radio group (A). Similarly, press F2 in the *Manager* column. This will display an up arrow icon (B) in the selected cell. Clicking this icon opens up a pop-up window carrying records of president and managers. Once again, click the *Manager* column, press F2, and then press the Tab key on your keyboard. The cursor's focus will move on to the *Hire Date* column and immediately the Date Picker window (C) will pop up. Keep pressing the Tab key to access the *On Leave* column, which will show a *Yes* and *No* switch (D). Access the *Tags* column, which should come up with a shuttle (E) carrying the five values defined in step 5. Using the arrow key in the shuttle, move all these values to the right pane and click the cross icon to close the shuttle. Click the **Save** button to write your changes to the database.

NOTE: The static list of values is defined using the following syntax:
STATIC[2]:Display Value[;Return Value],Display Value[;Return Value]

Where:
- The first keyword may be STATIC or STATIC2. STATIC results in the values being sorted alphabetically by display value. STATIC2 results in the values being displayed in the order they are entered in the list. See Chapter 10 - Section 10.14 - Step 10.
- A semicolon separates the display value from the return value in each entry.
- Return Value is optional. If a Return Value is not included, the return value equals the display value.

5.6.4 Protecting Rows in Interactive Grid

	Name	Job		Manager	Hire Date	Salary	Commission
			Identity			**Compensation**	
	KING	PRESIDENT			17-NOV-81	5000	--
	RIAZ	MANAGER		7902	22-JUN-16	1000	--
	BLAKE	MANAGER		KING	01-MAY-81	2850	--
	CLARK	MANAGER		KING	09-JUN-81	2450	--
	JONES	MANAGER		KING	02-APR-81	2975	--
	SCOTT	ANALYST		JONES	09-DEC-82	3000	-
✓	FORD|	ANALYST		JONES	03-DEC-81	3000	-
	ALLEN	SALESMAN		BLAKE	20-FEB-81	1600	300

Figure 5-8

In this example, you will see how to protect rows in an Interactive Grid. For this purpose, you need to add a column named CTRL to implement a simple rule that Managers and Presidents cannot be edited or deleted. This column is then selected in the *Allowed Row Operations Column* property in the *Attributes* folder.

1. With Page 100 being displayed in the Page Designer, click the *Column Groups* region and amend the SELECT statement as follows (the amendment is shown in bold):

```
SELECT empno, ename, job, mgr, hiredate, sal, comm, deptno, onleave,
        notes, flex4 as tags,
        case when JOB = 'MANAGER' or JOB = 'PRESIDENT' then ''
        else 'UD' end as CTRL
FROM EBA_DEMO_IG_EMP
```

2. After amending the SQL query you will see the *CTRL* column under the *Columns* folder. Click this column and set its *Type* to **Hidden**.

3. Click the *Attributes* folder under the *Column Groups* region and set *Allowed Row Operations Column* (under *Edit*) to the **CTRL** column.

4. Save the page and run it. Click the **Edit** button. Rows that cannot be edited or deleted are shown in a darker color (A) when in edit mode.

5.6.5 Scroll Paging

Another exciting feature of Interactive Grids is scroll paging (also known as infinite scrolling or virtual paging). It is enabled by setting *Pagination* attribute to *Scroll*. After enabling this attribute, the region appears to carry the entire result set but rows are rendered on demand as you scroll. When you scroll in the Interactive Grid, the model fetches data from the server as it is needed by the view. You can even drag the scroll bar handle all the way to the bottom and then scroll up. You need a database table with lots of records to assess this feature. In this exercise, you will use EBA_DEMO_IG_PEOPLE table, which carries over 4000 records.

1. Create a new page using the instructions mentioned earlier in Section 5.6.1. Set *Page Number* to **111**, set *Page Name* to **Scroll Paging**, and enter the following SELECT statement. Rest of the page properties will remain the same.

SELECT name, country, rating FROM EBA_DEMO_IG_PEOPLE

2. In the Page Designer, click the *Attributes* folder under the *Scroll Paging* region. Set *Type* under the *Pagination* section to **Scroll** and *Show Total Row Count* to **Yes**.

3. Save and run the page to test this amazing feature. You will see total number of records at the bottom of the Interactive Grid.

5.6.6 Master Detail. And Detail. And Detail.

Interactive Grid makes it effortless to create master-detail relationships and go any number of levels deep and across. You can create all types of master-detail-detail screens with ease. In this section, I'll demonstrate this new feature.

1. From the *SQL Workshop* menu, select **SQL Scripts** and click the **Upload** button. In the *Upload Script* screen, click the **Choose File** button. In the *Open* dialog box, select **master_detail_detail.sql** file from Chapter 5 folder in the book's source code and click **Open**. Enter **Master Detail Detail** in the *Script Name* box and click the **Upload** button. In the *SQL Scripts* interface click the **Run** button appearing in the last column. On the *Run Script* screen, click the **Run Now** button. The script will execute to create four tables (MD_continent, MD_country, MD_city, and MD_population) along with relevant data to demonstrate the new master detail detail feature. You can view these tables from the *SQL Workshop > Object Browser* interface.

2. Create a new page by clicking the **Create Page** button in the App Builder interface. This time, select the first **Blank Page** option and click **Next**. Set *Page Number* to **112**, *Name* to **Master Detail Detail**, *Page Mode* to **Normal**, and click **Next**. On the *Navigation Menu* screen, select the first *Navigation Preference* to not associate this page with any sales app navigation menu entry. On the final wizard screen, click **Finish**.

3. In the Page Designer, right-click the *Regions* node on the *Rendering* tab and select **Create Region**. Set the following properties for the new region. This region will display data from the *MD_continent* table.

Property	Value
Title	Continents
Type	Interactive Grid
SQL Query	select * from MD_continent

After entering the SQL query, click anywhere outside the query box. Expand the *Columns* folder under this region. Click the **CONTINENT_ID** column. Set its *Type* to **Hidden** and set *Primary Key* (under *Source*) to **Yes**. You must define a primary key column for an interactive grid region, which is required to establish a master detail relationship.

4. Create another region under the *Continents* region by right-clicking the main *Regions* node. This region will act as the detail for the *Continents* region. At run-time when you select a continent, this region will display a list of countries in the selected continent. Set the following properties for this new region.

Property	Value
Title	Countries
Type	Interactive Grid
SQL Query	select * from MD_country

Expand the *Columns* folder under the *Countries* region. Click the **COUNTRY_ID** column. Set its *Type* to **Hidden** and set *Primary Key* (under *Source*) to **Yes**. You set the *Primary Key* property to *Yes,* because this region will act as a master for the *Cities* region created in the next step. Now, associate this detail region to its master (*Continents*). Click the *Countries* region ▦▮ Countries and set the *Master Region* property (under *Master Detail*) to **Continents**. This should be set when this region is the detail region in a master-detail relationship with another region on the page. For the master-detail relationship to work correctly, you must also select the column(s) in the detail region, which are foreign keys to the master region, by setting the *Master Column* property. Click the **CONTINENT_ID** column (a foreign key) in the *Countries* region. Set its *Type* property to **Hidden** and *Master Column* (under *Master Detail*) to **CONTINENT_ID**, which references the same column in the master region.

5. Create another region and place it under the *Countries* region. This region will show a list of cities when you select a country from its master region. Set the following properties for this region:

Property	Value
Title	Cities
Type	Interactive Grid
SQL Query	select * from MD_city
Master Region	Countries

Expand the *Columns* folder under the *Cities* region. Click the **CITY_ID** column. Set its *Type* to **Hidden** and set *Primary Key* (under *Source*) to **Yes**. Click the **COUNTRY_ID** column in this region. Set the *Type* of this column to **Hidden** and *Master Column* to **COUNTRY_ID** to point to the same column in the *Countries* region.

6. Create the last region to display population of a city.

Property	Value
Title	Population
Type	Interactive Grid
SQL Query	select * from MD_population
Master Region	Cities

Expand the *Columns* folder under the *Population* region. Click the **POPULATION_ID** column. Set its *Type* to **Hidden**. Since this is the last region, you do not need to specify this column as a primary key. However, you have to set a couple of properties for the CITY_ID column in this region to associate it with its master. Click the **CITY_ID** column, set its *Type* property to **Hidden** and *Master Column* to **CITY_ID**. That's it!

Run the page and click the row representing Europe (A) in the first region. As you click this row, the second region will display countries in the Europe continent. Click Germany (B) in the second region. This will refresh the third region with a list of cities in Germany. Click the Berlin city (C) to see its population (D) in the forth region.

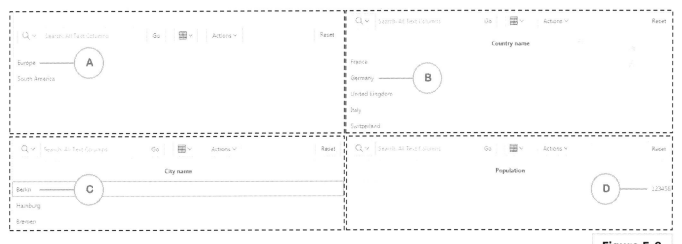

Figure 5-9

Summary

Here is a brief summary of this chapter to see what we grasped in it. We learned the following techniques while performing various exercises in this chapter:

- Declaratively created report and form pages and linked them together
- Placed form input items using 12 columns grid layout
- Changed the default type of an item and used list of values
- Used a dynamic action to automatically refresh a page
- Used various features of the new Interactive Grid
- Learned how to change types of columns
- Created validations to prevent customer record deletion with existing orders and to check customers' credit limits.
- Got hands-on exposure to Master Detail Detail feature.

Let's get back to our sales application. The next chapter discusses how to manage products in a database application with some more useful techniques to explore the exciting world of Oracle APEX.

Chapter 6

Set Up Products Catalog

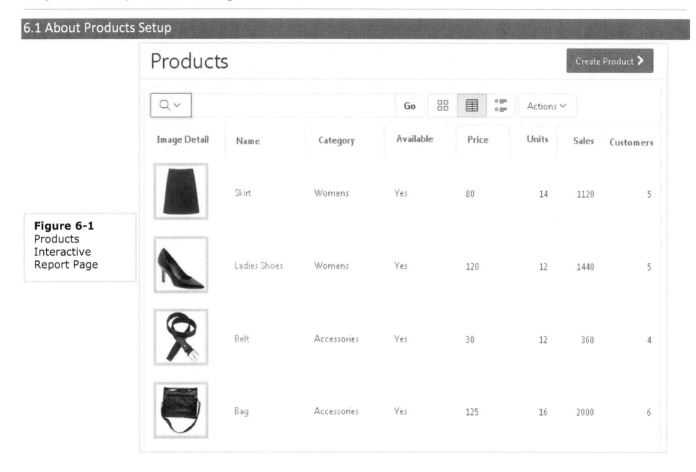

Figure 6-1
Products
Interactive
Report Page

Just like the Customers module, you'll create a Products setup to manage products information. This module will also have two pages: *Products* and *Product Details*. The main *Products* page (Page 3 – Figure 6-1) will have three different views: Icon, Report, and Details. Initially, the wizard will create the *Report View* version that you'll modify with a custom SQL statement. The remaining two views (*Detail* and *Icon*) are placed on the page by enabling respective properties found under the main Products region. Once you enable these views, their respective icons appear on the main Search bar. Using these icons you can switch among different views to browse products information. The *Product Details* page (Page 6) will be created to add, modify, and delete a product. To create these two pages you'll follow the same approach as you did in the previous chapter. Since most of the steps are similar to those already briefed in the Customers setup chapter, I'll elaborate the features new to this module.

The new stuff added to this module includes image handling and styling. This module is based on the DEMO_PRODUCT_INFO table in the database. Among conventional columns exists the following four special columns to handle images in the database. Normally, specialized processing is required to handle images in a database. The Oracle APEX environment has eliminated the need to perform all that specialized processing with these additional columns. Your Oracle APEX application will use these columns to properly process images in the BLOB column.

PRODUCT_IMAGE: This column uses BLOB data type. A BLOB (Binary Large Object) is an Oracle data type that can hold up to 4 GB of data. BLOBs are handy for storing digitized information, such as images, audio, and video.

MIMETYPE: A Multipurpose Internet Mail Extension (MIME) type identifies the format of a file. The MIME type enables applications to read the file. Applications such as Internet browsers and e-mail applications use the MIME type to handle files of different types. For example, an e-mail application can use the MIME type to detect what type of file is in a file attached to an e-mail. Many systems use MIME types to identify the format of arbitrary files on the file system. MIME types are composed of a top-level media type followed by a subtype identifier, separated by a forward slash character (/). An example of a MIME type is *image/jpeg*. The media type in this example is image and the subtype identifier is jpeg. The top-level media type is a general categorization about the content of the file, while the subtype identifier specifically identifies the format of the file.

FILENAME: A case-sensitive column name used to store the filename of the BLOB, such as bag.jpg.

IMAGE_LAST_UPDATE: A case-sensitive column name used to store the last update date of the BLOB.

Besides image handling, you'll also learn the technique to incorporate style sheet in an Oracle APEX page. Web browsers refer to Cascading Style Sheets (CSS) to define the appearance and layout of text and other material.

6.2 Create Pages for Products Setup

The following set of steps use the same approach you followed in the previous chapter to create a report along with an input form. Note that this time you will be creating an interactive report to display a list of products instead of an interactive grid–see Chapter 2 Section 2.3.3 for further details on the interactive report.

1. Click the **Create Page** Create Page > button in the App Builder interface.

2. Click the **Form** option ⊟, followed by the **Report with Form on Table** option. These two selections will create a report page (Figure 6-1) to display all product records from the table (selected in step 5) and a form page (Figure 6-2) to add, modify, and delete products.

3. On the *Page Attributes* wizard screen, set the following properties and click **Next**. The form page (Page 6) is named *Product Details* and it will be linked to the report page (*Products* - Page 3).

Property	Value
Report Type	Interactive Report
Report Page Number	3
Report Page Name	Products
Form Page Number	6
Form Page Name	Product Details
Form Page Mode	Modal Dialog
Breadcrumb	Breadcrumb
Parent Entry	No Parent Entry
Entry Name	Products

4. On the *Navigation Menu* screen, set *Navigation Preference* to **Identify an existing navigation menu entry for this page**, set *Existing Navigation Menu Entry* to **Setup**, and click **Next**. This step will highlight the *Setup* entry in the main navigation menu when you access the products setup.

5. On *Data Source* screen, accept the default schema in *Table/View Owner*, and select **DEMO_PRODUCT_INFO (table)** for *Table/View Name*. The columns from the selected table to be shown in the interactive report will appear in the right pane. In the next section, you will add a custom SQL query for the report page. For now, accept all the table columns and click **Next**.

6. On the **Form Page** screen, select the second option **Select Primary Key Column(s)** for *Primary Key Type*. In the *Select Column(s) to be included in Form* shuttle, add all columns from the DEMO_PRODUCT_INFO table to Page 6, except MIMETYPE, FILENAME, and IMAGE_LAST_UPDATE. These three columns are used in the background to handle images of products. Set *Primary Key Column 1* attribute to **PRODUCT_ID (Number)**. Set *Source for Primary Key Column 1* to **Existing Sequence**, and select **DEMO_PROD_SEQ** from the *Sequence* drop-down list. PRODUCT_ID is the primary key column, which uniquely identifies a product and is populated behind the scene using a database sequence object (DEMO_PROD_SEQ) when you add a new product. Click the **Create** button to finish the wizard.

This time, the wizard creates two pages (3 and 6) as an initial structure for this module. In the upcoming exercises you will undergo some new techniques to transform these wizard-generated pages and provide them a professional look.

6.3 Modify Products Page - Page 3

Execute the instructions provided in the following sub-sections to first modify the Products (interactive report) page.

6.3.1 Modify Region Properties

1. Call the **Products** page (Page 3) for some modifications.

2. Click the region named *Report 1* and set its *Title* to **Products**.

3. In *SQL Query*, replace the existing SELECT statement with the following:

```
select p.product_id, p.product_name, p.product_description, p.category,
       decode(p.product_avail, 'Y','Yes','N','No') product_avail, p.list_price,
       (select sum(quantity) from demo_order_items where product_id = p.product_id) units,
       (select sum(quantity * p.list_price) from demo_order_items where product_id = p.product_id) sales,
       (select count(o.customer_id) from demo_orders o, demo_order_items t
       where o.order_id = t.order_id and t.product_id = p.product_id group by p.product_id) customers,
       (select max(o.order_timestamp) od from demo_orders o, demo_order_items i where o.order_id =
       i.order_id and i.product_id = p.product_id) last_date_sold, p.product_id img,
       apex_util.prepare_url(p_url=>'f?p='||:app_id||':6:'||:app_session||
       ':::P6_PRODUCT_ID:'||p.product_id) icon_link,
       decode(nvl(dbms_lob.getlength(p.product_image),0),0,null,
       '<img alt="'||p.product_name||'" title="'||p.product_name||'" style="border: 4px solid #CCC;
       -moz-border-radius: 4px; -webkit-border-radius: 4px;"||
       'src="'||apex_util.get_blob_file_src('P6_PRODUCT_IMAGE',p.product_id)||'" height="75"
       width="75" />') detail_img,
       decode(nvl(dbms_lob.getlength(p.product_image),0),0,null,
       apex_util.get_blob_file_src('P6_PRODUCT_IMAGE',p.product_id)) detail_img_no_style,
       tags
from   demo_product_info p
```

The *icon_link* column in this query is formed using the PREPARE_URL function, which is a part of the APEX_UTIL package. It returns the f?p URL. The P_URL is a VARCHAR2 parameter passed on to this function. You will use this function throughout this book to form links – see f?p and APEX_UTIL.PREPARE_URL entries in the book's index. The link is formed to call the Product Details page – Page 6. The *detail_img* column holds images of products. The HTML <img> tag is used to display the images of products in conjunction with a built-in function named APEX_UTIL.GET_BLOB_FILE_SRC. This is an Oracle APEX function and it provides the ability to more specifically format the display of the image with height and width properties. The image is styled using CSS inline styling method. The *getlength* function of the *dbms_lob* package (*dbms_lob.getlength*) is used to estimate the size of a BLOB column in the table. The selection of the BLOB size is made to facilitate the inclusion of a download link in a report. If the length is 0, the BLOB is NULL and no download link is displayed.

4. Expand the *Columns* folder and set meaningful column headings as follows:
   Name, Description, Category, Available, Price, Units, Sales, Customers, Last Sold, Image, Icon Link, Image Detail, Detail Image No style, and **Tags**

5. Modify the following columns using the specified properties. These columns are marked as hidden to make them invisible at runtime. However, they will be visible to your application for handling images. These columns were also derived through the SQL SELECT statement defined in step 3. Note that you can use Ctrl+click or Shift+click keys combination to select multiple columns to change the *Type* properties at once. Each report column has the property *Escape special characters*. By default, this property is set to Yes. Selecting Yes for this property prevents Cross-Site Scripting (XSS) attacks and selecting *No* renders HTML tags stored in the page item or in the entries of a list of value.

Column	Property	Value
PRODUCT_ID	Type	Hidden Column
IMG	Type	Hidden Column
ICON_LINK	Type	Hidden Column
DETAIL_IMG	Escape special characters	No *(otherwise image will not appear)*
DETAIL_IMG_NO_STYLE	Type	Hidden Column

6. Click the **PRODUCT_NAME** column to transform it into a link. By selecting the Product Name column in the *Link Text* attribute you specify this report column to appear as a link. You created a similar kind of link in the previous chapter to call the Customer Details page. In Interactive Reports, you forward a value to the target page using special substitution strings (enclosed in # symbols) as compared to *&Item.* notation (for example, &CUSTOMER_ID.), which you use in the Interactive Grid–see Chapter 5 Section 5.3.1 Step 11.

Property	Value
Type	Link
Target *(under Link)*	Type = Page In this application Page = 6 Name = P6_PRODUCT_ID Value = #PRODUCT_ID#
Link Text	#PRODUCT_NAME#

7. If you save and run the report page at this stage, you will see a an EDIT column (identified with a pencil icon), which leads to the details page. Since we have already created a link (on the Name column through the SELECT statement in step 3), we will eliminate this column. Under the *Products* region, click its **Attributes** folder, and set *Link Column* to **Exclude Link Column**.

8. In the same *Attributes* folder, scroll down to the **Icon View** section and set the following properties. By default, most interactive reports display as a report. You can optionally display columns as icons. When configured, an icon (*View Icons*) appears on the Search bar. To use this view, you must specify the columns to identify the icon, the label, and the target (that is, the link). As a best practice the *Type* attribute of these columns is set to hidden (as you did in step 5), because they are typically not useful for end users.

116

Property	Value
Show	Yes
Columns Per Row	5 (*to display 5 images on a single row in View Icons interface*)
Link Column	ICON_LINK
Image Source Column	DETAIL_IMG_NO_STYLE
Label Column	PRODUCT_NAME
Image Attributes	width="75" height="75" (*styles height and width of images*)

9. Just under the Icon View section, there is another section named Detail View. In the **Detail View** section, set *Show* to **Yes**. When configured, a *View Details* icon appears on the Search bar.

10. In **Before Rows**, enter the following code. This attribute of the *Detail View* enables you to enter HTML code to be displayed before report rows. For example, you can use the <TABLE> element to put the database content in row/column format. Besides adding HTML code, styling information can also be incorporated using this attribute. The <style> tag is used to define style information for an HTML document. Inside the <style> element you specify how HTML elements should render in a browser. A cascading style sheet (CSS) provides a way to control the style of a web page without changing its structure. When used properly, a CSS separates visual properties such as color, margins, and fonts from the structure of the HTML document. Oracle Application Express includes themes containing templates to reference their own CSS. The style rules defined in each CSS for a particular theme also determine the way reports and regions display. The code below uses custom CSS rules to override the default Oracle APEX Interactive Report (apexir) styles.

```
<style>
  table.apexir_WORKSHEET_CUSTOM {
    border: none !important;
    box-shadow: none;
    -moz-box-shadow: none;
    -webkit-box-shadow: none;}

  .apexir_WORKSHEET_DATA td {
    border-bottom: none !important;}

  table.reportDetail td {
    padding: 2px 4px !important;
    border: none !important;
    font: 11px/16px Arial, sans-serif;}

  table.reportDetail td.separator {
    background: #F0F0F0 !important;
    padding: 0 !important;
    height: 1px !important;
    padding: 0;
    line-height: 2px !important;
```

NOTE: Remember that all APEX pages are HTML pages controlled by HTML properties and cascading style sheet (CSS) settings. When you create an interactive report, Oracle APEX renders it based on CSS classes associated with the current theme. Each APEX interactive report component has a CSS style definition that may be changed by applying standard CSS techniques to override the defaults. Such changes may be applied to a single interactive report, to a page template to effect changes across several interactive reports, or to all page templates of a theme to enforce a common look and feel for all reports in an application.

In the current step, you are changing the appearance of the report by overriding built-in styles for the table and subordinate elements.

```
overflow: hidden;}

table.reportDetail td h1 {margin: 0 !important}

table.reportDetail td img {
    margin-top: 8px;
    border: 4px solid #CCC;
    -moz-border-radius: 4px;
    -webkit-border-radius: 4px;}
  </style>
  <table class="reportDetail">
```

11. In **For Each Row**, enter the following code. The code is applied to each record. In every <td> element you are referencing interactive report columns and labels with the help of a special substitution string (#) and are styling each record using inline CSS method. You used the substitution string to reference table column names and labels of page items as #PRODUCT_NAME# and #CATEGORY_LABEL#, respectively.

```
<tr>
  <td rowspan="5" valign="top"><img width="75" height="75" src="#DETAIL_IMG_NO_STYLE#"></td>
  <td colspan="6"><h1><a href="#ICON_LINK#"><strong>#PRODUCT_NAME#</strong></a></h1></td>
</tr>
<tr>
  <td><strong>#CATEGORY_LABEL#:</strong></td><td>#CATEGORY#</td>
  <td><strong>#PRODUCT_AVAIL_LABEL#:</strong></td><td>#PRODUCT_AVAIL#</td>
  <td><strong>#LAST_DATE_SOLD_LABEL#:</strong></td><td>#LAST_DATE_SOLD#</td>
</tr>
<tr>
  <td align="left"><strong>#PRODUCT_DESCRIPTION_LABEL#:</strong></td>
  <td colspan="5">#PRODUCT_DESCRIPTION#</td>
</tr>
<tr>
  <td style="padding-bottom: 0px;"><strong>#LIST_PRICE_LABEL#</strong></td>
  <td style="padding-bottom: 0px;"><strong>#UNITS_LABEL#</strong></td>
  <td style="padding-bottom: 0px;"><strong>#SALES_LABEL#</strong></td>
  <td style="padding-bottom: 0px;"><strong>#CUSTOMERS_LABEL#</strong></td>
</tr>
<tr>
  <td style="padding-top: 0px;">#LIST_PRICE#</td>
  <td style="padding-top: 0px;">#UNITS#</td>
  <td style="padding-top: 0px;">#SALES#</td>
  <td style="padding-top: 0px;">#CUSTOMERS#</td>
</tr>
<tr>
  <td colspan="7" class="separator"></td>
</tr>
```

12. In **After Rows**, enter **</table>** to complete the HTML code. In this attribute you enter the HTML to be displayed after report rows. It is the closing table tag </TABLE> to end the table.

13. Save and run the page from the **Manage Products** option in the *Setup* menu. Click the **View Reports** icon ▦. Click the **Actions** menu and click **Columns**. Make sure all columns (except Description, Last Sold, and Tags) appear in *Display in Report section*. Use the arrow icons to arrange columns in a desired order and click the **Apply** button. Only the columns you selected will appear in the interactive report.

14. Click the **Actions** menu again and select **Save Report** (under *Report*). From the *Save* drop-down list, select **As Default Report Settings**. Set *Default Report Type* to **Primary** and click **Apply**. After modifying an interactive report you must save it using this procedure, otherwise you'll lose the applied settings when you subsequently view this report. Developers can save two types of default interactive report: primary and alternative. Both reports display on the Report list on the Search bar. The primary default report (you just saved) cannot be renamed or deleted.

6.3.2 Modify Button Properties

Modify the following attribute of the *Create* button. Currently it is lying under the Products region and is being switched to the Breadcrumb region to make it more visible. This button is used to add new products. Recall that in the Customers module you created it manually. This time, the wizard created it automatically for the interactive report along with a proper link, which leads you to the Product Details page–see the *Action* and *Target* properties of this button.

Property	Value
Label	Add Product
Region	**Breadcrumb**
Button Position	Create
Button Template	Text with Icon
Hot	Yes
Icon CSS Classes	fa-chevron-right

Click the **Save and Run Page** button to test Page 3. You will see three icons View Icon, View Report, and View Detail beside the Search Bar. Click each icon to see the corresponding output.

6.4 Modify Product Details Page - Page 6

The Page Designer toolbar carries a section called *Page Selector*. The Page Selector displays the current page. Click the down arrow (labeled *Page Finder*) to search for pages. Alternatively, enter a page number in the field and click *Go*. To navigate to the previous or next page, click *Navigate to Next Page* (up arrow) and *Navigate to Previous Page* (down arrow).

Using the Page Selector call **Page 6** in the Page Designer. Click the root node 📄 Page 6: Product Details and set the following properties to adjust the dimension of the Product Details page.

Property	Value
Title	Product Details
Width *(under Dialog)*	660
Height	530
Maximum Width	1000

6.4.1 Making Page Item Mandatory

Make the product name item (**P6_PRODUCT_NAME**) mandatory using the following properties:

Property	Value
Template *(under Appearance)*	Required
Value Required *(under Validation)*	Yes

The first property marks mandatory items on a page with an asterisk (*), while the second one ensures that the marked fields are not null. Set these two properties for **P6_CATEGORY, P6_PRODUCT_AVAIL,** and **P6_LIST_PRICE** page items, too.

6.4.2 Attach Categories LOV

We created a list of values (CATEGORIES) in Chapter 3 section 3.4.1. Here we're going to use that list to display predefined values of categories in a Select List. First, you will change the Category item from Text to a Select List, and then you'll define the list of values (LOV) to which the item will bound. Recall that you used this process in the Manage Customers module to display STATES LOV. In the Items folder under the Product Details region, click the **P6_CATEGORY** item and amend the following properties in the Property Editor:

Property	Value
Type *(under Identification)*	Select List
Type *(under List of Values)*	Shared Component
List of Values	CATEGORIES
Display Extra Values	No
Display Null Value	No

6.4.3 Attach LOV to Product Available Column

Next, you will change the *Product Available* field to a *Radio Group* comprising two options: *Yes* and *No*. This LOV was also created in Chapter 3 section 3.4.4. Just like the previous steps, here as well, you're changing the item type from Text to Radio Group. At runtime, this item will show two options (as shown in the Figure 6-2) to specify whether the selected product is available or not. If you ignore this exercise and leave the item to its default type, users can enter whatever value they like, resulting in compromising application's integrity. This is a good example to restrict users to select valid values. Select the **P6_PRODUCT_AVAIL** item and set the following properties. Note that the last two properties in the table set Y (which stands for Yes) as the default value for this item. You can also set the *Identification Type* of this page item to *Switch* to display the two options as a switch–see Chapter 10 Section 10.8.1.

Property	Value
Type *(under Identification)*	Radio Group
Label	Product Available
Number of Columns	2
Type *(under List of Values)*	Shared Component
List of Values	Y or N
Display Extra Values	No
Display Null Value	No
Type *(under Default)*	Static Value
Static Value	Y

6.4.4 Handling Image (Handle Image Exercise A)

Modify the following properties (in the *Settings* section) for the **P6_PRODUCT_IMAGE** item to handle the product image.

Property	Value
MIME Type Column	MIMETYPE
Filename Column	FILENAME
BLOB Last Update Column	IMAGE_LAST_UPDATE

In the *Settings* section, the attribute *Storage Type* is set to **BLOB column specified in item Source attribute** by default. The *Storage Type* attribute specifies where the uploaded file should be stored at. It has two values:

- *BLOB column specified in item source attribute*. Stores the uploaded file in the table used by the "Automatic Row Processing (DML)" process and the column specified in the item source attribute. The column has to be of data type BLOB.
- *Table APEX_APPLICATION_TEMP_FILE*. Stores the uploaded file in a table named APEX_APPLICATION_TEMP_FILE.

6.4.5 Create Region – Product Image (Handle Image Exercise B)

To show the images of selected products on Product Details page, we will create a *Static Content* sub-region. Note that this section will only create a blank region to hold an image. The image will be added to it in a subsequent section. To create a sub-region, right-click the sole region </> Form on DEMO_PRODUCT_INFO and select **Create Sub Region** from the context menu. A sub-region is a region that resides in a parent region. Select the new sub-region and modify the following properties. The region will be displayed only when there exists an image and this evaluation is made using a condition based on a PL/SQL function.

Property	Value
Title	Product Image
Type	Static Content
Parent Region	Form on DEMO_PRODUCT_INFO
Type (*under Server-side Condition*)	PL/SQL Function Body

PL/SQL Function Body	<pre>1 declare
	2 begin
	3 if :P6_PRODUCT_ID is not null then
	4 for c1 in (select nvl(dbms_lob.getlength(product_image),0) A
	5 from demo_product_info
	6 where product_id = :P6_PRODUCT_ID)
	7 loop
	8 if c1.A > 0 then
	9 return true;
	10 end if;
	11 end loop;
	12 end if;
	13 return false;
	14 end;</pre>

NOTE: Page items are referenced in a PL/SQL block using bind variables in which a colon(:) is prefixed to the item name – :P6_PRODUCT_ID, for example.

Code Explained

In Oracle APEX you make use of conditions to control the appearance of page components. The ability to dynamically show or hide a page component is referred to as *conditional rendering*. You define conditional rendering for regions, items, and buttons. These page components have a *Condition* section in the property editor, where you select a condition type from a list. In the current scenario, you set a condition based on a PL/SQL function, which returns a single Boolean value: True or False. If the code returns True, the region is displayed carrying the image of the selected product. After selecting a condition type, you inform Oracle APEX to execute the defined PL/SQL code. The code first executes an IF condition (line 3) to check whether the product ID is not null by evaluating the value of the page item P6_PRODUCT_ID. If the value is null, the flow of the code is transferred to line 13, where a false value is returned and the function is terminated. If there exists a value for the product ID, then line 4 is executed, which creates a FOR loop to loop through all records in the DEMO_PRODUCT_INFO table to find the record (and consequently the image) of the selected product (line 4-11). On line 8, another IF condition is used to assess whether the image is found. If so, a true value is returned on line 9 and the function is terminated.

6.4.6 Create Item (Handle Image Exercise C)

In this section, you will create a new item named P6_IMAGE to display the product image in the *Product Image* sub-region. Right-click the **Product Image** sub-region *Product Image* and select **Create Page Item** from the context menu. Set the following properties for the new item. The code defined in the PL/SQL Function Body fetches image of the selected product using a function (apex_util.get_blob_file_src). By setting the *Rows Returned* condition and using a SQL query we ensured the existence of an image in the table.

Property	Value
Name	P6_IMAGE
Type	Display Only
Label	*Clear the Label box to make it empty*
Region	Product Image
Template	No template (*Set it to -Select- placeholder*)
Type (*under Source*)	PL/SQL Function Body
PL/SQL Function Body	return '<img src="'||apex_util.get_blob_file_src('P6_PRODUCT_IMAGE',:P6_PRODUCT_ID)||'" />';
Type (*under Server-side Condition*)	Rows Returned
SQL Query	SELECT mimetype from demo_product_info WHERE product_id = :P6_PRODUCT_ID AND mimetype like 'image%'
Escape special characters	No (*Otherwise the image won't appear*)

6.4.7 Create Button to Remove Image (Handle Image Exercise D)

An image can be removed from the Product Details page and consequently from the underlying table by clicking this button. It is attached to a process (Delete Image) defined in the next section. Right-click the **Product Image** sub-region and select **Create Button**. Set the following properties for the new button. The Target value calls a confirmation box. This call is made using an Oracle APEX function (*apex.confirm*) by passing a message and the name of the Delete button. If you click Yes in the confirmation box, the process associated with the Delete button removes image references from the products table.

Property	Value
Name	DELETE_IMAGE
Label	Remove Image
Button Template	Text with Icon
Icon CSS Classes	fa-chevron-right
Action (*under Behavior*)	Redirect to URL
URL (*under Target*)	javascript:apex.confirm('Are you sure you want to delete this image? It will no longer be available for others to see if you continue.','DELETE_IMAGE');

6.5 Create Process Under Processing to Delete Image (Handle Image Exercise E)

This is the process I mentioned in the previous section. It will be associated with the Delete button to remove a product image. To remove an image stored in a database table, you are required to just replace the content of the relevant columns with a null. Click the **Processing** tab ⌞⌝ and then right-click the **Processing** folder. From the context menu select **Create Process**. Set the following properties for the new process:

Property	Value
Name	Delete Image Process
Type	PL/SQL Code

PL/SQL Code	UPDATE demo_product_info
	SET product_image=null,
	    mimetype=null,
	    filename=null,
	    image_last_update=null
	WHERE product_id = :P6_PRODUCT_ID;

Success Message	Product image deleted.
When Button Pressed	DELETE_IMAGE

Test Your Work

Save your work and run the application. From the main navigation menu, select **Manage Products** from the *Setup* menu. On the main interactive report page (Figure 6-1), click the three report icons ▦ ▤ ▥ individually to see different views of products information. Clicking **View Icons** will present small icons of products. Each product is presented as a linked icon. If you click any icon, you'll be taken to the form page (Page 6) where you'll see details of the selected product (Figure 6-2). Click the Report View icon. The Report View presents data in a table. Here, you can access the details page by clicking products' names. Click the Detail View icon. This View presents products information from a different perspective. You can access details of a product by clicking its name. This is the view that was styled in section 6.3.1 steps 9-12.

Click any product's name to call its details page (as illustrated in Figure 6-2). The main region (*Form on DEMO_PRODUCT_INFO*) was created by the wizard incorporating all relevant fields. The Product Image sub-region appears within the parent region. This region was created in section 6.4.5. Also, note that the Remove Image button (you created in section 6.4.7) appears within the child region.

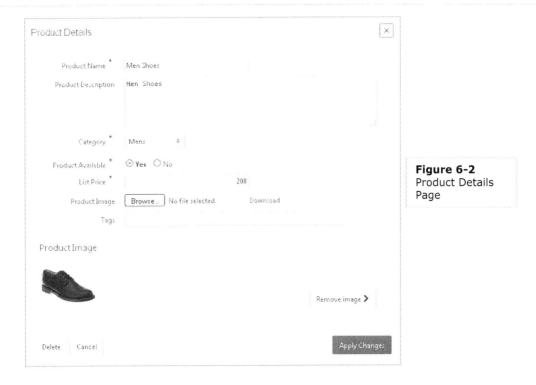

Figure 6-2
Product Details
Page

Create a new product record using the *Add Product* button on the Products report page. Click the *Browse* button and select any small image file to test image upload. You can use an existing product image by right-clicking the image and selecting *Save Image As* from the context menu. Or, use the *Download* link provided on the Product Details form page to get one for testing. Once you have an image in place, fill in all the fields except List Price. Try to save this record by clicking the *Create* button. A message will appear at the top of your screen informing you to provide some value for the List Price. Now, provide some alpha-numeric value like *abc123* in the List Price. Again, a message will come up reminding you to put a numeric value. These messages are fired when two auto-generated validations are violated. The wizard also takes care of data integrity and creates some validations (on the Processing tab) based on backend table's definitions. Finally, input a numeric value in the List Price field and save the record. You'll see the new product appears on the Products page among others with the image you uploaded. Edit this record and see the image appearing in the defined sub-region. Change the category of this product, switch availability to the other option and apply changes. Call the product again and observe the changes you just made to it. Click the *Remove Image* button and see what happens. Click the *Delete* button followed by *OK* in the confirmation box. The product will vanish from the list.

Summary

In this chapter, you were equipped with some more skills that will assist you in developing your own applications. Most importantly, you knew the techniques to handle, store, and retrieve images to and from database tables. Play around with this module by tweaking the saved properties to see resulting effects on the two pages. This way, you will learn some new things not covered in this chapter. Of course, you can always restore the properties to their original values by referencing the exercises provided in the chapter. An important point to consider here is that a module of this caliber would have taken plenty of time and effort to develop using conventional tools. With Oracle APEX declarative development, you created it in a couple of hours.

Chapter 7

Taking Orders

7.1 About Sale Orders

This chapter will teach you how to create professional looking order forms. Orders from customers will be taken through a sequence of wizard steps. The first wizard step will allow you to select an existing customer or create a new one. In the second step, you will select ordered products. After placing the order, the last step will show summary of the placed order. Once an order is created, you can view, modify, or delete it through Order Details page using a link in orders main page. The list presented below displays the application pages you will create in this chapter:

Page No.	Page Name	Purpose
4	Orders	The main page to display all existing orders
29	Order Details	Display a complete order with details for modification
11	Identify Customer (Wizard Step 1)	Select an existing customer or create a new one
12	Select Order Items (Wizard Step 2)	Add products to an order
14	Order Summary (Wizard Step 3)	Show summary of the placed order

You'll build this module sequentially in the sequence specified above. The first two pages (Page 4 and 29) will be created initially using a new wizard option: *Master Detail Form*. Both these pages are not part of the Order Wizard and will be utilized for order modification and deletion after recording an order. Page 4 is similar to the pages you created in Customer and Product modules and lists all placed orders, while Page 29 will be used to manipulate order details. For example, you can call an order in the usual way using the provided link in the master page. The called order will appear in the details page where you can:

- Add/Remove products to and from an order
- Delete the order itself

The purpose of each chapter in this book is to teach you some new features. Here as well, you'll get some new stuff. This chapter will walk you through to get detailed practical exposure to the techniques this module contains. After completing the two main pages, you will work on actual order wizard steps to create other pages of the module. Recall that in the previous chapter you modified the main interactive report (Page 3) to create a couple of views (Icon and Detail) and used the *Actions* menu to select and sort table columns. In this chapter, many other utilities covered under the Actions menu will be exposed. But first, let's create the two main pages using the conventional route.

1. Click the **Create Page** button in the App Builder.

2. On the first wizard screen, click the **Form** option.

3. This time, select the **Two Page Master Detail** option. A master detail form reflects a one-to-many relationship between two tables in a database. Typically, a master detail form displays a master row and multiple detail rows within a single HTML form. With this form, users can insert, update, and delete values from two tables or views. On the Master Detail page, the master record displays as a standard form and the detail records appear in an interactive grid region under the master section. This region, which used to be of Tabular Form type and supported images, is of Interactive Grid type in verion 5.1.

4. Fill in the next screen (*Page Attributes*) as illustrated below, and click **Next**.

* Master Page Number	4
* Master Page Name	Orders
* Detail Page Number	29
* Detail Page Name	Order Details
Breadcrumb	Breadcrumb
Parent Entry	No parent entry
* Master Page Entry Name	Orders
* Detail Page Entry Name	Order Details

5. On the *Navigation Menu* screen, set *Navigation Preference* to **Identify an existing navigation menu entry for this page**, set *Existing Navigation Menu Entry* to **Orders**, and click **Next**.

6. Select the values in the *Master Source* screen (as shown in the following figure), and click **Next**. In this step, you select the parent table, which contains the master information for each order. You also specify the primary key column, which will be populated automatically behind the scene using a trigger named *demo_orders_biu* along with a sequence named *demo_ord_seq*. You can view both these database objects from *SQL Workshop > Object Browser* interface–see Section 2.10 in Chapter 2. The ORDER_ID column selected in the *Form Navigation Order* list is the navigation order column used by the previous and next buttons on the *Order Details* page to navigate to a different master record.

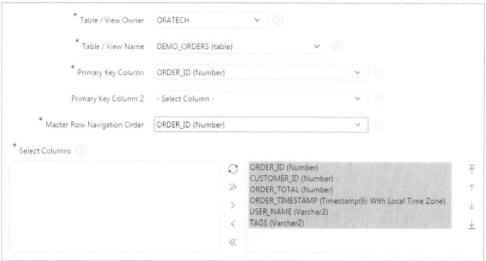

7. Set properties in the *Detail Source* screen as illustrated below and click **Create** to finish the wizard. On this screen, you specify the relational child table, which carries line item information for each order. The primary key column of this table will be populated automatically via a trigger named *demo_order_items_bi*, which gets the next primary key values from a sequence named *demo_order_items_seq*. In the *Master Detail Foreign Key* list you select the sole auto-generated foreign key, which creates a relationship between the master and detail tables.

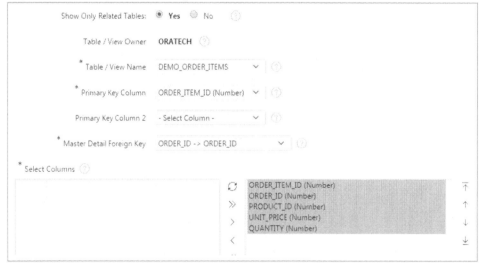

Before running these pages, let's see what the wizard has done for us. The following table lists all those components created automatically by the wizard with complete functionalities to execute this module. The master page (Page 4) is created with an Interactive Grid containing a list of all orders. Shortly, we will transform it into an Interactive Report to explore some more useful features. The details page (Page 29), on the other hand, has many things to reveal. The following table provides details of all those wizard-generated components.

Component: Pre-Rendering Process
Name: Fetch Row from DEMO_ORDERS
Description: Fetches master row from DEMO_ORDERS table. See *Test Your Work* section in Chapter 5 for further details on this process.

Component: Region
Name: Order Details
Description: The page has two regions. The upper region, which is a Static Content region, displays master information like customer ID, order date, and so on. The lower region shows product details along with quantity and price in an Interactive Grid.

Component: Buttons
Names: GET_NEXT_ORDER_ID and GET_PREVIOUS_ORDER_ID
Description: These buttons are added to the master region to fetch next and previous orders, respectively. For example, when you click the Next button `>` , the page is submitted to get the next order record from the server by triggering a process named *Get Next or Previous Primary Key Value* in the *Pre-Rendering* section of the page. This is a *Form Pagination* type process, which retrieves the previous or next record from a database table or view without navigating back to the report. If the form allows data to be updated (as in the current scenario), then you must save a record prior to this pagination process executing. If you don't, any updates made will be lost when you navigate to another record. Based on the currently fetched order number, which is held in the page item P29_ORDER_ID, the process dynamically obtains the next and previous order numbers and stores them in two hidden page items: P29_ORDER_ID_NEXT and P29_ORDER_ID_PREV – see *Primary Key Item*, *Next Primary Key Item*, and *Previous Primary Key Item* properties set for this process. The visibility of these buttons is controlled by a *Server-side Condition* (Item is NOT NULL), which says that these buttons will be visible only when their corresponding hidden items have some values.

Component: Button

Name: Cancel

Description: The Cancel button closes Page 29 and takes you back to Page 4 without saving an order. For this, a redirect action is generated in the *Behavior* section with Page 4 set as the target.

Component: Button

Name: Delete

Description: The Delete button removes a complete order. When this button is clicked, a confirmation dialog pops up using its *Target* property, which is set to: *javascript:apex.confirm(htmldb_delete_message,'DELETE');*
When you confirm the deletion, a *SQL DELETE action* (specified in *Database Action* property for this button) is executed within the built-in *Automatic Row Processing (DML)* processes–*Process Row of DEMO_ORDERS* and *Save Interactive Grid Data.*

Component: Button

Name: Save

Description: The Save button records updates to an existing order in the corresponding database table. This button is visible when you call an order for modification, in other words, P29_ORDER_ID is NOT NULL. The process behind this button is controlled by a *SQL UPDATE action* within the two built-in *Automatic Row Processing (DML)* processes.

Component: Button

Name: Create

Description: The Create button is used for new orders to handle the INSERT operation. This button is visible when you are creating a new order, that is, the page item P29_ORDER_ID is NULL. It uses the *SQL INSERT action* within the two built-in *Automatic Row Processing (DML)* processes.

Component: Process

Name: Process Row of DEMO_ORDERS

Description: This *Automatic Row Processing (DML)* type process is generated by the wizard to handle DML operations performed on the master row of an order, which gets into the DEMO_ORDERS table. It comes into action when you click Delete, Save, or Create buttons. To perform these operations successfully, ensure all the three operations (Insert, Update, and Delete) are checked in the *Supported Operations* property. Note that this process must precede the *Save Interactive Grid Data* process; otherwise, you will get "*Current version of data in database has changed since user initiated update process*" error. To avoid this error, drag and place this process before the *Save Interactive Grid Data* process or set its *Sequence* property to a number lower than that of *Save Interactive Grid Data* process. The three buttons and their associated actions are depicted in the following figure.

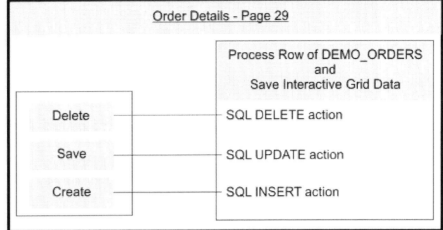

Component: Process

Name: Save Interactive Grid Data

Description: The *Save Interactive Grid Data* process is responsible to handle DML operations on the details table (DEMO_ORDER_ITEMS). This process is associated with the details section (Interactive Grid) to insert, update, or delete Interactive Grid rows.

Component: Branches

Name: Go To Page 29, Go To Page 29, and Go To Page 4

When you submit a page, the Oracle APEX server receives the submit request and performs the processes and validations associated with that request. After this, it evaluates where to land in the application via *branches*. By default, it selects the current page as the target page. For example, when you click the Next or Previous buttons on Page 29, you stay on the same page. If you want to land users to some other page, you can do this as well by creating branches. In the current scenario, you are moved back to Page 4 when you click Save, Delete, or Create buttons on Page 29. A branch has two important properties: *Behavior* and *Condition*. In the *Behavior* section you specify the page (or URL) to redirect to, and in *Condition* you specify when the branch is to be fired. Here, the first two branches appearing under the *After Submit* folder are created to keep you on Page 29. These branches are associated with *Next* and *Previous* buttons–see *When Button Pressed* properties of these branches. The third one (appearing in the *After Processing* folder) takes you back to Page 4 when you click *Save*, *Delete*, or *Create* buttons. An auto-generated condition (under the *Condition* section) evaluates the request, which comes from the three buttons to switch you to Page 4 - see the *Behavior* section that specifies the redirect.

Run Page 4 to check this module. The first page (Page 4) you see is an interactive grid. It is similar to the one you created in Chapter 6. It has a *Create* button, which is used to create a new order. Click the edit link (represented with a pencil icon) in front of any record to call the *Order Details* page (Page 29). The *Order Details* page has two regions. The upper region, which is called the master region, displays information from the DEMO_ORDERS table, while the lower interactive grid region shows relevant line item information from the DEMO_ORDER_ITEMS table. Besides usual buttons, the master region has two navigational buttons (on far right in the upper region). These buttons help you move forward and backward to browse orders. The *Order Timestamp* field is supplemented with a *Date Picker* control. You can add more products to the details section by clicking the *Add Row* button. From a professional viewpoint this page is not user friendly. If you try to add a new product, you have to enter its ID manually. Moreover, if you try to create a new order, you won't see the interactive grid. By default, this grid is visible only when you modify an existing order and hides when you try to create a new order. This behavior is controlled by a server side condition (Item is NOT NULL) set for the Interactive Grid region (Order Details). With this condition set, the region is rendered only when the page item P29_ORDER_ID has some value. Choosing the – *Select* – placeholder for the *Server-side Condition Type* property removes this condition and makes the interactive grid visible every time you access Page 29. Even after this adjustment, you will face some constraint issues related to a backend table. To avoid all such problems, execute the instructions provided in subsequent sections to make it easier for the end user.

7.3 Modify Orders Page - Page 4

Execute the instructions provided in the following sub-sections to modify the Orders page.

7.3.1 Delete and Re-Create the Default Orders Region

You need to delete the default *Orders* region to create a new one with the same name and with interactive functionality. The new region is being created to incorporate customers information in an interactive report to explore some exciting features of this useful tool.

1. Right-click the **Orders** region ⊞ Orders and select **Delete** from the context menu.

2. Create a new region by right-clicking the main *Regions* node and selecting the **Create Region** option.

3. Select the new region and modify it using the following table:

Property	Value
Title	Orders
Type	Interactive Report
SQL Query	select lpad(to_char(o.order_id),4,'0000') order_number, o.order_id, 　　to_char(o.order_timestamp,'Month YYYY') order_month, 　　trunc(o.order_timestamp) order_date, 　　o.user_name sales_rep, o.order_total, 　　c.cust_last_name||', '||c.cust_first_name customer_name, 　　(select count(*) from demo_order_items oi 　　 where oi.order_id = o.order_id and oi.quantity != 0) order_items, 　　o.tags tags from demo_orders o, demo_customers c where o.customer_id = c.customer_id

4. Expand the *Columns* folder under the new *Orders* region and set the *Type* property for the ORDER_ID column to **Hidden Column**.

5. Set meaningful headings for all interactive report columns as follows. Using drag and drop in the rendering tree you can arrange these columns in the defined order.

   Order #, Order Month, Order Date, Customer Name, Sales Rep, Order Items, Order Total, and Tags

6. Edit the **ORDER_TOTAL** column and select the value **$5,234.10** for its *Format Mask* property.

7. Select the **Order Number** column (not Order ID) and turn it into a link using the following properties:

Property	Value
Type	Link
Target *(under Link)*	Type = Page in this application Page = 29 Name = P29_ORDER_ID Value = #ORDER_ID# Clear Cache = 29
Link Text	#ORDER_NUMBER#

8. Click the **Attribute** folder (under the *Orders* region), scroll down to the *Actions Menu* section, and set *Save Public Report* to **Yes** to include this option in the *Actions* menu at runtime. By enabling this option you will be able to create a public report in section 7.3.4.

9. Save your modifications.

7.3.2 Modify the Interactive Report

Perform the following steps to change the look and feel of the initial interactive report. After performing these steps, the interactive report will be saved as the *Default Primary Report*, which cannot be renamed or deleted. Note that these modifications are made using the *Actions* menu at runtime.

1. Click the **Save and Run Page** button to run Page 4.

2. Click the **Actions** menu `Actions ∨` and then click **Columns** in the Actions menu.

3. Using the arrow buttons to your right, arrange the columns appearing in *Display in Report* section as follows. If you do not want to see a column in the report, move it to the *Do Not Display* pane.

   Order #, Order Month, Order Date, Customer Name, Sales Rep, Order Items, Order Total, and **Tags**

4. Click the **Apply** button.

5. To display most current orders on top, click the **Actions** menu and select **Data | Sort**. In the *Sort* grid, select the **Order #** column in the first row, set the corresponding *Direction* to **Descending**, and click **Apply**.

6. Click **Actions | Report | Save Report**. In the *Save Report* dialog box, select **As Default Report Settings** from the *Save* list, select **Primary** for *Default Report Type*, and click **Apply**. Perform this step whenever you make changes to a report via the *Actions* menu; otherwise, your modifications will not be reflected the next time you log in to the application. In Interactive Reports, you can apply a number of filters, highlights, and other customizations. Rather than having to re-enter these customizations each time you run the report, you tell Oracle APEX to remember them so that they are applied automatically on every next run. The application users can save multiple reports based on the default primary report, as discussed in the next couple of sections.

7.3.3 Create Alternative Report

Alternative report enables developers to create multiple report layouts. Only developers can save, rename, or delete an Alternative Report. This report (named Monthly Review) is based on the default primary report and will be rendered in a different layout using the *Control Break* utility on Order Month column. Execute the following steps on the primary interactive report on Page 4 to create three different views of the report.

A. Report View

1. From the **Actions** menu, select **Save Report** (under *Report*). In the *Save Report* dialog box, select **As Default Report Settings** from the *Save* list. This time, select

the **Alternative** option for *Default Report Type*, enter **Monthly Review** in the *Name* box, and click **Apply**. You will see a drop down list between the *Search* bar and the *Actions* menu carrying two reports: *Primary Report* and *Monthly Review*.

2. From the list, select the alternative report named **2. Monthly Review**.

3. Click **Actions | Format | Control Break**. Under *Column*, select **Order Month** in the first row, set *Status* to **Enabled**, and click **Apply**. The *Control Break* feature enables grouping to be added to your report on one or more columns. The *Column* attribute defines which column to group on and the *Status* attribute determines whether the control break is active. When you click the *Apply* button, you will see the report results are grouped by the *Order Month* column and the *Control Break* column rule is listed under the toolbar, as shown in the following illustration. A checkbox is displayed next to the *Control Break* column and is used to turn the control break on or off. The control break can be deleted from the report by clicking the small cross icon.

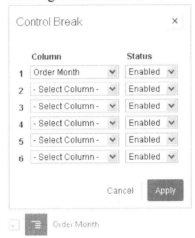

4. Click **Actions | Format | Highlight**. Type **Orders > $2,000** in the *Name* box, set *Highlight Type* to **Cell**, click **[green]** for *Background Color*, click **[red]** for *Text Color*, in *Highlight Condition* set *Column* to **Order Total**, *Operator* to **>** (greater than), *Expression* to **2000**, and click **Apply**. To distinguish important data from the rest, Oracle APEX provides you with conditional highlighting feature in interactive reports. The highlight feature in Interactive Reports enables users to display data in different colors based on a condition. You can define multiple highlight conditions for a report. In this step, you're instructing to highlight the Order Total column in the report with green background and red text color where the value of this column is greater than 2000. Since you set the *Highlight Type* to *Cell*, the condition will apply only to the Order Total column. To modify an existing condition, click it under the toolbar.

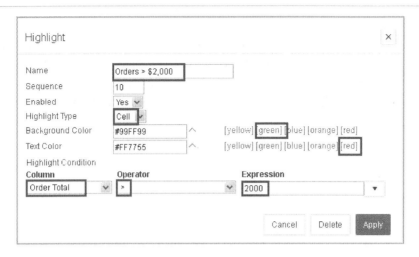

5. Click **Actions | Format | Highlight**. Type **Orders <= $900** in the *Name* field, set *Highlight Type* to **Row**, click **[yellow]** for *Background Color*, click **[Red]** for *Text Color*, in *Highlight Condition* set *Column* to **Order Total**, *Operator* to <= (less than or equal to), *Expression* to **900** and click **Apply**. This step is similar to the previous one with different parameters. In contrast to the previous action, where only a single cell was highlighted, this one highlights a complete row with yellow background and red text color and applies it to all rows in the report that have Order Total equaling $900 or less.

The resulting output should resemble Figure 7-1.

Order Month : December 2016

Order # ↓⁼	Order Date	Customer Name	Sales Rep	Order Items	Order Total	Tags
0010	27-DEC-2016	Bradley, Eugene	DEMO	3	$870.00	-
0009	24-DEC-2016	Hartsfield, William	DEMO	3	$730.00	-
0008	18-DEC-2016	OHare, Frank	DEMO	4	$1,060.00	-
0007	10-DEC-2016	Logan, Edward	DEMO	7	$905.00	-
0006	05-DEC-2016	Logan, Edward	DEMO	4	$1,515.00	-

Order Month : November 2016

Order #	Order Date	Customer Name	Sales Rep	Order Items	Order Total	Tags
0005	30-NOV-2016	Lambert, Albert	DEMO	5	$950.00	-
0004	20-NOV-2016	LaGuardia, Fiorello	DEMO	5	$1,090.00	-
0003	18-NOV-2016	Hartsfield, William	DEMO	5	$1,640.00	-
0002	07-NOV-2016	Dulles, John	DEMO	10	$2,350.00	LARGE ORDER

Order Month : October 2016

Order #	Order Date	Customer Name	Sales Rep	Order Items	Order Total	Tags
0001	24-OCT-2016	Bradley, Eugene	DEMO	3	$1,890.00	-

Figure 7-1
Monthly Order Review Report

B. Chart View

You can generate charts in Interactive Reports based on the results of a report. You can specify the type of chart together with the data in the report you want to chart. In the following exercise, you will create a horizontal bar chart to present monthly sales figures using the Order Month column for the chart labels and a sum of the Order Total column for the chart values.

1. Click **Actions | Chart**.

2. Select the first option (horizontal bar) for the *Chart Type*.

3. Select **Order Month** for *Label*.

4. Enter **Period** in *Axis Title for Label*.

5. Select **Order Total** for *Value*.

6. Enter **Total Orders Amount** in *Axis Title for Value*.

7. Select **Sum** for *Function*.

8. Select **Label-Ascending** for *Sort*.

9. Click **Apply**.

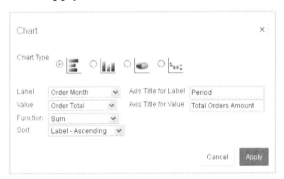

The chart should look like Figure 7-2. Note that the toolbar now has two icons: View Report and View Chart. If the chart doesn't appear, click the View Chart icon <img> in the search bar. Move your mouse over each bar to see total amount for the month.

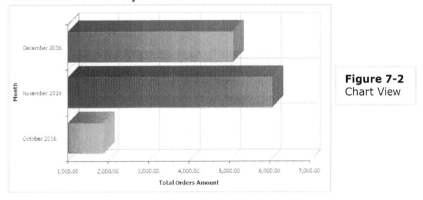

Figure 7-2
Chart View

C. Group By View

Group By enables users to group the result set by one or more columns and perform mathematical computations against the columns. Once users define the group by, a corresponding icon is placed in the Search bar, which they can use to switch among the three report views.

1. Click the **View Report** icon ⊞ in the interactive report toolbar to switch back to the report view interface.

2. Click **Actions | Group By**.

3. Set the properties as show in the following figure and click **Apply**. Use the *Add Function* link to add the second function (Count). The first function calculates the monthly average of orders, while the second function counts the number of orders placed in each month.

4. Click **Actions | Report | Save Report**. Select **As Default Report Setting** followed by the **Alternative** option. Click the **Apply** button.

The output should look like the figure illustrated below. Note that a third icon (*View Group By*) will be added to the toolbar.

Order Month	Average Order Total	Number of Orders
October 2016	$1,890.00	1
December 2016	$1,016.00	5
November 2016	$1,515.00	4
		1 - 3

7.3.4 Create Public Report

This type of report can be saved, renamed, or deleted by end users who created it. Other users can view and save the layout as another report. Execute the following instructions to create the three views Report, Chart, and Group by of a public report. The Alternative report created in the previous section focused on orders, while this one is created from customers perspective.

A. Report View

1. Select the default **1. Primary Report** from the *Reports* drop-down list.

2. From the **Actions** menu, select **Save Report** (under *Report*).

3. From the *Save* drop-down list select **As Named Report**. Users can create multiple variations of a report and save them as named reports for either public or private viewing. For report *Name*, enter **Customer Review**, put a check on **Public** and click the **Apply** button. A new report group (Public) will be added to the reports list in the Search bar, carrying a new report named *Customer Review*. When you click the Apply button, the report is displayed on your screen.

4. With report **1. Customer Review** being displayed on your screen, click **Actions | Format | Control Break**. Select **Customer Name** in the first row under *Column*, set *Status* to **Enabled**, and click **Apply** to see the following output.

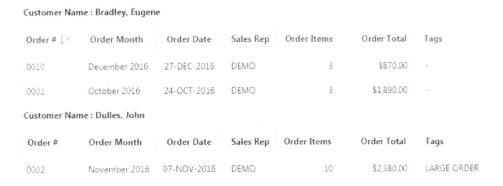

Customer Name : Bradley, Eugene

Order # ↓≡	Order Month	Order Date	Sales Rep	Order Items	Order Total	Tags
0010	December 2016	27-DEC-2016	DEMO	3	$870.00	-
0001	October 2016	24-OCT-2016	DEMO	3	$1,890.00	-

Customer Name : Dulles, John

Order #	Order Month	Order Date	Sales Rep	Order Items	Order Total	Tags
0002	November 2016	07-NOV-2016	DEMO	10	$2,380.00	LARGE ORDER

B. Chart View

1. Click **Actions | Chart**.

2. Fill in the Chart parameters as shown below:

3. Click the **Apply** button. The output should resemble Figure 7-3.

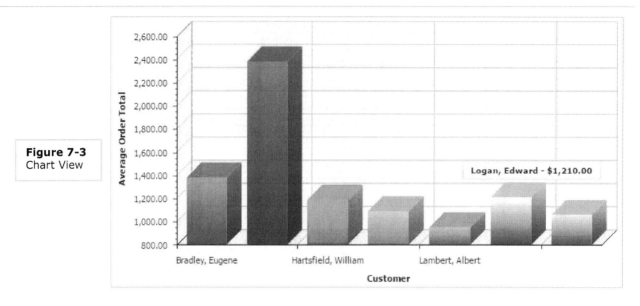

Figure 7-3
Chart View

NOTE: The chart uses an Average function (as compared to the Sum function used in the previous exercise). A customer (Edward Logan) has placed two orders amounting to $2,420. The average for this customer comes to $1,210 (2,420/2) and this is what you see when you move your mouse over the bar representing this customer.

C. **Group By View**

1. Click the **View Report** icon to switch back.

2. Click **Actions | Group By**.

3. Set properties as show in the following illustration. Don't forget to put check marks in the Sum columns to produce grand totals on the page. If you are not able to add more functions initially, click the Apply button and edit the Group By view.

4. Click **Apply**.

5. Save your work using the **Actions** menu.

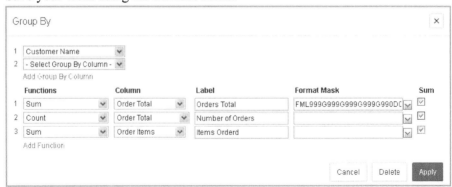

The following is the output for the selections you just made. In this view, you utilized Sum and Count functions on two columns: Order Total and Order Items. This view displays total amount of orders placed by each customer with number of orders and the total number of items ordered.

Customer Name	Orders Total	Number of Orders	Items Ordered
Dulles, John	$2,380.00	1	10
OHare, Frank	$1,060.00	1	4
Logan, Edward	$2,420.00	2	11
Lambert, Albert	$950.00	1	5
Hartsfield, William	$2,370.00	2	8
LaGuardia, Fiorello	$1,090.00	1	5
Bradley, Eugene	$2,760.00	2	6
	$13,030.00	10	49

D. Pivot View

The Pivot option is the Actions menu is used to create a cross tab view based on the data in the report. Let's see an instance of this option, too.

1. Click the **View Report** icon to switch back.

2. Click **Actions | Pivot**.

3. Set properties as show in the following illustration. Don't forget to put check mark in the Sum columns to produce grand totals on the page.

4. Click **Apply**.

5. Save your work using the **Actions** menu. The following figure illustrates the output of your work.

	December 2016	November 2016	October 2016
Customer Name	Order Total	Order Total	Order Total
Bradley, Eugene	$870.00	-	$1,890.00
Dulles, John	-	$2,380.00	-
Hartsfield, William	$730.00	$1,640.00	-
LaGuardia, Fiorello	-	$1,090.00	-
Lambert, Albert	-	$950.00	-
Logan, Edward	$2,420.00	-	-
OHare, Frank	$1,060.00	-	-
	$5,080.00	$6,060.00	$1,890.00

In the previous few sections you used some options from the *Actions* menu to customize the interactive report. However, the menu contains a few more, as listed below:

- **Select Columns** specifies which columns to display and in what order.
- **Filter** focuses the report by adding or modifying the WHERE clause on the query.
- **Rows Per Page** determines how many rows display in the current report.
- **Format** contains the following submenu:
  - **Sort**. Changes the columns to sort on and determines whether to sort in ascending or descending order.
  - **Compute**. Enables users to add computed columns to a report.
- **Flashback** enables you to view the data as it existed at a previous point in time by specifying number of minutes. To use this option, the Oracle database FLASHBACK feature must be turned on.
- **Reset** is used to reorganize the report back to the default report settings.
- **Help** provides descriptions of how to customize interactive reports.
- **Download** enables users to download a report. Available download formats depend upon your installation and report definition. To see these formats, click a region's *Attribute* folder and check the *Download* section in the Property Editor.
- **Subscription** enables users to set a schedule to send an interactive report by e-mail.

7.3.5 Create Button

You deleted and re-created the default region in section 7.3.1 and due to which you lost the Create button associated with it that was there to create new orders. In this section, you will create a new button for the same purpose.

On the *Rendering* tab in Page 4 right-click the *Breadcrumb* region (under the Breadcrumb Bar folder) and select **Create Button**. Set the following properties for the new button. The value (P11_CUSTOMER_OPTIONS) set for the *Name* property is an item on Page 11 (to be created in section 7.5.4). The link sets the value of this item to EXISTING on the target page. Note that you cannot use the LOVs to pick values for the *Name* and *Value* properties, because you haven't created Page 11 yet. These LOVs are populated with page items only when you specify an existing page number (after the *Target Type* property).

Property	Value
Button Name	ENTER_NEW_ORDER
Label	Enter New Order
Button Template	Text with Icon
Hot	Yes
Icon CSS Classes	fa-chevron-right
Action	Redirect to Page in this Application
Target	Type = Page in this Application Page = 11 Name = P11_CUSTOMER_OPTIONS Value = EXISTING Clear Cache = 11

7.4 Modify Order Details Page - Page 29

7.4.1 Modify Master Region Properties

Page 29 contains two regions. The master region is of *Static Content* type and carries order header information, while the second region is an interactive grid, which contains line item details. Modify the master region using the following steps:

1. In Page 29, click the root node (**Page 29: Order Details**) and set the *Page Mode* property to **Modal Dialog** to open it on top of Page 4. Set *Width, Height,* and *Maximum Width* properties to **900, 800,** and **1200,** respectively. Also, set *Dialog Template* (in the *Appearance* section) to **Wizard Modal Dialog**. Dialog templates are defined in the application theme. When a dialog page is created, the template is automatically set to *Theme Default*, which will render the page using the default page template defined in the current theme. The *Wizard Modal Dialog* provides a streamlined user interface suitable for input forms. When you switch to this template, the name of *Content Body* changes to *Wizard Body* and a new folder named *Wizard Buttons* is added. We will use this folder to place all our page buttons to make them visible all the time.

2. Click the **Order Details** region </> Order Details and enter **Order #&P29_ORDER_ID.** (including the terminating period) for its *Title*. The expression consists of two parts. The first one (Order #), is a string concatenated to a page item (P29_ORDER_ID), which carries the order number. The string, when combined, would be presented as: *Order # 1*. Make sure that region's *Template* attribute (under *Appearance*) is set to **Standard** to show this title.

3. Create a new page item in the *Items* folder under the master region and set the following properties. This item will present customer information on each order as display-only text. *Display Only* items are shown as non-enterable text item. Note that you may get an invalid query error message when you enter the SQL query specified in the table. Save the page by clicking the Save button to get rid of this message. Moreover, if you keep the default value (*Yes*) for *Escape Special Characters* property, the customer information appears on a single line with <br/> tags. The *Save Session State* property is set to *No* to clear the value of this item from the session state when the page gets submitted.

Property	Value
Name	P29_CUSTOMER_INFO
Type	Display Only
Label	Customer
Save Session State	No
Type *(under Source)*	SQL Query (return single value)

SQL Query	select apex_escape.html(cust_first_name) || ' ' ||
	     apex_escape.html(cust_last_name) || '
	' ||
	     apex_escape.html(cust_street_address1) ||
	     decode(cust_street_address2, null, null, '
	' ||
	     apex_escape.html(cust_street_address2)) || '</br>' ||
	     apex_escape.html(cust_city) || ', ' ||
	     apex_escape.html(cust_state) || ' ' ||
	     apex_escape.html(cust_postal_code)
	 from demo_customers
	 where customer_id = :P29_CUSTOMER_ID

Escape Special Characters	No

4. Using drag and drop arrange the columns (in the *Rendering* tree) as follows: P29_CUSTOMER_INFO, P29_ORDER_TIMESTAMP, P29_ORDER_TOTAL, P29_USER_NAME, P29_TAGS, and P29_CUSTOMER_ID.

5. Edit the following items individually and set the corresponding properties shown under each item.

a. **P29_ORDER_TIMESTAMP**

Property	Value
Type	Display Only
Label	Order Date
Format Mask	DD-MON-YYYY HH:MIPM

b. **P29_ORDER_TOTAL**

Property	Value
Type	Display Only
Format Mask	$5,234.10

c. **P29_USER_NAME**

Property	Value
Type	Select List
Label	Sales Rep
Type (*List of Values*)	SQL Query
SQL Query	select distinct user_name d, user_name r from demo_orders union select upper(:APP_USER) d, upper(:APP_USER) r from dual order by 1
Display Extra Values	No
Display Null Value	No
Help Text	Use to change the Sales Rep associated with this order.

In the *Help Text* attribute you specify help text for an item. The help text may be used to provide field level, context sensitive help. At run-time you will see a small help icon ⓘ in-front of this item. When you click this icon, a window pops up to show the help text.

d. **P29_TAGS**

Property	Value
Type	Text Field

e. **P29_CUSTOMER_ID**

Property	Value
Type	Hidden
Value Protected	No

f. **P29_ORDER_ID**

Property	Value
Type	Hidden
Value Protected	No

6. In the *Region Buttons* folder, set *Button Position* property to **Edit** for GET_PREVIOUS_ORDER_ID and GET_NEXT_ORDER_ID buttons to place them on top of the region.

7.4.2 Modify Details Region's Properties

After setting the master region, let's modify the details region to give it a desirable look.

1. Click the **Order Details** interactive grid *Order Details* and set its *Title* to **Items for Order #&P29_ORDER_ID.** (including the terminating period). Also, replace existing SQL Query with the one that follows: This region (which used to be of Tabular Form type that supported images) is switched to the new Interactive Grid type in version 5.1.

```
select oi.order_item_id, oi.order_id, oi.product_id, oi.unit_price, oi.quantity,
       (oi.unit_price * oi.quantity) extended_price
from DEMO_ORDER_ITEMS oi, DEMO_PRODUCT_INFO pi
where oi.ORDER_ID = :P29_ORDER_ID
and oi.product_id = pi.product_id (+)
```

2. Save the page using the **Save** button to reflect the impact of the SQL statement in the details region.

3. Under the *Columns* folder, edit the following columns using the specified properties. The default *Type* for UNIT_PRICE is *Number Field*, which allows end user to modify the price of a product. It is changed to *Display Only* type to eliminate price alteration. With this value set, the values in the price column are not editable. The *Alignment* property sets the heading alignment, while the *Column Alignment* specifies the column display alignment. For product ID column, we changed two properties. First, we set its *Type* property to *Select List*. Secondly, we associated an LOV (*Products with Price*) to it. This LOV was created in Chapter 3 section 3.4.2 to display a list of products along with respective prices. The *Query Only* property (under *Source* section) set for the *Extended Price* column specifies whether to exclude the column from DML operations. If set to *Yes*, Application Express will not utilize the column when executing the *Interactive Grid - Automatic Row Processing (DML)* process. In the current scenario, you excluded the *Extended Price* column, because it is not a physical table column and is calculated in the SELECT query stated above. If you keep the default value of this property for the *Extended Price* column, you will get "*Virtual column not allowed here*" error message when you try to save an existing order. All columns whose

definitions include concatenations, inner selects, function calls, or a column in an updateable view that is based on an expression should be excluded. All columns that need to be included in any INSERT or UPDATE statements must have this option set to *No*. Note that columns of type *Display Only* are also included in the *Automatic Row Processing* unless this option is set to *Yes*.

Column	Property	Value
PRODUCT_ID	Type Heading Alignment Type *(LOV)* List of Values Display Null Value	Select List Product Start Shared Components Products With Price No
UNIT_PRICE	Type Alignment Column Alignment Format Mask	Display Only end end $5,234.10
QUANTITY	Width *(Appearance)* Type *(Default)* PL/SQL Expression	5 PL/SQL Expression 1 *(sets 1 as the default quantity)*
EXTENDED_PRICE	Type Heading Alignment Column Alignment Format Mask Query Only *(Source)*	Display Only Price end end $5,234.10 Yes

4. Using drag and drop arrange the five visible columns in the following order: PRODUCT_ID, UNIT_PRICE, QUANTITY, and EXTENDED_PRICE

5. Right-click the *Wizard Buttons* folder and select **Create Region**. Set *Title* of the new region to **Buttons** and *Template* to **Buttons Container**. In the *Regions Buttons* folder, click the **Cancel** button, and set its *Region* property to **Buttons**. Set the same Buttons region for **Delete**, **Save**, and **Create** buttons, too. This action will place the four buttons under the Buttons region in the interactive grid–see Figure 7-5.

6. On the *Processing* tab, drag and place the process "*Process Row of DEMO_ORDERS*" before the *Save Interactive Grid Data* process or set its *Sequence* property to a number lower than that of the *Save Interactive Grid Data* process. Note that this process must precede the *Save Interactive Grid Data* process; otherwise, you will get the error "*Current version of data in database has changed since user initiated update process*" when you try to manipulate data in the interactive grid.

7. Save the changes.

Run the application and click the *Orders* option in the main navigation menu. The page that comes up should look like Figure 7-4. Click any order number to call the *Order Details* page (Figure 7-5). Try to navigate forward and backward using the Next and Previous ⊠⊠ buttons. At the moment, you can only use these two pages to manipulate existing orders. In the next sections, you will create some more pages to enter new orders. Call order number **0002** and click the **Add Row** button appearing in the Interactive Grid's toolbar. A new row will be added to the grid with the Product column appearing as a list of values carrying all products with their respective prices. Select **Belt** from this list, enter some value in the *Quantity* column (or accept the default quantity 1), and click the **Save** button. You will see an error message that pops up due to the violation of a unique constraint (DEMO_ORDER_ITEMS_UK), which is implemented for DEMO_ORDER_ITEMS table. Now, remove the checkmark appearing in the first column of the new record and put a check on the previous Belt record. From the *Row Actions* menu (second column in the interactive gird), select **Delete Row**. The previous Belt record will be marked as deleted. Click the **Save** button again. Call the order again. The new record will be added to the table and the previous Belt record will be removed.

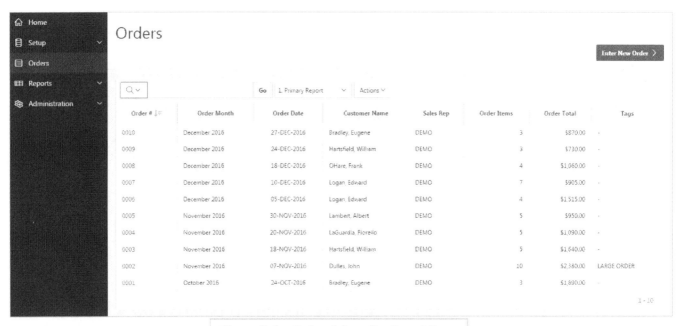

Figure 7-4 – Orders Interactive Report Page

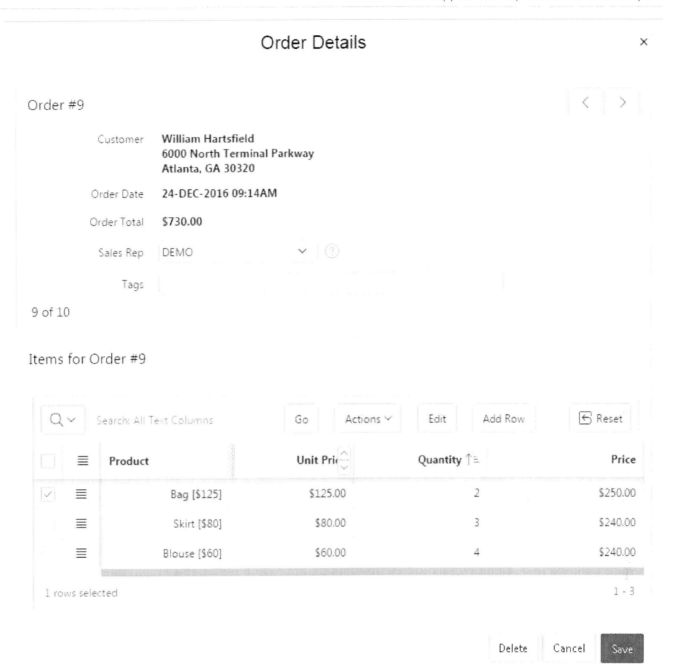

Figure 7-5 – Order Details Page

7.5 Create a Page to Enter a New Order - Page 11

As mentioned earlier, you will go through a series of steps to enter a new order. You identified and created these steps in *Order Wizard* list in Chapter 3 section 3.2.3. The top region (A) in Figure 7-6 reflects those steps. Each step will be associated to an application page. The rest of this chapter will guide you to create those three pages individually. In this exercise, you will create Page 11 - *Enter New Order*. The order recording process initiates when you click the button *Enter New Order* on the *Orders* page (Page 4). This button was created in Section 7.3.5 to call Page 11, where you will select a customer who placed the order. Besides selecting an existing customer, you can also create record of a new customer on this page. The LOV button (B) corresponding to the *Customer* box calls a list of existing customers from which you can select one for the order. If you select the *New Customer* option (C), a region (*New Customer Details*) will be shown under the existing region. By default, this region is hidden and becomes visible when you click the *New Customer* option. This functionality is controlled by a dynamic action (*Hide/Show Customer*), which will also be created for this page. In addition to various techniques taught in this part, you'll create this page from an existing page - *Customer Details* (Page 7) - to generate a new customer record. Here, you'll make a copy of that page and will tweak it for the current scenario. Let's see how it is done.

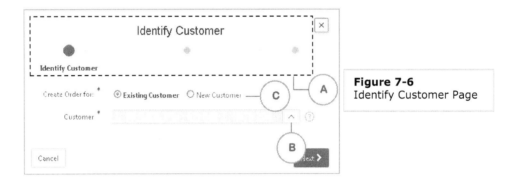

Figure 7-6
Identify Customer Page

1. In the App Builder interface, click the **Customer Details - Page 7** to open its definitions in the Page Designer.

2. Click the **Create** menu ⌊ +∨ ⌋ at top-right in the toolbar and select **Page as copy**.

3. On the first wizard screen, select the option **Page in this application** for *Create a page as a copy of* and click **Next**.

4. Fill in the following values on *Page To Copy* screen and click **Next**.

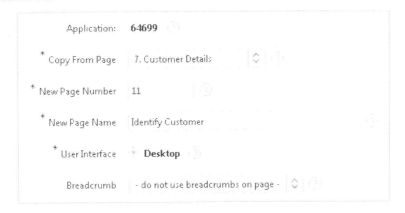

5. On the *Navigation Menu* screen select **Identify an existing navigation menu entry for this page**, select **Orders** for *Existing Navigation Menu*, and click **Next.**

6. Accept the names of existing page buttons and items on the *New Names* screen and click the **Copy** button to finish the wizard.

Look at the Page Designer. All the elements from Page 7 appear on the new page, especially the items section, which carries all input elements (with P11 prefix) to create a new customer record. This is the section we needed on our new page to spare some time.

7.5.1 Modify Page Properties

1. In Page 11, click the root node (**Page 11: Identify Customer**).

2. Set *Dialog Template* (under *Appearance*) to **Wizard Modal Dialog**. The template creates a region (*Wizard Progress Bar*) to hold the order progress list (A), as shown in Figure 7-6, and alters the name of the main region from *Content Body* to *Wizard Body*.

3. Set *Width* and *Height* properties to **700** and **500**, respectively.

4. Remove **htmldb_delete_message** variable from *Function and Global Variable Declaration* property. Save the page after removing the variable. This is an auto-generated variable associated with the customer record deletion process handled transparently by Oracle APEX. It is removed because the customer record deletion process is not required here.

7.5.2 Create Region – Order Progress

Right-click the *Wizard Progress Bar* folder (under *Regions*) and select **Create Region**. Set the following properties for the new region. The *Order Wizard* list used here was created in Chapter 3 - section 3.2.3. The *Wizard Progress* value specified for the *List Template* property displays a progress train based on the list items and is well suited for wizards and multi-step flows.

Property	Value
Title	Order Progress
Type	List
List	Order Wizard
Template	Blank with Attributes
List Template (*under Attributes node*)	Wizard Progress
Label Display (*under Template Options*)	All Steps (*displays labels of all wizard steps*)

7.5.3 Create Region – Identify Customer

Right-click the *Wizard Body* folder and select **Create Region**. Drag the new region and place it above the *Customer Details* region. Set the following properties for it. This region is created to act as a main container to hold a radio group item and a couple of sub-regions.

Property	Value
Title	Identify Customer
Type	Static Content
Template	Standard

7.5.4 Create Item

Right-click the new *Identify Customer* region and select **Create Page Item**. Set the following properties for the new item, which is a *Radio Group*. The list of values attached to this radio group item (*NEW OR EXISTING CUSTOMER*) was created in Chapter 3 - section 3.4.5 with two static values to create a new customer or select an existing one for a new order. The value set for the *Number of Columns* property displays these values in two separate columns. The first *Type* and *Static Value* properties (under *Source*) specify the source type the value of this item will based on when you access this page, whereas the second pair sets the EXISTING value as the default choice.

Property	Value
Name	P11_CUSTOMER_OPTIONS
Type	Radio Group
Label	Create Order for:
Number of Columns	2
Label Column Span	3
Template	Required
Type *(under List of Values)*	Shared Component
List of Values	NEW OR EXISTING CUSTOMER
Display Null Value	No
Type (Source)	Static Value
Static Value (Source)	EXISTING
Type (Default)	Static Value
Static Value (Default)	EXISTING

7.5.5 Create a Sub Region – Existing Customer

Right-click the *Identify Customer* region and select **Create Sub Region**. This will add a sub region under the page item P11_CUSTOMER_OPTIONS. Set the following properties from the sub region.

Property	Value
Title	Existing Customer
Type	Static Content
Template	Blank with Attributes

7.5.6 Modify Item – P11_CUSTOMER_ID

In the *Items* section, click **P11_CUSTOMER_ID**. Set the *Name* property of this hidden item to **P11_CUSTOMER_ID_XYZ**. Set *Server-side Condition Type* to **Never** (last in the list). This item is renamed and suppressed from being rendered because a new item (of Popup LOV type) with the same name is created in the next section to display a list of customers, instead. By selecting the *Never* value for the *Server-side Condition Type* property, you permanently disable a page component. That is, the component is never rendered.

7.5.7 Add LOV

Right-click the *Existing Customer* sub-region and select **Create Page Item**. Set the following properties for this item. The *Type* value (under *Source*) is set to *Null*, because the IDs and names of customers are retreived using a SQL query and displayed in a Popup LOV.

Property	Value
Name	P11_CUSTOMER_ID
Type	Popup LOV
Label	Customer
Template	Required
Width	70
Value Required	No
Type *(under List of Values)*	SQL Query
SQL Query	select cust_last_name || ', ' || cust_first_name d, customer_id r from demo_customers order by cust_last_name
Display Extra Values	No
Display Null Value	No
Type *(under Source)*	Null
Help Text	Choose a customer using the pop-up selector, or to create a new customer, select the New customer option.

7.5.8 Modify Customer Details Region

Click the *Customer Details* region and set the following properties for this region. When you specify a parent region you make a region child of a parent region.

Property	Value
Title	New Customer Details
Parent Region	Identify Customer

7.5.9 Delete Validation, Processes, and Buttons

1. On the *Processing* tab, right-click the entry **Can't Delete Customer with Orders** under *Validations*, and select **Delete** from the context menu. Similarly, delete **Get PK**, **Process Row of DEMO_CUSTOMERS**, and **reset page** processes.

2. Also, remove **Delete**, **Save**, and **Create** buttons from the *Buttons* region on the *Rendering* tab.

7.5.10 Delete Process

On the *Rendering* tab, expand the *Pre-Rendering | After Header | Processes* node and delete the process named **Fetch Row from DEMO CUSTOMERS**. This is a default process created in the Customers module and is not required in the current scenario.

7.5.11 Create Button – Next

Create a new button in the *Buttons* region and set the following properties for it. After identifying a customer, you click this button to advance to the second order wizard step. This button will appear under the *Cancel* button in the Page Designer. When this button is clicked, the *Action* property submits the page and a branch (created in section 7.5.18) takes control of the application flow and moves you on to the next wizard step.

Property	Value
Button Name	NEXT
Label	Next
Button Position	Next
Button Template	Text with Icon
Hot	Yes
Icon CSS Classes	fa-chevron-right
Action	Submit Page *(default)*

7.5.12 Create Process - Create or Truncate Order Collection

When developing web applications in Oracle APEX, you often need a mechanism to store an unknown number of items in a temporary location. The most common example of this is an online shopping cart where a user can add a large number of items. To cope with this situation in Oracle APEX, you use Collections to store variable information. Before using a collection, it is necessary to initialize it in the context of the current application session. After clicking the *Enter New Order* button, you're brought to this page (Page 11) and this is where your collection (named *ORDER*) is initialized using a PL/SQL process that fires *Before Header* when the user enters into the interface of Page 11. See sections 7.6.7 and 7.6.8 for relevant details on collections.

On the *Rendering* tab, expand the *Pre-Rendering* folder. Right-click the *Before Header* node and select **Create Process**. Set the following properties for the new process.

Property	Value
Name	Create or Truncate ORDER Collection
Type	PL/SQL Code
PL/SQL Code	apex_collection.create_or_truncate_collection (p_collection_name => 'ORDER');

7.5.13 Create Dynamic Action

Click the *Dynamic Actions* tab. Right-click the *Change* folder and select **Create Dynamic Action**. Click the *New* node and set the following properties. The following settings inform Oracle APEX to fire the dynamic action when user changes (*Event*) the radio group item (*Selection Type*) P11_CUSTOMER_OPTIONS (*Item*) from *New Customer* to *Existing*.

Property	Value
Name	Hide / Show Customers
Event	Change
Selection Type	Item(s)
Item(s)	P11_CUSTOMER_OPTIONS
Type *(under Client-side Condition)*	Item = value
Item *(under Client-side Condition)*	P11_CUSTOMER_OPTIONS
Value	EXISTING

Click the *Show* node to set the following properties. The values for these properties are set to show the *Existing Customer* region when the EXISTING option is selected from the radio group. The *Yes* value set for the *Fire on Initialization* property specifies to fire the action when the page loads.

Property	Value
Action	Show
Selection Type	Region
Region	Existing Customer
Fire When Event Result is	True
Fire on Initialization	Yes

Right-click the *Show* node and select **Create Action**. Set the following properties for it. This action is also assoicated with the previous two and is added to hide *New Customer Details* region when the EXISTING option is selected.

Property	Value
Action	Hide
Selection Type	Region
Region	New Customer Details
Fire When Event Result is	True
Fire on Initialization	Yes

Right-click the *Show* folder again and select **Create Opposite Action**. This will add an opposite *Hide* action under the *False* folder (with all properties set) to hide the *Existing Customer* region.

Right-click the *Hide* node under the *True* folder and select **Create Opposite Action**. This will add a *Show* action under the *False* folder to show the *New Customer Details* region.

If you run the page at this stage (by clicking the *Enter New Order* button on Page 4), you'll see the P11_CUSTOMER_ID item (in the *Existing Customer* region) is shown on the page. Now, select the *New Customer* option. The item P11_CUSTOMER_ID disappears from the page and the *New Customer Details* region becomes visible. Select the *Existing Customer* option again, the item becomes visible and the *New Customer Details* region hides.

7.5.14 Modify Validation – Check Credit Limit

On the Processing tab, click the **Check Credit Limit** validation. Set its *Sequence* to **100** and save the change to place this validation in a proper sequence after the following validations. Note that the *Sequence* property determines the order of evaluation.

7.5.15 Create Validation – Customer ID Not Null

Right-click the *Validations* folder and select **Create Validation**. Set the following properties for the new validation. You can control when and if a validation is performed by configuring its *Condition Type* property (7). Select a condition type from the list that must meet in order for a validation to process. In the current scenario, the condition (*item=value*) is formed like this: P11_CUSTOMER_OPTIONS = EXISTING. The validation fires when you select the *Existing Customer* option on the application page, and do not select a customer from the provided list. In case of an error at runtime, the #LABEL# substitution string specified in the *Error Message* property is replaced with the label of the associated item P11_CUSTOMER_ID–that is, *Customer*.

Property	Value
Name	Customer ID Not Null
Sequence	10
Type *(Validation)*	Item is NOT NULL
Item	P11_CUSTOMER_ID
Error Message	#LABEL# must have some value.
Associated Item	P11_CUSTOMER_ID
Type *(Server-side Condition)*	Item = Value
Item	P11_CUSTOMER_OPTIONS
Value	EXISTING

7.5.16 Create Validation – First Name Not Null

Create another validation. This validation will check whether the first name of a new customer is provided. It is fired only when the *New Customer* option is selected.

Property	Value
Name	First Name is Not Null
Sequence	20
Type *(Validation)*	Item is NOT NULL
Item	P11_CUST_FIRST_NAME
Error Message	#LABEL# must have some value.
Type *(Server-side Condition)*	Item = Value
Item	P11_CUSTOMER_OPTIONS
Value	NEW

Using the previous table, create NOT NULL validations for Last Name, State, Postal Code, and Credit Limit items.

7.5.17 Create Validation – Phone Number

Create the following validation to check input of proper phone numbers. *Regular Expressions* enable you to search for patterns in string data by using standardized syntax conventions, rather than just a straight character comparisons. The validation passes if the phone numbers matches the regular expression attribute and fails if the item value does not match the regular expression. The last three properties inform Oracle APEX to execute the validation only when a new customer is created.

Property	Value
Name	Phone Number Format
Type *(Validation)*	Item matches Regular Expression
Item	P11_PHONE_NUMBER1
Regular Expression	^\(?[[:digit:]]{3}\)?[-.][[:digit:]]{3}[-.][[:digit:]]{4}$
Error Message	Phone number format not recognized
Associated Item	P11_PHONE_NUMBER1
Type *(Server-side Condition)*	Item = Value
Item	P11_CUSTOMER_OPTIONS
Value	NEW

Create a similar validation for **P11_PHONE_NUMBER2** item.

Next, you have to set the *Value Required* attribute to **No** for P11_CUSTOMER_ID (in *Existing Customer* Region), P11_CUST_FIRST_NAME, P11_CUST_LAST_NAME, P11_CUST_STATE, P11_CUST_POSTAL_CODE, and P11_CREDIT_LIMIT. The *Value Required* properties for these items were inherited from Page 7 where they were set to *Yes*, to mark them as mandatory. In the previous two sections, you used an alternate method to manually control the validation process for these items. If you don't reverse the *Value Required* status, then the application will throw NOT NULL errors for these items, even if you select an existing customer.

7.5.18 Create Branch

When the *Next* button is clicked, the defined button action (*Submit Page*) triggers after performing all validations. The submit page process executes instructions specified in this branch and moves the user to the next order wizard step. On the *Processing* tab, right-click the *After Processing* node and select **Create Branch**. Set the following properties for the new branch.

Property	Value
Name	Go To Page 12
Type *(under Behavior)*	Page or URL (Redirect)
Target	Type = Page in this Application Page = 12 Clear Cache = 12
When Button Pressed	NEXT

Test Your Work

From the main menu, select *Orders* and click the *Enter New Order* button. Your page should look like Figure 7-6. Select *Existing Customer* and click the LOV button to call the list of customers. Note that each customer name is displayed as a link. Click a link to select a customer. The name of the selected customer appears in the *Customer* box. This is how an existing customer is selected for an order. Now, click the *New Customer* option, the Dynamic Action created in section 7.5.13 invokes and performs two actions. First, it hides the *Customer* box and the LOV. Second, it shows a form similar to the one you created in Chapter 5 to add a new customer record. Click the *Next* button without putting any value in the provided form. You'll see an inline message box appearing with five errors. This is the procedure you handled in the validation sections. After correcting all the form errors if you click *Next*, the message "*Sorry, this page isn't available*" pops up indicating that Page 12 doesn't exist. Your next task is to create Page 12 where you'll select products for an order.

7.6 Create Select Items Page - Pages 12

Having identified the customer, the second step in the order wizard is to add products to the order. In this exercise, you will create Page 12 of the application to select ordered items and input the required quantities.

1. Click the **Create Page** button in the App Builder interface.

2. This time, select the **Blank Page** option. This option is selected to create an application page from scratch. Using this option you can create and customize a page according to your own specific needs.

3. Complete the first wizard step as show in the following figure and click **Next**.

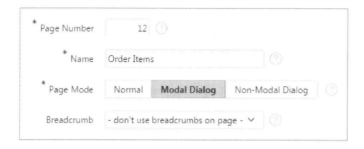

4. On the *Navigation Menu* screen, set *Navigation Preference* to **Identify an existing navigation menu entry for this page**, *Existing Navigation Menu Entry* to **Orders**, and click **Next**.

5. Click **Finish** to end the wizard.

7.6.1 Modify Page Properties

You styled the *Detail View* of an interactive report to customize its look in the previous chapter. Here as well, you will apply some styling rules to give the page a professional touch. Previously, you added rules to a single page element: HTML table. In the following exercise you'll apply rules to the whole page. Before getting your feet wet, go through the following topic to understand Cascading Style Sheets (CSS).

Cascading Style Sheets

A cascading style sheet (CSS) provides a way to control the style of a web page without changing its structure. When used properly, a CSS separates visual properties such as color, margins, and fonts from the structure of the HTML document.

In this chapter, you will use CSS to style Page 12 (Select Items - Figure 7-7). On this page you will add class properties to PL/SQL code and will reference them in CSS in the HTML Head section. Before moving on to understand the actual functionality, let's first take a look at a simple example on how to use class attribute in an HTML document. The class attribute is mostly used to point to a class in a style sheet. The syntax is *<element class="classname">*.

```
<html>
  <head>
    <style type="text/css">
      h1.header {color:blue;}
      p.styledpara {color:red;}
    </style>
  </head>
  <body>
    <h1 class="header">Class Referenced in CSS</h1>
    <p>A normal paragraph.</p>
    <p class="styledpara">Note that this is an important paragraph.</p>
  </body>
</html>
```

> I wrote a complete book titled *"The Web Book – Build Static & Dynamic Websites"* (ISBN-13: 978-1483929279) that teaches five core web technologies including HTML and CSS from scratch.

The body of this web page contains three sections:

- **<h1 class="header">Class Referenced in CSS</h1>** – The text "*Class Referenced in CSS*" is enclosed in h1 html tag. It is called level 1 heading and is the most important heading in a document. It is usually used to indicate the title of the document. The text is preceded by a class named "header".

- Considering the class syntax, *h1* is the *element* and *header* is the *classname*. This class is referenced in the style section using a CSS rule – *h1.header {color:blue;}* – to present the heading in blue color. A CSS rule has two main parts: a selector and one or more declarations. The selector is normally the HTML element you want to style. Each declaration consists of a property and a value. The property is the style attribute you want to change. Each property has a value. In the *h1.header {color:blue;}* rule, *h1* is the selector, *header* is the classname, and *{color:blue;}* is the declaration.

- **<p>A normal paragraph.</p>** – It is a plain paragraph without any style applied to it. HTML documents are divided into paragraphs and paragraphs are defined with the <p> tag. The <p> tag is called the start tag or opening tag, while </p> is called the end or closing tag.

- **<p class="styledpara">Note that this is an important paragraph.</p>** – It is a paragraph with a class named "*styledpara*". In the style section, the selector "*p*" followed by the classname "*styledpara*" with the declaration*{color:red;}* is referencing this section to present the paragraph text in red color.

Now that you have understood how CSS is used in web pages, let's figure out how it is used in Oracle APEX.

1. Click the root node – **Page 12: Order Items**.

2. Set *Dialog Template* to **Wizard Modal Dialog**.

3. Set *Width* and *Height* to 500 and 600, respectively.

4. Enter the following code for **inline** property under CSS section and save your work. You can find this code in *BookCode\Chapter7\7.6.1.txt* file. CSS rules entered in this box will be applied to all the referenced elements on the current page, as illustrated in Figure 7-7.

Rule #	Rule	PL/SQL Ref.
	A - CustomerInfo	
1	div.CustomerInfo strong{font:bold 12px/16px Arial,sans-serif;display:block;width:120px;}	11,22
2	div.CustomerInfo p{display:block;margin:0; font: normal 12px/16px Arial, sans-serif;}	12-19,23-30
	B - Products	
3	div.Products{clear:both;margin:16px 0 0 0;padding:0 8px 0 0;}	36-42
4	div.Products table{border:1px solid #CCC;border-bottom:none;}	37,47
5	div.Products table th{background-color:#DDD;color:#000;font:bold 12px/16px Arial,sans-serif;padding:4px 10px;text-align:right;border-bottom:1px solid #CCC;}	37,47
6	div.Products table td{border-bottom:1px solid #CCC;font:normal 12px/16px Arial,sans-serif; padding:4px 10px;text-align:right;}	39
7	div.Products table td a{color:#000;}	39
8	div.Products .left{text-align:left;}	37,39,47
	C - CartItem	
9	div.CartItem{padding:8px 8px 0 8px;font:normal 11px/14px Arial,sans-serif;}	53-59
10	div.CartItem a{color:#000;}	54-55
11	div.CartItem span{display:block;text-align:right;padding:8px 0 0;}	56-57
12	div.CartItem span.subtotal{font-weight:bold;}	58
	D - CartTotal	
13	div.CartTotal{margin-top:8px;padding:8px;border-top:1px dotted #AAA;}	65-68
14	div.CartTotal span{display:block;text-align:right;font:normal 11px/14px Arial,sans-serif;padding:0 0 4px 0;}	66
15	div.CartTotal p{padding:0;margin:0;font:normal 11px/14px Arial,sans-serif;position:relative;}	66
16	div.CartTotal p.CartTotal{font:bold 12px/14px Arial,sans-serif;padding:8px 0 0;}	67
17	div.CartTotal p.CartTotal span{font:bold 12px/14px Arial,sans-serif;padding:8px 0 0 0;}	67
18	div.CartTotal p span{padding:0;position:absolute;right:0;top:0;}	66

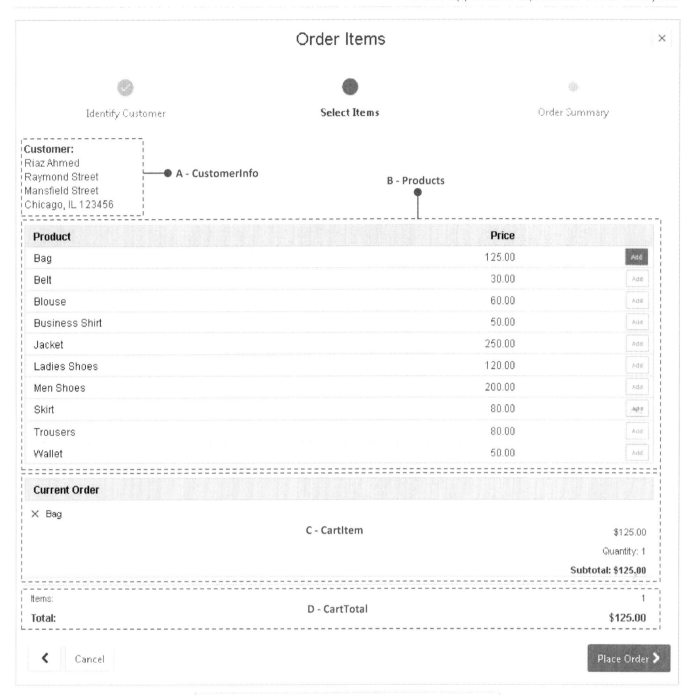

Figure 7-7 – CSS Rules Applied to Select Items Page

7.6.2 Create Region – Order Progress

Right-click the *Wizard Progress Bar* folder and select **Create Region**. Set the following properties for the new region. A similar region was added previously to Page 11 to display the Order Progress bar.

Property	Value
Title	Order Progress
Type	List
List	Order Wizard
Template	Blank with Attributes
List Template (*under Attributes node*)	Wizard Progress

7.6.3 Create Region – Select Items

The region being created in this section is based on a custom PL/SQL code. The code references CSS rules (defined in the previous section) to design the *Select Items* page, as illustrated in Figure 7-7.

What is PL/SQL?

PL/SQL stands for Procedural Language/Structured Query Language. It is a programming language that uses detailed sequential instructions to process data. A PL/SQL program combines SQL command (such as Select and Update) with procedural commands for tasks, such as manipulating variable values, evaluating IF/THEN logic structure, and creating loop structures that repeat instructions multiple times until the condition satisfies the defined criteria. PL/SQL was expressly designed for this purpose.

The structure of a PL/SQL program block is:

```
Declare
    Variable declaration
Begin
    Program statements
Exception
    Error-handling statements
End;
```

PL/SQL program variables are declared in the program's declaration section. The beginning of the declaration section is marked with the reserved word DECLARE. You can declare multiple variables in the declaration section. The body of a PL/SQL block consists of program statements, which can be assigned statements, conditional statements, loop statements, and so on. The body lies between the BEGIN and EXCEPTION statements. The exception section contains program statements for error handling. Finally, PL/SQL programs end with the END; statement. Comments in PL/SQL code are added by prefixing them with double hyphens.

In a PL/SQL program block, the DECLARE and EXCEPTION sections are optional. If there are no variables to declare, you can omit the DECLARE section and start the program with the BEGIN command.

1. Right-click the *Order Progress* region and select **Create Sub Region** from the context menu.

2. Enter **Select Items** for its *Title* and set its *Type* to **PL/SQL Dynamic Content** to display the page content using PL/SQL code. PL/SQL Dynamic Content displays the HTML output from the PL/SQL code.

3. Do not set any option for the *Template* property (in other words, change it from the default *Standard* value to the **-Select-** placeholder).

4. Add the code defined in the *PL/SQL Code* column in the *PL/SQL Code* property (in the *Source* section). You can find this code in *BookCode\Chapter7\7.6.4.txt* file. The first column (CSS Rule) in the following table references the rules defined in the previous section. These rules are applied to the injected HTML elements in the PL/SQL code. The second table column is populated with a serial number assigned to each PL/SQL code. These numbers are referenced in the explanation section underneath.

CSS Rule	Line No.	PL/SQL Code
	1	declare
	2	l_customer_id varchar2(30) := :P11_CUSTOMER_ID;
	3	begin
	4	--
	5	-- **display customer information**
	6	--
	7	sys.htp.p('<div class="CustomerInfo">');
	8	if :P11_CUSTOMER_OPTIONS = 'EXISTING' then
	9	for x in (select * from demo_customers where customer_id = l_customer_id) loop
	10	sys.htp.p('<div class="CustomerInfo">');
1	11	sys.htp.p('<strong>Customer:</strong>');
	12	sys.htp.p('<p>');
	13	sys.htp.p(sys.htf.escape_sc(x.cust_first_name) || ' ' || sys.htf.escape_sc(x.cust_last_name) || ' ');
	14	sys.htp.p(sys.htf.escape_sc(x.cust_street_address1) || ' ');
	15	if x.cust_street_address2 is not null then
2	16	sys.htp.p(sys.htf.escape_sc(x.cust_street_address2) || ' ');
	17	end if;
	18	sys.htp.p(sys.htf.escape_sc(x.cust_city) || ', ' || sys.htf.escape_sc(x.cust_state) || ' ' || sys.htf.escape_sc(x.cust_postal_code));
	19	sys.htp.p('</p>');
	20	end loop;
	21	else
1	22	sys.htp.p('<strong>Customer:</strong>');
	23	sys.htp.p('<p>');
	24	sys.htp.p(sys.htf.escape_sc(:P11_CUST_FIRST_NAME) || ' ' || sys.htf.escape_sc(:P11_CUST_LAST_NAME) || ' ');
	25	sys.htp.p(sys.htf.escape_sc(:P11_CUST_STREET_ADDRESS1) || ' ');
	26	if :P11_CUST_STREET_ADDRESS2 is not null then
2	27	sys.htp.p(sys.htf.escape_sc(:P11_CUST_STREET_ADDRESS2) || ' ');
	28	end if;
	29	sys.htp.p(sys.htf.escape_sc(:P11_CUST_CITY) || ', ' || sys.htf.escape_sc(:P11_CUST_STATE) || ' ' || sys.htf.escape_sc(:P11_CUST_POSTAL_CODE));
	30	sys.htp.p('</p>');
	31	end if;
	32	sys.htp.p(' </div>');

CSS Rule	Line	PL/SQL Code
	33	--
	34	**-- display products**
	35	--
3	36	sys.htp.p('<div class="Products" >');
4	37	sys.htp.p('<table width="100%" cellspacing="0" cellpadding="0" border="0">
		<thead>
5,8		<tr><th class="left">Product</th><th>Price</th><th></th></tr>
		</thead>
		<tbody>');
	38	for c1 in (select product_id, product_name, list_price, 'Add to Cart' add_to_order
		from demo_product_info
		where product_avail = 'Y'
		order by product_name) loop
6, 7, 8	39	sys.htp.p('<tr><td class="left">' ||sys.htf.escape_sc(c1.product_name)||'</td>
		<td>'||trim(to_char(c1.list_price,'999G999G990D00')) || '</td>
		<td><a
		href="'||apex_util.prepare_url('f?p=&APP_ID.:12:'||:app_session||':**ADD**:::P12_PRODUCT_ID:'|| c1.product_id)||'" class="t-Button t-Button--simple t-Button--hot"><span>Add<i
		class="iR"></i></span></a></td>
		</tr>');
	40	end loop;
	41	sys.htp.p('</tbody></table>');
	42	sys.htp.p('</div>');

CSS Rule	Line	PL/SQL Code
	43	--
	44	-- **display current order**
	45	--
3	46	sys.htp.p('<div class="Products" >');
4	47	sys.htp.p('<table width="100%" cellspacing="0" cellpadding="0" border="0">
		<thead>
8		<tr><th class="left">Current Order</th></tr>
		</thead>
		</table>
4		<table width="100%" cellspacing="0" cellpadding="0" border="0">
		<tbody>');
	48	declare
	49	c number := 0; t number := 0;
	50	begin
	51	-- loop over cart values
	52	for c1 in (select c001 pid, c002 i, to_number(c003) p, count(c002) q, sum(c003) ep, 'Remove' remove
		from apex_collections
		where collection_name = 'ORDER'
		group by c001, c002, c003
		order by c002)
		loop
9	53	sys.htp.p('<div class="CartItem">
10	54	<a href="'||
		apex_util.prepare_url('f?p=&APP_ID.:12:&SESSION.:**REMOVE**:::P12_PRODUCT_ID:'||sys.htf.esca
		pe_sc(c1.pid))||'"><img src="#IMAGE_PREFIX#delete.gif" alt="Remove from cart" title="Remove
		from cart" /></a>
10	55	'||sys.htf.escape_sc(c1.i)||'
	56	<span>'||trim(to_char(c1.p,'$999G999G999D00'))||'</span>
	57	<span>Quantity: '||c1.q||'</span>
	58	<span class="subtotal">Subtotal: '||trim(to_char(c1.ep,'$999G999G999D00'))||'</span>
11	59	</div>');
	60	c := c + 1;
12	61	t := t + c1.ep;
	62	end loop;
	63	sys.htp.p('</tbody></table>');

CSS Rule	Line	PL/SQL Code
	64	if c > 0 then
13,14	65	sys.htp.p('<div class="CartTotal">
15,16	66	<p>Items: <span>'||c||'</span></p>
17,18	67	<p class="CartTotal">Total: <span>'||trim(to_char(t,'$999G999G999D00'))||'</span></p>
	68	</div>');
	69	else
	70	sys.htp.p('<div class="alertMessage info" style="margin-top: 8px;">');
	71	sys.htp.p('<img src="#IMAGE_PREFIX#f_spacer.gif">');
	72	sys.htp.p('<div class="innerMessage">');
	73	sys.htp.p('<h3>Note</h3>');
	74	sys.htp.p('<p>You have no items in your current order.</p>');
	75	sys.htp.p('</div>');
	76	sys.htp.p('</div>');
	77	end if;
	78	end;
	79	sys.htp.p('</div>');
	80	end;

> **NOTE:** The ELSE block (lines 70-76) executes when the user tries to move on without selecting a product in the current order. The block uses a built-in class (*alertMessage info*) that carries an image (f_spacer.gif) followed by the message specified on lines 73-74.

Table 7-1 – PL/SQL Code

In this PL/SQL code you merged some HTML elements to deliver the page in your browser. Before getting into the code details, let's first acquaint ourselves with some specific terms and objects used in the PL/SQL code.

Using HTML in PL/SQL Code

Oracle Application Express installs with your Oracle database and is comprised of data in tables and PL/SQL code. Whether you are running the Oracle Application Express development environment or an application you built using Oracle Application Express, the process is the same. Your browser sends a URL request, which is translated into an appropriate Oracle Application Express PL/SQL call. After the database processes the PL/SQL, the results are relayed back to your browser as HTML. This cycle happens each time you either request or submit a page.

Specific HTML content not handled by Oracle Application Express (forms, reports, and charts) are generated using the PL/SQL region type. You can use PL/SQL to have more control over dynamically generated HTML within a region, as you do here. Let's see how these two core technologies are used together.

htp and htf Packages:

htp (hypertext procedures) and htf (hypertext functions) are part of PL/SQL Web Toolkit package to generate HTML tags. These packages translate PL/SQL into HTML understood by a web browser. For instance, the *htp.anchor* procedure generates the HTML anchor tag, <a>. The following PL/SQL block generate a simple HTML document:

```
CREATE OR REPLACE PROCEDURE hello AS
BEGIN
    htp.htmlopen;                      -- generates <HTML>
    htp.headopen;                      -- generates <HEAD>
    htp.title('Hello');                -- generates <TITLE>Hello</TITLE>
    htp.headclose;                     -- generates </HEAD>
    htp.bodyopen;                      -- generates <BODY>
    htp.header(1, 'Hello');            -- generates <H1>Hello</H1>
    htp.bodyclose;                     -- generates </BODY>
    htp.htmlclose;                     -- generates </HTML>
END;
```

Oracle provided the htp.p tag to allow you to override any PL/SQL-HTML procedure or even a tag that did not exist. If a developer wishes to use a new HTML tag or simply is unaware of the PL/SQL analog to the html tag, s/he can use the htp.p procedure.

For every htp procedure that generates HTML tags, there is a corresponding htf function with identical parameters. The function versions do not directly generate output in your web page. Instead, they pass their output as return values to the statements that invoked them.

htp.p / htp.print:
Generates the specified parameter as a string

htp.p('<p>'):
Indicates that the text coming after the tag is to be formatted as a paragraph

Customer::
Renders the text they surround in bold

htf.escape_sc:
Escape_sc is a function, which replaces characters that have special meaning in HTML with their escape sequence.

converts occurrence of & to &amp
converts occurrence of " to &quot
converts occurrence of < to &lt
converts occurrence of > to &gt

172

To prevent XSS (Cross Site Scripting) attacks, you must call SYS.HTF.ESCAPE_SC to prevent embedded JavaScript code from being executed when you inject the string into an HTML page. The SYS prefix is used to signify Oracle's SYS schema. The HTP and HTF packages normally exist in the SYS schema and Oracle APEX relies on them.

Cursor FOR LOOP Statement

The cursor FOR LOOP statement implicitly declares its loop index as a record variable of the row type that a specified cursor returns and then opens a cursor. With each iteration, the cursor FOR LOOP statement fetches a row from the result set into the record. When there are no more rows to fetch, the cursor FOR LOOP statement closes the cursor. The cursor also closes if a statement inside the loop transfers control outside the loop or raises an exception.

The cursor FOR LOOP statement lets you run a SELECT statement and then immediately loop through the rows of the result set. This statement can use either an implicit or explicit cursor.

If you use the SELECT statement only in the cursor FOR LOOP statement, then specify the SELECT statement inside the cursor FOR LOOP statement, as in Example A. This form of the cursor FOR LOOP statement uses an implicit cursor and is called an implicit cursor FOR LOOP statement. Because the implicit cursor is internal to the statement, you cannot reference it with the name SQL.

Example A - Implicit Cursor FOR LOOP Statement

```
BEGIN
  FOR item IN (
    SELECT last_name, job_id
    FROM employees
    WHERE job_id LIKE '%CLERK%' AND manager_id > 120
    ORDER BY last_name
  )
  LOOP
    DBMS_OUTPUT.PUT_LINE ('Name = ' || item.last_name || ', Job = ' || item.job_id);
  END LOOP;
END;
/
```

Output:

Name = Atkinson, Job = ST_CLERK

Name = Bell, Job = SH_CLERK

Name = Bissot, Job = ST_CLERK

...

Name = Walsh, Job = SH_CLERK

If you use the SELECT statement multiple times in the same PL/SQL unit, define an explicit cursor for it and specify that cursor in the cursor FOR LOOP statement, as shown in Example B. This form of the cursor FOR LOOP statement is called an explicit cursor FOR LOOP statement. You can use the same explicit cursor elsewhere in the same PL/SQL unit.

Example B - Explicit Cursor FOR LOOP Statement

```
DECLARE
  CURSOR c1 IS
    SELECT last_name, job_id FROM employees
    WHERE job_id LIKE '%CLERK%' AND manager_id > 120
    ORDER BY last_name;
BEGIN
  FOR item IN c1
  LOOP
    DBMS_OUTPUT.PUT_LINE ('Name = ' || item.last_name || ', Job = ' || item.job_id);
  END LOOP;
END;
/
```

Output:
Name = Atkinson, Job = ST_CLERK
Name = Bell, Job = SH_CLERK
Name = Bissot, Job = ST_CLERK
...
Name = Walsh, Job = SH_CLERK

TABLE 7-1 PL/SQL CODE EXPLAINED

Display Customer Information (Lines 7-32)
This procedure fetches information of the selected customer and presents it in a desirable format (as shown in Figure 7-7) using the CSS rules defined under the class *CustomerInfo*.

Declare (Line: 1)
This is the parent PL/SQL block. A nested block is also used under the *Display Current Order* section on line:48.

l_customer_id varchar2(30) := :P11_CUSTOMER_ID; (Line: 2)
Assigns customer ID, which is retrieved from the previous order wizard step (Page 11), to the variable *l_customer_id*. This variable is used in a SQL statement (on Line No. 9) to fetch details of the selected customer. In PL/SQL, the symbol := is called the assignment operator. The variable, which is being assigned the new value, is placed on the left side of the assignment operator and the value is placed on the right side of the operator.

:P11_CUSTOMER_ID is called a bind variable. Bind variables are substituion variables that are used in place of literals. You can use bind variables syntax anywhere in Oracle Application Express where you are using SQL or PL/SQL to reference session state of a specified item. For example:

```
SELECT * FROM employees WHERE last_name like '%' || :P99_SEARCH_STRING || '%'
```

In this example, the search string is a page item. If the region type is defined as SQL Query, then you can reference the value using standard SQL bind variable syntax. Using bind variables ensures that parsed representations of SQL queries are reused by the database, optimizing memory usage by the server.

The use of bind variables is encouraged in Oracle APEX. Bind variables help you protect your Oracle APEX application from SQL injection attacks. Bind variables work in much the same way as passing data to a stored procedure. Bind variables automatically treat all input data as "flat" data and never mistake it for SQL code. Besides the prevention of SQL injection attacks, there are other performance-related benefits to its use.

You declare a page item as a bind variable by prefixing a colon character (:) like this: :P11_CUSTOMER_OPTIONS.

When using bind variable syntax, remember the following rules:

- Bind variable names must correspond to an item name
- Bind variable names are not case-sensitive
- Bind variable names cannot be longer than 30 characters

Although page item and application item names can be up to 255 characters, if you intend to use an application item within SQL using bind variable syntax, the item name must be 30 characters or less.

Begin (Line: 3)
Read *What is PL/SQL* at the beginning of this section.
The code block from line number 7 to 32 creates the first section on the page (marked as A in Figure 7-7) using the <div> HTML element and styles it using Rule 1 and 2. The code between lines 9-20 is executed when the user selects an existing customer from the previous wizard step.

sys.htp.p('<div class="CustomerInfo">'); (Line: 7)
The <div> tag defines a division or a section in an HTML document. This is the opening tag, which references the *CustomerInfo* class in CSS rules to format the following elements. The ending tag is defined on Line 32.

for x in (select * from demo_customers where customer_id = l_customer_id) loop (Line: 9)
Initiates the FOR loop to locate and fetch record of the selected customer from the demo_customers table.

sys.htp.p('<strong>Customer:</strong>'); (Line: 11)
Displays the label "Customer:" in bold.

sys.htp.p('<p>'); (Line: 12)
The paragraph opening tag. It ends on Line 19.

sys.htp.p(sys.htf.escape_sc(x.cust_first_name) || ' '
||sys.htf.escape_sc(x.cust_last_name) || '<br />'); (Line: 13)
Concatenates customer's first and last names using the concatenation characters (||). The <br /> tag inserts a single line break.

sys.htp.p(sys.htf.escape_sc(x.cust_street_address1) || '<br />'); (Line: 14)
Show customer's first address on a new line.

if x.cust_street_address2 is not null then (Lines: 15-17)
  sys.htp.p(sys.htf.escape_sc(x.cust_street_address2) || '<br />');
end if;
It's a condition to check whether the customer's second address is not null. If it's not, print it on a new line.

sys.htp.p(sys.htf.escape_sc(x.cust_city) || ', ' || sys.htf.escapte_sc(x.cust_state) ||
' ' || sys.htf.escape_sc(x.cust_postal_code)); (Line: 18)
Displays city, state, and postal code data on the same row separating each other with a comma and a blank space.

sys.htp.p('</p>'); (Line: 19)
The paragraph end tag.

end loop; (Line: 20)
The loop terminates here after fetching details of an existing customer from the database table.

sys.htp.p('</div>'); (Line: 32)
The div tag terminates here. The output of this section is illustrated in Figure 7-7: A - CustomerInfo. The ELSE block (line 22-30) is executed when a new customer is added to the database from the order interface. In that situation, all values on the current page are fetched from the previous wizard step (Page 11).

Display Products (Lines: 36-42)
Here you create a section on your web page to display all products along with their prices and include an option, which allows users to add products to their cart.

sys.htp.p('<div class="Products" >'); (Line: 36)
Creates a division based on the Products class. HTML elements under this division are styled using rules 3-8.

```
sys.htp.p('<table width="100%" cellspacing="0" cellpadding="0" border="0"> (Line:
37)
```

Here you are initiating to draw an HTML table. The <table> tag defines an HTML table. An HTML table consists of the <table> element and one or more <tr>, <th>, and <td> elements. The <tr> element defines a table row, the <th> element defines a table header, and the <td> element defines a table cell. The Width attribute specifies the width of the table. Setting 100% width instructs the browser to consume the full screen width to display the table element.

```
<thead> (Line: 37)
   <tr><th class="left">Product</th><th>Price</th><th></th></tr>
</thead>
```

The <thead> tag is used to group header content in an HTML table. The <thead> element is used in conjunction with the <tbody> and <tfoot> elements to specify each part of a table (header, body, footer). The <tr> tag creates a row for column heading. The three <th> tags specify the headings. The first two columns are labeled Product and Price, respectively. The third column heading is left blank. A specific declaration (class="left") is included that points toward the CSS rule (8) *div.Products .left{text-align:left;}* to align the title of the first column (Product) to the left. The second column (Price) is styled using a general rule (5).

```
<tbody>'); (Line: 37)
```

The <tbody> tag is used to group the body content in an HTML table. This section spans up to line 41 and is marked as B in Figure 7-7.

```
for c1 in (select product_id, product_name,  list_price, 'Add to Cart' add_to_order
from demo_product_info
where product_avail = 'Y'
order by product_name) loop  (Line: 38)
```

The FOR loop fetches Product ID, Product Name, and List Price columns from the products table. To display a button (Add) in the table, we appended a column aliased add_to_order and populated all rows with a constant value 'Add to Cart'. For further information on FOR LOOP, see the *Cursor FOR LOOP Statement* section earlier in this section.

```
sys.htp.p('<tr><td class="left">' || sys.htf.escape_sc(c1.product_name)||'</td>
          <td>'||trim(to_char(c1.list_price,'999G999G990D00')) || '</td>
          <td><a href="'||apex_util.prepare_url('f?p=&APP_ID.:12:'||:app_session||'
                  :ADD:::P12_PRODUCT_ID:'|| c1.product_id)||'"
               class="t-Button t-Button--simple t-Button--hot">
               <span>Add<i class="iR"></i></span></a>
          </td>
      </tr>'); (Line: 39)
```

This line displays product names with respective prices in two separate columns. The product column is styled using Rule 8, while the price column is styled using Rule 5.

There is an *Add* button in the third column of the table, which is presented as a link using the HTML anchor tag <a> and is styled using a built-in class (t-Button). An anchor can be used in two ways:

1. To create a link to another document by using the href attribute.
2. To create a bookmark inside a document by using the name attribute.

It is usually referred to as a link or a hyperlink. The most important attribute of the <a> element is the *href* attribute, which specifies the URL of the page to which the link goes. When this button is clicked, the product it represents is moved to the Current Order section with the help of a process (*Add Product to the Order Collection*) defined in section 7.6.7.

The c1 prefix in front of column names, points to the FOR LOOP cursor. The TRIM function in the expression, *trim(to_char(c1.list_price,'999G999G990D00'))*, takes a character expression and returns that expression with leading and/or trailing pad characters removed. This expression initially formats the list price column to add thousand separators and decimal place. Next, it converts the numeric price value to text expression using the TO_CHAR function and finally applies the TRIM function. The TO_CHAR function converts a DATETIME, number, or NTEXT expression to a TEXT expression in a specified format. The table that follows lists the elements of a number format model with some examples.

Element	Example	Description
0	0999	Returns leading zeros.
	9990	Returns trailing zeros.
9	9999	Returns value with the specified number of digits with a leading space if positive or with a leading minus if negative. Leading zeros are blank, except for a zero value, which returns a zero for the integer part of the fixed-point number.
D	99D99	Returns in the specified position the decimal character, which is the current value of the NLS_NUMERIC_CHARACTER parameter. The default is a period (.).
G	9G999	Returns the group separator (which is usually comma) in the specified position. You can specify multiple group separators in a number format model. Use the following SQL statement to check the current value for decimal and group separator characters: SELECT value FROM v$nls_parameters WHERE parameter='NLS_NUMERIC_CHARACTERS';

The code,

```
<a
href="'||apex_util.prepare_url('f?p=&APP_ID.:12:'||:app_session||':ADD:::P12_PRODUCT_ID
:'|| c1.product_id)||'" class="t-Button t-Button--simple t-Button--hot">
<span>Add<iclass="iR"></i></span></a>,
```

creates a link with an ADD request. The value of REQUEST is the name of the button the user clicks. For example, suppose you have a button with a name of CHANGE and a label *Apply Changes*. When a user clicks the button, the value of REQUEST is

CHANGE. In section 7.6.7, you will create the following process named *Add Product to the order collection.*

```
for x in (select p.rowid, p.* from demo_product_info p where product_id=:P12_PRODUCT_ID)
loop
  select count(*)
  into l_count
  from wwv_flow_collections
  where collection_name = 'ORDER'
  and c001 = x.product_id;
  if l_count >= 10 then
    exit;
  end if;
  apex_collection.add_member(p_collection_name => 'ORDER',
    p_c001 => x.product_id,
    p_c002 => x.product_name,
    p_c003 => x.list_price,
    p_c004 => 1,
    p_c010 => x.rowid);
end loop;
```

During the process creation, you'll select Request=Value in Condition Type and will enter ADD for Value. The ADD request in the <a> tag is referencing the same expression. When a user clicks the ADD button on the web page, the URL sends the ADD request to the process along with the selected product ID using a hidden item named P12_PRODUCT_ID to be created in Section 7.6.4. In turn, the process adds the product to the Current Order section. The URL generated from this code looks something like this at runtime:

```
f?p=64699:12:13238397476902:ADD:::P12_PRODUCT_ID:10
```

end loop; (Line: 40)
End of FOR loop.

sys.htp.p('</tbody></table>'); (Line: 41)
Table and body closing tags.

sys.htp.p('</div>'); (Line: 42)
The closing div tag.

Display Current Order (Lines: 46-79)
This section acts as a shopping cart. The products selected by a user are placed in this section.

sys.htp.p('<div class="Products" >'); (Line: 46)
Defines the <div> tag and utilizes the Products class referenced in rules 3-8.

```
sys.htp.p('<table width="100%" cellspacing="0" cellpadding="0" border="0">
 <thead>
  <tr><th class="left">Current Order</th></tr>
 </thead>
</table>  (Line: 47)
```

Displays section heading as follows in the first row of a separate table.

Current Order

Declare (Line: 48)

This is a nested or child block. To nest a block means to embed one or more PL/SQL block inside another PL/SQL block to have better control over program's execution.

c number := 0; t number := 0; (Line: 49)

Declared two numeric counter variables and initialized them with zero. The variable c is used to evaluate whether any product is selected in the current order, while the variable t stores total value for the order.

Begin (Line: 50)

```
for c1 in (select c001 pid, c002 i, to_number(c003) p, count(c002) q, sum(c003) ep,
'Remove' remove
        from apex_collections
        where collection_name = 'ORDER'
        group by c001, c002, c003
        order by c001)
```
loop (Line: 52)

APEX Collection enables you to temporarily capture one or more non-scalar values. You can use collections to store rows and columns currently in session state so they can be accessed, manipulated, or processed during a user's specific session. You can think of a collection as a bucket in which you temporarily store and name rows of information.

Every collection contains a named list of data elements (or members), which can have up to 50 character properties (varchar2 (4000)), 5 number, 5 date, 1 XML type, 1 BLOB, and 1 CLOB attribute. You insert, update, and delete collection information using the PL/SQL API APEX_COLLECTION.

When you create a new collection, you must give it a name that cannot exceed 255 characters. Note that collection names are not case-sensitive and will be converted to uppercase. Once the collection is named, you can access the values (members of a collection) in the collection by running a SQL query against the database view APEX_COLLECTIONS.

The APEX_COLLECTIONS view has the following definition:

COLLECTION_NAME	NOT NULL VARCHAR2(255)
SEQ_ID	NOT NULL NUMBER
C001	VARCHAR2(4000)
C002	VARCHAR2(4000)
C003	VARCHAR2(4000)
C004	VARCHAR2(4000)
C005	VARCHAR2(4000)
...	
C050	VARCHAR2(4000)
N001	NUMBER
N002	NUMBER
N003	NUMBER
N004	NUMBER
N005	NUMBER
CLOB001	CLOB
BLOB001	BLOB
XMLTYPE001	XMLTYPE
MD5_ORIGINAL	VARCHAR2(4000)

Use the APEX_COLLECTIONS view in an application just as you would use any other table or view in an application, for example:

```
SELECT c001, c002, c003, n001, clob001   FROM APEX_collections WHERE
collection_name = 'DEPARTMENTS'
```

Note that you can't read apex_collection using external tools. A collection is related to an Oracle APEX session and not available outside of it. However, using the following statement you can query WWV_FLOW_COLLECTION_MEMBERS$. It is into this table that Oracle APEX stores its collection data. To view the collection data (after completing this chapter), add Men Shoes to the Current Order section on the Select Items page. Connect to the SQL Command Line utility using SYS user's credentials and issue the following statement:

```
Select c001,c002,c003,c004 from APEX_040200.wwv_flow_collection_members$;
```

Output:
```
c001=9 (product id), c002=Men Shoes (product), c003=110 (list price), and
c004=1 (quantity)
```

The CREATE_OR_TRUNCATE_COLLECTION method creates a new collection if the named collection does not exist. If the named collection already exists, this method truncates it. Truncating a collection empties it, but leaves it in place.

In section 7.5.12, we created a process named *Create or Truncate Order Collection* under the page rendering section and used the following statement to create a collection named ORDER:

```
apex_collection.create_or_truncate_collection (p_collection_name => 'ORDER');
```

In the "For C1 in" loop, we're selecting records from the same ORDER collection. Columns from apex_collections in the SELECT statement correspond to:

Column	Corresponds To
C001 – pid	Product ID (9)
C002 – i	Product Name (Men Shoes)
C003 – p	List Price (110)
C002 - q	Quantity (1)
C003 - ep	Extended Price (110) This value will increase with each Add button click to accumulate total cost of a product.

sys.htp.p('<div class="CartItem"> (Line: 53)
This line references another class (CartItem) to style the actual Current Order section.

<a
href="'||apex_util.prepare_url('f?p=&APP_ID.:12:&SESSION.:REMOVE:::P12_PROD
UCT_ID:'||sys.htf.escape_sc(c1.pid))||'"><img src="#IMAGE_PREFIX#delete.gif"
alt="Remove from cart" title="Remove from cart" />
</a>   (Line: 54)
The <a> tag creates a link with a REMOVE request. This time, it uses product ID from the collection. In section 7.6.7 (B), there is a process named Remove product from the order collection (as shown below) where the request expression is set to REMOVE.

```
for x in
  (select seq_id, c001 from apex_collections
    where collection_name = 'ORDER' and c001 = :P12_PRODUCT_ID)
loop
apex_collection.delete_member(p_collection_name => 'ORDER', p_seq => x.seq_id);
end loop;
```

In HTML, images are defined with the <img> tag. The <img> tag has no closing tag. To display an image on a page, you need to use the src attribute. Src stands for "source". The value of the src attribute is the URL of the image you want to display.

Syntax for defining an image:
<img src="url" alt="some_text"/>

The URL points to the location where the image is stored. The value of IMAGE_PREFIX determines the virtual path the web server uses to point to the images directory distributed with Oracle Application Express. We used "delete.gif" that is displayed in front of the product name. The required *alt* attribute specifies an alternate text for an image, if the image cannot be displayed.

When a user clicks the remove link [**X**] in the Current Order section, the URL sends a REMOVE request to the process along with the product ID. The DELETE_MEMBER procedure deletes a specified member from a given named collection using the *p_seq* => *x.seq_id* parameter, which is the sequence ID of the collection member to be deleted.

'||sys.htf.escape_sc(c1.i)||' (Line: 55)
Displays name of the selected product in the Current Order section.

<span>'||trim(to_char(c1.p,'$999G999G999D00'))||'</span> (Line: 56)
<span>Quantity: '||c1.q||'</span> (Line: 57)
<span class="subtotal">Subtotal:
'||trim(to_char(c1.ep,'$999G999G999D00'))||'</span> (Line: 58)
The three lines display price, quantity, and sub-total of the selected product in the Current Order section, as shown below:

```
            $125.00
        Quantity: 10
Subtotal: $1,250.00
```

</div>'); (Line: 59)
The ending div tag.

c := c + 1; (Line: 60)
This counter increments the value of c with 1 at the end of each loop. The variable c is used to calculate number of items selected in the current order.

t := t + c1.ep; (Line: 61)
Similar to the variable c, t is also incremented to sum up extended price (**c1.ep**) to calculate total order value.

```
if c > 0 then
  sys.htp.p('<div class="CartTotal">
   <p>Items: <span>'||c||'</span></p>
   <p class="CartTotal">Total:
<span>'||trim(to_char(t,'$999G999G999D00'))||'</span></p>
   </div>');
else
  sys.htp.p('<div class="alertMessage info" style="margin-top: 8px;">');
   sys.htp.p('<img src="#IMAGE_PREFIX#f_spacer.gif">');
   sys.htp.p('<div class="innerMessage">');
    sys.htp.p('<h3>Note</h3>');
    sys.htp.p('<p>You have no items in your current order.</p>');
   sys.htp.p('</div>');
  sys.htp.p('</div>');
end if; (Line: 64-77)
```

The condition (IF c > 0) evaluates whether a product is selected in the current order. A value other than zero in this variable indicates addition of product(s). If the current order has some items added, the label *Total:* along with the value is displayed, which is stored in the variable t. If no items are selected, the message defined in the else block is shown using a couple of built-in classes.

7.6.4 Create Hidden Item

Create a hidden item in the *Select Items* region. When you click the Add button on Page 12 to add a product to an order, the ID of that product is stored in this hidden item using a URL specified in the PL/SQL code on line 39.

Property	Value
Name	P12_PRODUCT_ID
Type	Hidden

7.6.5 Create Region to hold Buttons

Right-click the *Wizard Buttons* folder and select **Create Region**. Enter **Buttons** for the *Title* of this region and set its *Template* to **Buttons Container**. The region will hold three buttons: Cancel, Previous, and Next. These buttons are created in the next section.

7.6.6 Create Buttons

All the three buttons created in this section have one thing in common, the *Action* property, which is set to *Submit Page*. When you click any of these three buttons, the page is submitted and a corresponding branch (created in section 7.6.9) is fired to take you to the specified location. For example, if you click the *Cancel* button, the corresponding branch takes you back to the main Orders page (Page 4). Right-click the new *Buttons* region and select **Create Button**. Set the following properties for the new button:

Property	Value
Button Name	CANCEL
Label	Cancel
Button Position	Close
Action	Submit Page

Create another button under the *Cancel* button and set the following properties:

Property	Value
Button Name	PREVIOUS
Label	Previous
Button Position	Previous
Button Template	Icon
Icon CSS Classes	fa-chevron-left
Action	Submit Page

Create the final button under the *Previous* button and set the following properties:

Property	Value
Button Name	NEXT
Label	Place Order
Button Position	Next
Button Template	Text with Icon
Hot	Yes
Icon CSS Classes	fa-chevron-right
Action	Submit Page

7.6.7 Create Processes

The two processes created in this section handle the routine to either add a product to the *Current Order* section or remove one from it. The *add_member* function references the collection (*ORDER* created in section 7.5.12) to populate the collection with a new product. In Table 7-1, the link defined on line 39 in the PL/SQL code forwards an ADD request, which is entertained here after evaluating the request in step 4 below.

A. Add Product to the Order Collection

1. Expand the *Pre-Rendering* node (on the *Rendering* tab) and create a process under *Before Header* folder.

2. Enter **Add Product to the ORDER Collection** for the name of the new process and set its *Type* to **PL/SQL Code**.

3. Enter the following code in the *PL/SQL Code* box. Locate this code under *BookCode\Chapter7\7.6.7A.txt* file.

```
declare
  l_count number := 0;
begin
for x in (select p.rowid, p.* from demo_product_info p
          where product_id = :P12_PRODUCT_ID)
loop
  select count(*)
  into l_count
  from wwv_flow_collections
  where collection_name = 'ORDER'
  and c001 = x.product_id;
  if l_count >= 10 then
    exit;
  end if;
  apex_collection.add_member(p_collection_name => 'ORDER',
    p_c001 => x.product_id,
    p_c002 => x.product_name,
    p_c003 => x.list_price,
    p_c004 => 1,
    p_c010 => x.rowid);
end loop;
end;
```

4. In *Server-side Condition* section, set *Type* to **Request=Value**, and enter **ADD** in the *Value* property box.

B. Remove Product from the Order Collection

The *delete_member* function is just opposite to the *add_member* function. It is called by a link (Table 7-1 line 54), which carries a *REMOVE* request. The request is evaluated by a condition set in Step 3 below. If the request matches, the selected product is deleted from the ORDER collection.

1. **Create** another process under the previous one. *Name* it **Remove Product from the ORDER Collection** and set its *Type* to **PL/SQL Code**.

2. Enter the following code in the *PL/SQL Code* property box. Get this code from *BookCode\Chapter7\7.6.7B.txt* file.

```
for x in
  (select seq_id, c001 from apex_collections
    where collection_name = 'ORDER' and c001 = :P12_PRODUCT_ID)
loop
  apex_collection.delete_member(p_collection_name => 'ORDER', p_seq =>
x.seq_id);
end loop;
```

3. In *Server-side Condition* section, set *Type* to **Request=Value**, and enter **REMOVE** in the *Value* property box.

7.6.8 Create Process – Place Order

After selecting products for an order, you click the *Next* button. The process defined in this section is associated with this button. The PL/SQL code specified in this process adds new customer and order information in relevant database tables using a few SQL INSERT statements. After committing the DML statement, the process truncates the *ORDER* collection.

1. On the *Processing* tab, create a new process under the *Processing* folder.

2. Enter **Place Order** for the name of the new process and set its *Type* to **PL/SQL Code**. Enter the following code in the *PL/SQL Code* box. Also, select **NEXT** for *When Button Pressed* property. The code is stored under *BookCode\Chapter7\7.6.8.txt* file

```
declare
  l_order_id    number;
  l_customer_id varchar2(30) := :P11_CUSTOMER_ID;
begin
-- Create New Customer
  if :P11_CUSTOMER_OPTIONS = 'NEW' then
    insert into DEMO_CUSTOMERS (
      CUST_FIRST_NAME, CUST_LAST_NAME, CUST_STREET_ADDRESS1,
      CUST_STREET_ADDRESS2, CUST_CITY, CUST_STATE, CUST_POSTAL_CODE,
      CUST_EMAIL, PHONE_NUMBER1, PHONE_NUMBER2, URL, CREDIT_LIMIT, TAGS)
    values (
      :P11_CUST_FIRST_NAME, :P11_CUST_LAST_NAME, :P11_CUST_STREET_ADDRESS1,
      :P11_CUST_STREET_ADDRESS2, :P11_CUST_CITY, :P11_CUST_STATE,
      :P11_CUST_POSTAL_CODE, :P11_CUST_EMAIL, :P11_PHONE_NUMBER1,
      :P11_PHONE_NUMBER2, :P11_URL, :P11_CREDIT_LIMIT, :P11_TAGS)
    returning customer_id into l_customer_id;
    :P11_CUSTOMER_ID := l_customer_id;
  end if;
-- Insert a row into the Order Header table
-- The statement returning order_id into l_order_id stores the primary key value for
   the order_id column (generated by the DEMO_ORD_SEQ sequence) into the local
   variable l_order_id. This value is used in the INSERT statements to
   populate the order_id column in DEMO_ORDER_ITEMS table.
  insert into demo_orders(customer_id, order_total, order_timestamp, user_name)
  values  (l_customer_id, null, systimestamp, upper(:APP_USER))
  returning order_id into l_order_id;
  commit;
-- Loop through the ORDER collection and insert rows into the Order Line Item table
  for x in (select c001, c003, sum(c004) c004 from apex_collections
            where collection_name = 'ORDER' group by c001, c003) loop
    insert into demo_order_items(order_item_id, order_id, product_id, unit_price, quantity)
    values (null, l_order_id, to_number(x.c001), to_number(x.c003),to_number(x.c004));
```

```
  end loop;
  commit;
```
-- Set the item P14_ORDER_ID to the order which was just placed
```
  :P14_ORDER_ID := l_order_id;
```
-- Truncate the collection after the order has been placed
```
  apex_collection.truncate_collection(p_collection_name => 'ORDER');
end;
```

7.6.9 Create Branches

Create the following three branches under the *After Processing* folder on the *Processing* tab. The buttons referenced in these branches were created in section 7.6.6.

Property	Value
Name	Go To Page 14
Type (under *Bahavior*)	Page or URL (Redirect)
Target	Type = Page in this Application Page = 14
When Button Pressed	NEXT

Property	Value
Name	Go To Page 4
Type (under *Bahavior*)	Page or URL (Redirect)
Target	Type = Page in this Application Page = 4
When Button Pressed	CANCEL

Property	Value
Name	Go To Page 11
Type (under *Bahavior*)	Page or URL (Redirect)
Target	Type = Page in this Application Page = 11
When Button Pressed	PREVIOUS

Test Your Work

Navigate to the Orders page using the main menu route and click the **Enter New Order** button. Select a customer using the *Existing Customer* option and click *Next*. Click the *Add* button next to Business Shirt to add this product to the *Current Order* pane. Click the *Add* button for the Business Shirt again and see increase in Quantity and Total. Add some more products and observe the change in the *Current Order* section. Click the cross sign ✕ to remove this product from the Current Order section. Click *Cancel* to return to Page 4 without saving the order.

After adding products to the Order form, you click the *Place Order* button. The next page, *Order Summary*, comes up to show details of the placed order. In this section, you will create this page. It is the last step in the order creation wizard.

1. Create one more **Blank Page**.

2. Complete the first wizard step as show in the following and click **Next**.

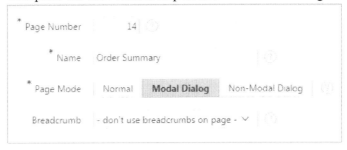

3. On the *Navigation Menu* screen, set *Navigation Preference* to **Identify an existing navigation menu entry for this page**, and set *Existing Navigation Menu Entry* to **Orders**. Click **Next**.

4. Click **Finish** to end the wizard.

5. Click the root node (**Page 14: Order Summary**) and set *Dialog Template* to **Wizard Modal Dialog**.

7.7.1 Create Region – Order Progress

Right-click the *Wizard Progress Bar* folder and select **Create Region**. Set the following properties for the new region.

Property	Value
Title	Order Progress
Type	List
List	Order Wizard
Template	Blank with Attributes
List Template (*under Attributes node*)	Wizard Progress

7.7.2 Create Region – Order Header

Right-click the *Wizard Body* folder and select **Create Region**. Set the following properties for this region. Just like section 7.6.3, you defined the region as *PL/SQL Dynamic Content*, which is based on PL/SQL that enables you to render any HTML or text.

Property	Value
Title	Order Header
Type	PL/SQL Dynamic Content
PL/SQL Code	begin

```
begin
for x in (select c.cust_first_name, c.cust_last_name, cust_street_address1,
cust_street_address2, cust_city, cust_state, cust_postal_code from demo_customers c,
demo_orders o
where c.customer_id = o.customer_id and o.order_id = :P14_ORDER_ID)
loop
  htp.p('<span style="font-size:16px;font-weight:bold;">ORDER #' ||
      sys.htf.escape_sc(:P14_ORDER_ID) || '</span><br />');
  htp.p(sys.htf.escape_sc(x.cust_first_name) || ' ' || sys.htf.escape_sc(x.cust_last_name) ||
      '<br />');
  htp.p(sys.htf.escape_sc(x.cust_street_address1) || '<br />');
  if x.cust_street_address2 is not null then
    htp.p(sys.htf.escape_sc(x.cust_street_address2) || '<br />');
  end if;
  htp.p(sys.htf.escape_sc(x.cust_city) || ', ' || sys.htf.escape_sc(x.cust_state) || ' ' ||
      sys.htf.escape_sc(x.cust_postal_code) || '<br /><br />');
end loop;
end;
```

7.7.3 Create Region – Order Lines

Add another region under the *Wizard Body* folder and set the following properties for this region. After creating this region expand its *Columns* node and set suitable heading for each column. This region will carry line item information.

Property	Value
Title	Order Lines
Type	Classic Report
SQL Query	select p.product_name, oi.unit_price, oi.quantity, (oi.unit_price * oi.quantity) extended_price from demo_order_items oi, demo_product_info p where oi.product_id = p.product_id and oi.order_id = :P14_ORDER_ID

7.7.4 Create Item

Right-click the *Order Lines* region and select **Create Page Item**. Set the following properties for the new item. The value for this item was set in the PL/SQL code defined in section 7.6.8 and was utilized in the codes defined in section 7.7.2 and in section 7.7.3 to fetch order information.

Property	Value
Name	P14_ORDER_ID
Type	Hidden

7.7.5 Create Region – Buttons

Right-click the *Wizard Buttons* folder and select **Create Region**. Enter **Buttons** for its *Name* and set its *Template* to **Buttons Container**. The region will hold the following button.

7.7.6 Create Button

Right-click the new *Buttons* region node and select **Create Button**. Set the following properties for the new button:

Property	Value
Button Name	BACK
Label	Back To Orders
Button Position	Next
Hot	Yes
Action	Redirect to Page in this Application
Target	Type = Page in this application Page = 4

Complete Testing

Congratulation! You have completed the most tiresome but interesting chapter of the book in which you learned numerous techniques. Now you are in a position to test the whole work you performed in this chapter.

1. Move to the application's **Home page**.

2. Click the **Orders** menu and then click the **Enter New Order** button.

3. Select **New Customer**.

4. **Fill in the New Customer form** using your own name, address, and so on. Click **Next** to proceed.

5. On the *Select Item* page **add some products** to the *Current Order* pane.

6. Click the **Place Order** button to see the *Order Summary* page resembling Figure 7-8.

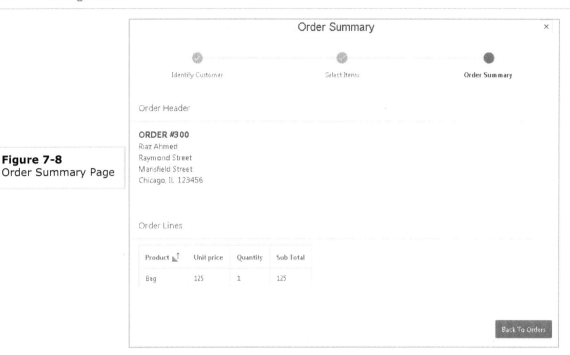

Figure 7-8
Order Summary Page

7. Click the **Back To Orders** button in the *Order Summary* page to return to the orders main page. The newly created order will appear in the orders list.

8. Click the number of the new order to modify it in *Order Details* page (Page 29). Try to add or remove products on this page and save your modifications.

9. Also, try the delete operation by deleting this new order.

7.8 A More Simple Approach

I know as a beginner you might be confused with the stuff described in section 7.5 onward. I added this stuff purposely to present something that would be helpful to you in your future endeavors. However, in this section I'll demonstrate a simpler approach to add, modify, and delete orders using just one interface.

1. Execute all the steps mentioned in section 7.2 to create the two master and details pages. In step 4, set number of the *Master Page* to **404**, and number of the *Details Page* to **429**. Also, make the Interactive Grid visible on the Order Details page (Page 429), as instructed at the end of section 7.2.

2. Execute the instructions provided in section **7.3.1** to delete and re-create the default *Orders* region on the Order Master page–Page 404. In step 7 of section 7.3.1, set *Page* and *Clear Cache* properties to **429** to point to the correct page number and set the *Name* property to **P429_ORDER_ID**. Skip the optional report sections (spanning from 7.3.2 to 7.3.4) at this stage to preserve some time.

3. Create the *Enter New Order* button as follows. On the **Rendering** in Page 404 right-click the *Breadcrumb* region (under *Breadcrumb Bar*) and click **Create**

Button. Set the following attributes for this button. Note that previously this buttons was used to initiate the order wizard by calling Page 11. Here, we are calling Page 429 to directly enter a new order.

Property	Value
Button Name	ENTER_NEW_ORDER
Label	Enter New Order
Button Template	Text with Icon
Hot	Yes
Icon CSS Classes	fa-chevron-right
Action	Redirect to Page in this Application
Target	Type = Page in this Application Page = 429 Clear Cache = 429

4. Save Page 404.

5. In the *Page Finder* box (far left on the toolbar), enter **429** and click **Go** to call **Page 429** in the Page Designer.

6. Click the root node (*Page 429: Order Details*) and set the *Page Mode* property to **Modal Dialog**. Set *Width, Height,* and *Maximum Width* properties to **900**, **800**, and **1200**, respectively. Also, set *Dialog Template* (in the *Appearance* section) to **Wizard Modal Dialog**.

7. Edit the following items individually and set the corresponding properties shown under each item. The customer ID item, which was displayed as *Display Only* item in the previous method, will now be rendered as a Select List carrying the names of all customers. The SQL query defined for the Select List automatically shows the correct customer name when you navigate from one order to another.

P429_CUSTOMER_ID

Property	Value
Type	Select List
Label	Customer
Type (*List of Values*)	SQL Query
SQL Query	select cust_first_name ||' '|| cust_last_name d, customer_id r from demo_customers

P429_USER_NAME

Property	Value
Type	Select List
Label	Sales Rep
Type *(List of Values)*	SQL Query
SQL Query	select distinct user_name d, user_name r from demo_orders union select upper(:APP_USER) d, upper(:APP_USER) r from dual order by 1
Display Extra Values	No
Display Null Value	No
Help Text	Use to change the Sales Rep associated with this order.

P429_TAG

Property	Value
Type	Text Field

8. In the *Region Buttons* folder, set *Button Position* property to **Edit** for GET_PREVIOUS_ORDER_ID and GET_NEXT_ORDER_ID buttons to place them on top of the region.

9. Click the **Order Details** interactive grid *Order Details* and replace the existing source *SQL Query* with the one that follows:

```
select oi.order_item_id, oi.order_id, oi.product_id, oi.unit_price,
       oi.quantity, (oi.unit_price * oi.quantity) extended_price
from DEMO_ORDER_ITEMS oi, DEMO_PRODUCT_INFO pi
where oi.ORDER_ID = :P429_ORDER_ID
and oi.product_id = pi.product_id (+)
```

10. Under the *Columns* folder, edit the following columns using the specified properties and values.

Column	Property	Value
PRODUCT_ID	Type Heading Alignment Type *(LOV)* List of Values Display Null Value	Select List Product Start Shared Components Products With Price No
UNIT_PRICE	Type Alignment Column Alignment	Display Only end end
QUANTITY	Width *(Appearance)* Type *(Default)* PL/SQL Expression	5 PL/SQL Expression 1 *(sets 1 as the default quantity)*
EXTENDED_PRICE	Type Heading Alignment Column Alignment Format Mask Query Only *(Source)*	Display Only Price end end $5,234.10 Yes

11. Right-click the *Wizard Buttons* folder and select **Create Region**. Set *Title* of the new region to **Buttons** and *Template* to **Buttons Container**. In *Regions Buttons* folder, click the **Cancel** button and set its *Region* property (under *Layout*) to **Buttons**. Set this region for **Delete**, **Save**, and **Create** buttons, too. This action will place all the four buttons under the *Buttons* region–see Figure 7-5.

12. Save the changes. Call **Page 404** in the Page Designer and click **Save and Run Page** button. Click the **Enter New Order** button–you will see Page 429. Select a Customer from the Select List and pick a date from the Date Picker. In the *Order Details* section, click the **Edit** button. The first product (Bag) will appear in the Product column with 1 as its default quantity. Click the **Create** button to save the order. You will get *cannot insert NULL into ("DEMO_ORDER_ITEMS"."ORDER_ID")* error. The ORDER_ID column in the order items table acts as a foreign key to create a relationship between master and detail order records. The error is generated because there is no way to pass the order ID information to the *Save Interactive Grid Data* process, which is responsible to handle order items data. In the next couple of steps, you will make this provision. Click the **Cancel** button on *Order Details* page to move back.

13. In the Page Designer, call Page 429. On the *Processing* tab, click the **Process Row of DEMO_ORDERS** process. **Drag and place** this process before the *Save Interactive Grid Data*. Next, set the *Return Key Into Item* property of the

Process Row of DEMO_ORDERS process to **P429_ORDER_ID**. This is the page item that will hold the primary key column value returned from a SQL INSERT statement. You can type in the item name or pick it from the list of available items. When a new order record is inserted, this item will get back the primary key value generated by the sequences and database triggers. This value will be set into session state and a process (created in the next step) will utilize it to perform DML operations on the order items table.

14. Click the **Save Interactive Grid Data** process under the *Process Row of DEMO_ORDERS* and switch its *Type* from *Interactive Grid - Automatic Row Processing (DML)* to **PL/SQL Code**. Enter the following code in the *PL/SQL Code* box. In this code, you specify SQL Insert, Update, and Delete statements to manually handle the three operations for the Interactive Grid data. The *:APEX$ROW_STATUS* is a built-in substitution string, which is used to refer to the row status in an Interactive Grid. This placeholder returns the status of *C* if created, *U* if updated, or *D* if deleted for the currently processed interactive grid row. Enter "**The DML operation performed successfully**" in the *Success Message* box. Similarly, enter "**Could not perform the DML operation**" in the *Error Message* box, and **save** your work.

```
begin
  case :APEX$ROW_STATUS
  when 'C' then
    insert into DEMO_ORDER_ITEMS
        (order_item_id, order_id, product_id, unit_price, quantity)
    values (null, :P429_ORDER_ID, :PRODUCT_ID, :UNIT_PRICE, :QUANTITY);
  when 'U' then
    update DEMO_ORDER_ITEMS
      set product_id  = :PRODUCT_ID,
          unit_price = :UNIT_PRICE,
          quantity = :QUANTITY
          where order_item_id = :ORDER_ITEM_ID and order_id = :ORDER_ID;
  when 'D' then
    delete DEMO_ORDER_ITEMS
    where order_item_id = :ORDER_ITEM_ID and order_id = :P429_ORDER_ID;
  end case;
end;
```

Test Your Work

Click the **Enter New Order** button on Page 404. As usual, select a customer and pick an order date. Click the **Edit** button in the *Order Details* region. With a product appearing in the first row along with its default quantity, click the **Create** button. This time, the order will be saved and you will see the success message. In the interactive report, click the order number you just saved, and then click **Add Row** to add some more products. Just select a product, enter some value in the *Quantity* column, and click **Save**. The modified order will be saved as well. Try to remove a product from this order using the **Delete Rows** option in the *Row Actions* menu. Finally, click the **Delete** button on the Order Details page to test order deletion. You're done!

Summary

Here are the highlights of this chapter:

- *Master Detail Form* – You learned how to implement Master Detail Form feature to handle data in two relational tables and went through the auto-generated page components added by the wizard to transparently manage the order processing module.

- *Interactive Report* – Created an interactive report from scratch based on a custom SQL SELECT statement and learned how to alter the report layout by applying highlighting, sorting, and using aggregate functions. You also applied Control Breaks to group related data and added Chart and Group By Views.

- *Primary, Public, and Alternative Interactive Report* – You created three variants of the interactive report and went through the concepts behind these variants.

- *Wizard Steps* – Learned how to create wizard-like interfaces to perform related tasks in a sequence.

- *Copy Page Utility* – The chapter provided a shortcut to utilize an existing page with all functionalities using a different number and for a different scenario.

- *Oracle APEX Collection* – You learned how to use collections to store and retrieve rows and columns information in session state.

- *Custom Processes and Dynamic Actions* – In addition to the auto-generated components and processes, you learned how to manually add your own processes and other components.

- *Using HTML in PL/SQL Code* – You used PL/SQL to have more control over dynamically generated HTML within a region.

- *Using CSS in Oracle APEX Pages* – You applied styling rules to give the page a more professional look.

- *Simple Approach* – Besides the advance techniques, you also learned how to create this module using a simple approach.

Chapter 8

Present Data Graphically

8.1 About Graphical Reports

Presenting data in Oracle APEX, either graphically or in text format, is as easy as creating the input forms. You have had a taste of this feature when you designed the Home page of the application and also had some hands-on exposure to charts while creating the Order module in the previous chapter. Again, the built-in wizards make it so easy to create flexible and powerful graphical reports in Oracle Application Express. In this chapter, you will take a step forward to create the following reports to graphically present the sales application data:

Report	Purpose	Page No.
Customer Orders	Show total orders placed by each customer	17
Sales By Category and Product	Display sales for category and products	16
Sales by Category / Month	Total monthly sales for each category	5
Order Calendar	Show orders in a calendar view	10
Customer Map	Show orders in different states with the help of a map	15
Product Order Tree	Display orders data in a tree view	19

8.2 Create Reports List Page

Prior to creating reports, you will create a page to list all the reports available in the application. The page carrying the reports list (as illustrated in Figure 8-1) will appear when you click the *Reports* entry in the main navigation menu.

Figure 8-1
Reports Page

1. Create a **Blank Page** and set the following properties for it:

Property	Value
Page Number	26
Name	Reports
Page Mode	Normal
Breadcrumb	don't use breadcrumb on page
Navigation Preference	Identify an existing navigation menu entry for this page
Existing Navigation Menu Entry	Reports

2. Right-click the *Content Body* folder and select **Create Region**. Set the following properties for the new region. The region will display the *Reports List* you created in Chapter 3 section 3.2.2.

Property	Value
Title	Reports
Type	List
List	Reports List

3. Click the *Attributes* node under the *Reports* region. Set *List Template* to **Cards** and the *Template Options* according to the followings illustration. By choosing the *Cards* option, the images you set for the *Reports List* in Chapter 3 section 3.2.2 will be presented as cards–see Figure 8-1. *Template Options* allow for selecting a number of CSS customization settings to be applied directly against the component. Template options are defined as CSS classes in the associated templates. The best way to understand these attribute is to select, apply, and test the available options.

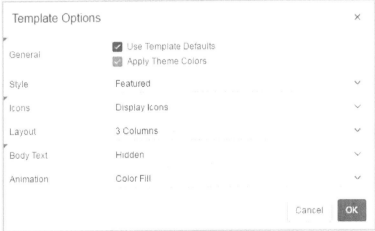

This graphical report is based on Oracle JET bar chart to display amount of orders by category placed by customers. Each bar in the chart has multiple slices representing amounts of different orders. When you move your mouse over these slices a tooltip (A) displays the corresponding amount. The chart will be created with drill-down functionality. That is, when you click a bar, you'll be taken to Page 7 where you will see profile of the selected customer. You will also make provision to change the chart's orientation (B) and will provide options to present it as either stacked or un-stacked (C).

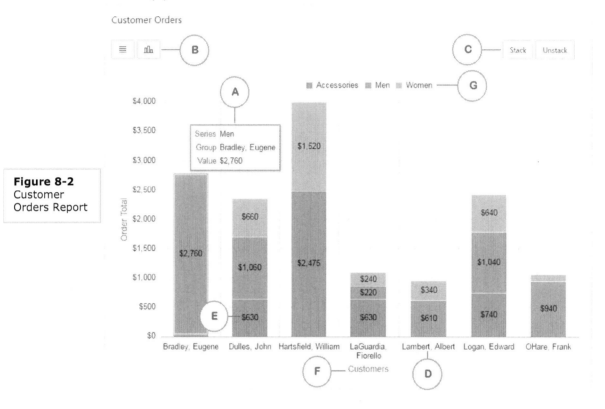

Figure 8-2
Customer
Orders Report

1. Create a **Blank Page** and set the following properties for it:

Property	Value
Page Number	17
Name	Customer Orders
Page Mode	Normal
Breadcrumb	don't use breadcrumb on page
Navigation Preference	Identify an existing navigation menu entry for this page
Existing Navigation Menu Entry	Reports

2. Right-click the *Content Body* folder and select **Create Region**. Set the following properties for the new region. Immediately after switching the region's *Type*, a new folder named *Series* along with a child node (*New*) is added under the region. Each product in this app is associated with one of the three categories: Accessories, Men, and Women. The query below fetches summarized order figures by customers for each category.

Property	Value
Title	Customer Orders
Type	Chart
SQL Query	select c.customer_id, c.cust_last_name||', '||c.cust_first_name Customer_Name, 　　　sum (decode(p.category,'Accessories',oi.quantity * oi.unit_price,0)) "Accessories", 　　　sum (decode(p.category,'Mens',oi.quantity * oi.unit_price,0)) "Men", 　　　sum (decode(p.category,'Womens',oi.quantity * oi.unit_price,0)) "Women" from demo_customers c, demo_orders o, demo_order_items oi, demo_product_info p where c.customer_id = o.customer_id and o.order_id = oi.order_id and 　　　oi.product_id = p.product_id group by c.customer_id, c.cust_last_name, c.cust_first_name order by c.cust_last_name

3. Click the **Attributes** folder under the *Customer Orders* chart region and set the following properties. The *Stack* property specifies whether the data items are stacked. We defined *Automatic* animation setting for the chart, which applies the Oracle JET's default animation settings. It specifies whether animation is shown when data is changed on the chart. A data change can occur if the chart gets automatically refreshed. In the current scenario, the animation takes place when you click of the four buttons (B & C): Horizontal, Vertical, Stack, or Unstack. These buttons will be created in subsequent steps. The *Hide and Show Behavior* is performed when you click a legend item (G). For example, deselecting a legend item will hide its associated data series on the chart. With the value set to *Rescale* for this property, the chart rescales as you select or de-select a legend. This is useful for series with largely varying values.

Property	Value
Type	Bar
Title	*Leave it blank*
Orientation	Vertical
Stack	Yes
Maximum Width	800
Height	500
On Data Change *(under Animation)*	Automatic
Position *(under Legend)*	Top
Hide and Show Behavior	Rescale

4. Click the **New** node (under *Series*) and set the following properties. Each series you create for your chart appears in a unique color to represent product category and displays sales figures for each category (using the *Value* property) that is derived from the SELECT statement specified in step 2. You set *Source Type* (on row 2) to *Region Source*, which specifies that the data of this series is to be extracted from the SQL query defined for the *Customer Orders* region (in step 2). In the *Label* attribute you select a column name that is used for defining the label(s) of the x-axis (D) on the chart, while the *Accessories* column selected for the *Value* property is used for defining the ordered value (E) on this chart. When you click a chart bar (representing *Accessories*), you're drilled down to Page 7 to browse customer details.

Property	Value
Name	Accessories
Type *(under Source)*	Region Source
Label *(under Column Mapping)*	CUSTOMER_NAME
Value	Accessories
Type *(under Link)*	Redirect to Page in this Application
Target	Type = Page in this Application Page = 7 Name = P7_CUSTOMER_ID Value = &CUSTOMER_ID. Clear Cache = 7

5. Right-click the *Series* folder and select **Create Series** from the context menu to add another series. Set the following properties for the new series. Use the same values as defined for the *Target* property in Step 4 to transform this series into a link to access Page 7.

Property	Value
Name	Men
Type *(under Source)*	Region Source
Label *(under Column Mapping)*	CUSTOMER_NAME
Value	Men

6. Create one more series and set the following properties. Create a link as you did for the previous two steps.

Property	Value
Name	Women
Type *(under Source)*	Region Source
Label *(under Column Mapping)*	CUSTOMER_NAME
Value	Women

7. Click the x-axis node (under *Axes*) and enter **Customers** for the *Title* attribute. The title will appear at the bottom of the chart (F).

8. Click the y-axis node and set the following properties. When you format a number as currency, the *Currency* property is required to be set to specify the currency that will be used when formatting the number. You enter a currency that is used when formatting the value on the chart. The value should be a ISO 4217 alphabetic currency code. If the format type is set to Currency, it is required that the *Currency* property also be specified. Visit http://www.xe.com/iso4217.php to see a list of standard currency codes.

Property	Value
Title	Order Total
Format Type	Currency
Decimal Places	0
Currency	USD

9. In this step, you will add two buttons (B) to the *Customer Orders* region. When clicked, these buttons will change the chart's orientation using the default animation set in step 3. Right-click the *Customer Orders* region and select **Create Button** from the context menu. A new folder named *Region Buttons* will be added with a button labeled *New*. Set the following properties for this button. The *Action* attribute says that this button is associated with a dynamic action (step 10), which fires when the button is clicked.

Property	Value
Button Name	Horizontal
Label	Horizontal
Button Position	Previous
Button Template	Icon
Icon CSS Classes	fa-bars
Action	Defined by Dynamic Action

Right-click *Region Button* and select **Create Button** to add a new button. Set the following properties for the new button.

Property	Value
Button Name	Vertical
Label	Vertical
Button Position	Previous
Button Template	Icon
Icon CSS Classes	fa-bar-chart
Action	Defined by Dynamic Action

10. Now add two dynamic actions for the two buttons. Click the *Dynamic Actions* tab, right-click the *Click* folder, and select **Create Dynamic Action**. Click the **New** node and set the following properties. This dynamic action is named *Horizontal Orientation* – you are free to give it any other name you deem suitable. The next three properties specify that this dynamic action should trigger when the *Horizontal* button is clicked.

Property	Value
Name	Horizontal Orientation
Event	Click
Selection Type	Button
Button	Horizontal

205

Click the **Show** node under the *True* folder to set the following properties. When the *Horizontal* button is clicked, the JavaScript code (defined on row 2) is fired. In this code, *dualChart* is a static ID you will set in step 12 for the *Customer Orders* region. You control chart's orientation through the *ojChart* class, which has two options (*Horizontal* and *Vertical*), where Vertical is the default option. In this step, you inform the Oracle APEX engine to display the chart horizontally when the *Horizontal* button is clicked. Note that the chart orientation only applies to bar, line, area, combo, and funnel charts.

Property	Value
Action	Execute JavaScript Code
Code	$("#dualChart_jet").ojChart({orientation: **'horizontal'**});
Selection Type	Region
Region	Customer Orders
Event	Horizontal Orientation
Fire on Initialization	No

11. Right-click the *Click* folder and select **Create Dynamic Action** to add one more for vertical orientation, as follows. Click the **New** node and set the following properties:

Property	Value
Name	Vertical Orientation
Event	Click
Selection Type	Button
Button	Vertical

Click the **Show** node under the *True* folder and set the following properties:

Property	Value
Action	Execute JavaScript Code
Code	$("#dualChart_jet").ojChart({orientation: **'vertical'**});
Selection Type	Region
Region	Customer Orders
Event	Vertical Orientation
Fire on Initialization	No

12. If you run the pages at this stage, you will not see the orientation effect if you click any of the two buttons. This is because of the static ID (*dualChart*), which is mentioned in the JavaScript code to reference the *Customer Orders* region but has not been assigned to the region itself. Switch back to the *Rendering* tab, click the **Customer Orders** region, and in the *Advanced* section enter **dualChart** as the value for the *Static ID* property. Now the region can be recognized by this static ID.

13. Add two more buttons to *Region Buttons*. These buttons will be used to render the series data as stacked or unstacked (C). Set the following properties for the two buttons:

Property	Value (Button1)	Value (Button2)
Button Name	Stack	Unstack
Label	Stack	Unstack
Button Position	Next	Next

14. Create two dynamic actions for the two buttons as follows. Set the **New** nodes' properties as defined in the first table below:

Property	Value (New node)	Value (New node)
Name	Stack Chart	Unstack Chart
Event	Click	Click
Selection Type	Button	Button
Button	Stack	Unstack

The *Stack Chart* dynamic event's **Show** node properties:

Property	Value
Action	Execute JavaScript Code
Code	$("#dualChart_jet").ojChart({stack: 'on'});
Selection Type	Region
Region	Customer Orders
Event	Stack Chart
Fire on Initialization	No

The *Unstack Chart* dynamic event's **Show** node properties:

Property	Value
Action	Execute JavaScript Code
Code	$("#dualChart_jet").ojChart({stack: 'off'});
Selection Type	Region
Region	Customer Orders
Event	Unstack Chart
Fire on Initialization	No

Save your work. Run the application and click *Reports* in the navigation menu. You will see the *Reports* page created in section 8.2. Click the first *Customer Orders* card to access Page 17. You will see a chart, as shown in Figure 8-2. Move your cursor over the chart bars and different portions within a particular bar. You will see a tooltip (A) showing order amount of the corresponding customer. Click the *Vertical* and *Horizontal* buttons (B) to change the chart's orientation. Similarly, click the *Stack* and *Unstack* buttons (C) to see respective animated effects.

In this report, you'll present Category and Products sales data in two separate page regions using different charting options, as illustrated in Figure 8-3.

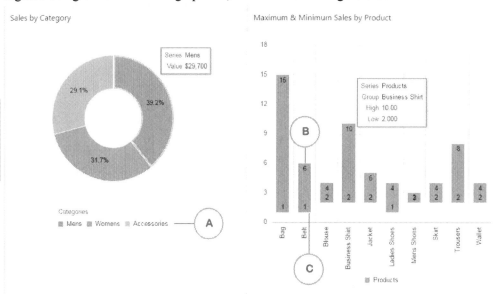

Figure 8-3
Sales by Category and Products Report

1. Create a **Blank Page** and set the following properties for it:

Property	Value
Page Number	16
Name	Sales by Category and Product
Page Mode	Normal
Breadcrumb	don't use breadcrumbs on page
Navigation Preference	Identify an existing navigation menu entry for this page
Existing Navigation Menu Entry	Reports

2. In the Page Designer, right-click the *Content Body* folder and select **Create Region**. Set the following properties for the new region.

Property	Value
Title	Sales by Category
Type	Chart

3. Click the **Attributes** folder under the *Sales by Category* region and set the following properties. Selecting *Yes* for *Dim on Hover* dims all data items when not currently hovered over and highlights only the current data item hovered over with respective order figures in US dollars. The *Hide and Show Behavior* is performed when you click a legend item (A). For example, deselecting a legend item will hide its associated data series on the chart. With the value set to *Rescale* for this property, the chart rescales as you select or de-select a legend. This is useful for series with largely varying values.

Property	Value
Type	Donut
Height	400
Dim on Hover	Yes
Format Type	Currency
Decimal Places	0
Currency	USD
Title *(under Legend)*	Categories
Hide and Show Behavior	Rescale

4. Click the **New** node under *Series* and enter the following properties.

Property	Value
Name	Donut Chart Series
Type *(under Source)*	SQL Query

SQL Query	select p.category label,
	        sum(o.order_total) total_sales
	from demo_orders o,
	        demo_order_items oi,
	        demo_product_info p
	where o.order_id = oi.order_id and
	        oi.product_id = p.product_id
	group by category order by 2 desc

Label *(under Column Mapping)*	LABEL
Value	TOTAL_SALES
Show *(under Label)*	Yes

5. Right-click the *Content Body* folder and select **Create Region** to add another region. This region will carry a *Range* chart to display maximum (B) and minimum (C) ordered quantities for each product. Set the following properties for the new region:

Property	Value
Title	Maximum & Minimum Sales by Product
Type	Chart

SQL Query	select p.product_id, p.product_name,
	        min(oi.quantity), max(oi.quantity)
	from demo_product_info p,
	        demo_order_items oi
	where p.product_id = oi.product_id
	group by p.product_id, p.product_name
	order by p.product_name asc

6. Click the **Attributes** folder under the *Maximum & Minimum Sales by Product* region and set the following properties:

Property	Value
Type	Range
Maximum Width	500
Height	500

7. Click the **New** node under *Series* to set the following properties. The PRODUCT_NAME column will be used for defining the label(s) of the x-axis on the chart. Then, you specify *Low* and *High* column names to be used for defining the low and high values on this chart. In the last six properties you create a link to access Page 6 to browse details of the selected product.

Property	Value
Name	Products
Type *(under Source)*	Region Source
Label *(under Column Mapping)*	PRODUCT_NAME
Low	MIN(OI.QUANTITY)
High	MAX(OI.QUANTITY)
Type *(under Link)*	Redirect to Page in this Application
Target	Type = Page in this application Page = 6 Name = P6_PRODUCT_ID Value = &PRODUCT_ID. Clear Cache = 6
Show *(under Label)*	Yes

Save and access this page from *Sales by Category and Product* card on the *Reports* page. You will see the two charts, as illustrated in Figure 8-3. The page has two regions containing graphical data for category and product sales. Move the mouse cursor over each chart and see respective sales figures. Click the bar representing Bag, the system will drill you down to Page 6 to show the details of this product.

8.5 Sales by Category / Month Report - Page 5

This chart is added to present category sales in different months. In this graphical report, you will make use of *Region Display Selector* (A) to display two different views of category sales data. *Region Display Selector* region enables you to include show and hide controls for each region on a page. This page will have two regions containing two different chart types. After adding the *Region Display Selector* and the two regions, you can switch the regions using the selector appearing on top of the page, as shown in Figure 8-4. The page displays three tabs: *Show All*, *Sales by Category (Line)*, and *Sales by Month (Bar)*. If you click the *Show All* tab, the page displays all the regions. If you click any of the other two tabs, the page shows only the chosen region.

Show All   Sales by Category (Line)   Sales by Month (Bar) ─── (A)

Sales by Category (Line)

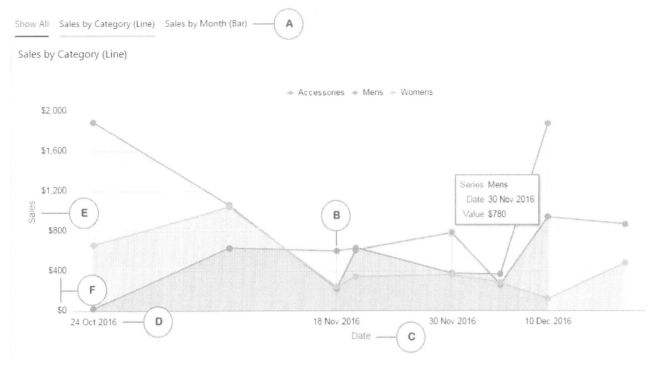

Sales by Month (Bar)

Figure 8-4

1. Create a **Blank Page** and set the following properties for it:

Property	Value
Page Number	5
Name	Sales by Category Per Month
Page Mode	Normal
Breadcrumb	don't use breadcrumbs on page
Navigation Preference	Identify an existing navigation menu entry for this page
Existing Navigation Menu Entry	Reports

2. Right-click the *Content Body* folder and select **Create Region**. Set the following properties for this region. As mentioned earlier, this region will display other regions on the page as horizontal tabs (A). By removing the *Standard Template* (in the third property), the region looks as a part of existing regions.

Property	Value
Title	Region Display Selector
Type	Region Display Selector
Template	-Select- *(that is, no template selected)*

3. Create another region under *Content Body* and set the following properties. This region will hold a Line with Area chart.

Property	Value
Title	Sales by Category (Line)
Type	Chart

4. Click the **Attributes** folder under the *Sales by Category (Line)* chart region and set the following properties. The *Time Axis Type* property automatically renders the chart data in chronological order.

Property	Value
Type	Line with Area
Height	400
Time Axis Type	Enabled
Position *(under Legend)*	Top
Hide and Show Behavior	Rescale

5. Click the **New** node under *Series* and set the following properties. The last two properties will show markers in shape of circles (B). The *Show* property (last in the table) specifies whether the label(s) should be rendered on the chart. By setting it to *No*, we suppressed the visibility of the sales figures.

Property	Value
Type *(under Source)*	SQL Query

SQL Query	select p.category **type**,
	        trunc(o.order_timestamp) **when**,
	        sum (oi.quantity * oi.unit_price) **sales**
	from demo_product_info p,
	        demo_order_items oi,
	        demo_orders o
	where oi.product_id = p.product_id and
	        o.order_id = oi.order_id
	group by p.category, trunc(o.order_timestamp),
	        to_char(o.order_timestamp, 'YYYYMM')
	order by to_char(o.order_timestamp, 'YYYYMM')

Series Name	TYPE
Label	WHEN
Value	SALES
Show *(under Marker)*	Yes
Shape	Circle
Show *(under Label)*	No

6. Click the x-axis node to set the following properties. In these properties, we set a title (C) and date format (D) for X-axis.

Property	Value
Title	Date
Format Type	Date - Medium
Pattern	dd MMM yyyy

7. Set the following properties for y-axis. The *Sales* title (E) appears to the left of the chart. Sale values are displayed as currency in US dollars. In the *Step* property we enter the increment (F) between major tick marks.

Property	Value
Title	Sales
Format Type	Currency
Decimal Places	0
Currency	USD
Step *(under Value)*	400

8. Create another region under the *Content Body* folder to hold a bar chart. Set the following properties for this new region:

Property	Value
Title	Sales by Month (Bar)
Type	Chart

9. Click the **Attributes** node under the *Sales by Month chart* region and set the following properties. The *Show Group Name* specifies whether the group name should be displayed in the tooltip rendered on the chart. We set it to *No* to suppress the *order_timestamp* group mentioned in the SQL Query in step 10.

Property	Value
Type	Bar
Stack	Yes
Height	400
Show Group Name	No

10. Click the **New** node under *Series* and set the following properties:

Property	Value
Source Type	SQL Query

SQL Query	select p.category **type** ,
	        to_char(o.order_timestamp, 'MON RRRR') **month**,
	        sum (oi.quantity * oi.unit_price) **sales**
	from demo_product_info p,
	        demo_order_items oi,
	        demo_orders o
	where oi.product_id = p.product_id and
	        o.order_id = oi.order_id
	group by p.category, to_char(o.order_timestamp, 'MON RRRR'),
	        to_char(o.order_timestamp, 'YYYYMM')
	order by to_char(o.order_timestamp, 'YYYYMM')

Series Name	TYPE
Label	MONTH
Value	SALES
Show *(under Label)*	Yes

11. Set the following properties for y-axis:

Property	Value
Format Type	Currency
Decimal Places	0
Currency	USD

Save and then run this page from the *Reports* page. The output of this report should resemble Figure 8-4. The two charts display comparative sales figures for each category during a month. Click all the three options (individually) in the *Region Selector Toolbar* and observe the change.

In this report orders will be displayed in a calendar. Oracle APEX includes a built-in wizard for generating a calendar, which offers two options to view orders: *month* (C) and *list* (D). Using the two buttons provided at top left (A), you can switch between months. The *today* button (B) brings you back to the current date. The placed orders are displayed in respective date cells. Clicking an order in a cell (E) takes you to Page 29 to see its detail.

Figure 8-5 – Order Calendar Report

Execute the following steps to create a calendar report.

1. Click the **Create Page** button to create a new page.

2. One the first wizard screen, click the **Calendar** icon ⊞.

3. Fill in the next couple of pages according to the following table and click **Next**.

Property	Value
Page Number	10
Name	Order Calendar
Page Mode	Normal
Breadcrumb	do not use breadcrumbs on page
Navigation Preference	Identify an existing navigation menu entry for this page
Existing Navigation Menu Entry	Reports

4. On the *Source* wizard screen, select the second option **SQL Query**, put the following query in the *Enter Region Source* box and move on. In this query, order value is concatenated to each customer's name and is presented in $999,999,999,999.99 format. You can test this query in *SQL Commands* to see its output.

```
select order_id,
    (select cust_first_name||' '||cust_last_name
      from demo_customers c
      where c.customer_id = o.customer_id ) ||' ['||
      to_char(order_total,'FML999G999G999G999G990D00')||']' customer,
      order_timestamp
from demo_orders o
```

5. Set properties on the *Settings* screen as follows. The *Display Column* specifies the column to be displayed on the calendar, while the *Start Date Column* attribute specifies which column is to be used as the date to place an entry on the calendar. If you want to manage events through Calendar, then select the column that holds the start date for events displayed on this calendar in the *Start Date Column*. Next, select the column that holds the end date for events displayed on this calendar in the *End Date Column* attribute. If this attribute is specified, the calendar displays duration based events. The *Show Time* attribute specifies whether the time portion of the date should be displayed. The *Week* and *Day* views will be displayed on the calendar only when *Show Time* is set to *Yes*. If the start date or end date columns do not include time components, they will be shown as 12:00 am. Click **Create** to finish the wizard.

Display Column	CUSTOMER
Start Date Column	ORDER_TIMESTAMP
End Date Column	- Select -
Show Time	No

6. Click the **Attributes** node under the *Order Calendar* region in the Page Designer. In the Properties pane, click the **View/Edit Link** attribute and set the following properties to create a link. The link will drill-down to the *Order Details* page (Page 29) to show the details when the user clicks an existing order.

Property	Value
Target Type	Page in this application
Page	29
Name	P29_ORDER_ID
Value	&ORDER_ID.
Clear Cache	29

7. In the *Attributes* node, click the **Create Link** property and set the following properties to create another link. This property is used to create a link to call Page 11 to enter a new order when the user clicks an empty calendar cell.

Property	Value
Target Type	Page in this application
Page	11

Save and run this page from the *Order Calendar* card on the *Reports* page–the page should look like Figure 8-5. If you don't see orders in the calendar, use the buttons available at top-left to switch back and forth. Click any name link in the calendar report to drill-down and browse order details. Click any blank date cell. This will start the Order Wizard to take new order entry. Note that a new order is created in the current date, irrespective of the month in view or the date cell you clicked.

8.7 Customer Map Report - Page 15

In this exercise you'll create a map report, which shows number of customers in any particular state. Clicking any state link will take you to the Customers interactive grid page (Page 2). You define a map in the App Builder using a wizard. For most chart wizards, you select a map type, map source, and provide a SQL query using the following syntax:

```
SELECT link, label, value
FROM ...
```

Where:
- *link* is a URL.
- *label* is the text that identifies the point on the map with which you want to associate data. The *Region ID* or *Region Name* of the map will be used as the label.
- *value* is the numeric column that defines the data to be associated with a point on the map.

Map support in Oracle Application Express is based on the AnyChart AnyMap Interactive Maps Component. AnyMap is a flexible Macromedia Flash-based solution that enables developers to visualize geographical related data. Flash maps are rendered by a browser and require Flash Player 9 or later. AnyChart stores map data in files with a *.amap extension and supports 300 map files for the United States of America, Europe, Asia, Africa, Oceania, North America, and South America. To render the desired map, you select the map source in the wizard (for example, Germany) and the map XML automatically references the desired map source .amap file, germany.amap.

Customer Map

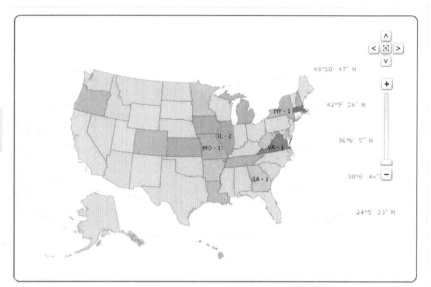

Figure 8-6
Customer Map

Follow the instructions listed below to create a map report.

1. In the *App Builder*, click the **Create Page** button to create a new page.

2. On the first wizard screen, select the **Chart** option.

3. On the next screen, select **Map Chart**.

4. For map type, select the default **United States of America** option and click **Next**.

5. Expand the *Country Maps* folder and click the **States** node to proceed.

6. Fill in the next screen as shown in the following table and click **Next**.

Property	Value
Page Number	15
Page Name	Customer Map
Page Mode	Normal
Breadcrumb	do not use breadcrumbs on page
Navigation Preference	Identify an existing navigation menu entry for this page
Existing Navigation Menu Entry	Reports

7. On the *Map Attributes* wizard screen, enter **Customer Map** for *Map Title*. Accept all other default properties and click **Next**. You can click the help icon (represented by a small question mark) to see the purpose of each property.

8. In the *Enter SQL Query* text area, enter the following statement and click **Create** to finish the wizard.

select apex_util.prepare_url('f?p='||:APP_ID||':2:'||:app_session||
':::2,RIR:IR_CUST_STATE:'||cust_state) click_link,
cust_state region_id, count(*) count_of_customers
from demo_customers
group by cust_state

9. In the Page Designer, click the **Attributes** node under the *Customer Map* region, and set *Map Region Column* to **REGION_ID**. The attribute sets the map region column for the selected map. By default, *Map Region Column* is set to *REGION_NAME*. This is the reference column holding the data that corresponds with the information returned via the LABEL parameter of the map series query. Selecting the REGION_ID column will highlight corresponding states with number of customers, as illustrated in Figure 8-6.

10. Save the page and run it from the *Customer Map* card under *Reports*. Click the Illinois state marked as IL-2. This will call the Customers page (Page 2).

8.8 Product Order Tree - Page 19

App Builder includes a built-in wizard for generating a tree. You can create a tree from a query that specifies a hierarchical relationship by identifying an ID and parent ID column in a table or view. The tree query utilizes a START WITH .. CONNECT BY clause to generate the hierarchy.

In this exercise you'll be guided to create a tree view of orders. The root node will show the three product categories you've been dealing with throughout this book. Level 1 node will be populated with individual categories and each category will have corresponding products at Level 2. The final node (Level 3) will hold names of all customers who placed some orders for the selected product along with quantity.

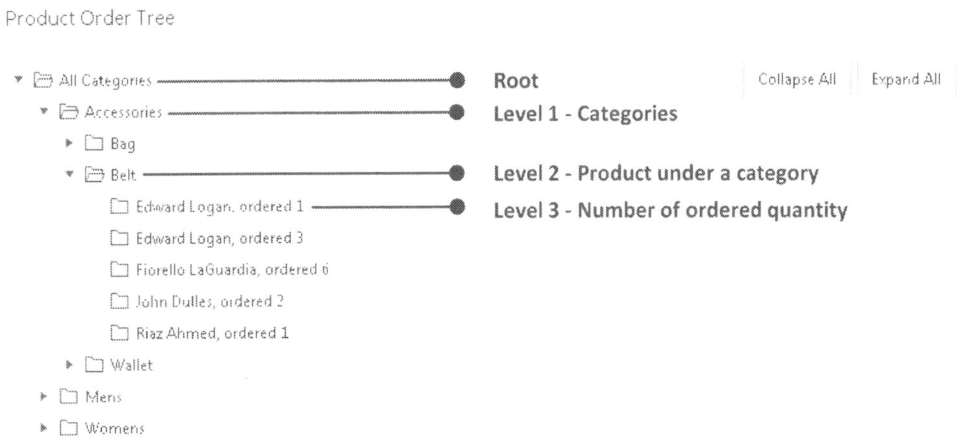

Figure 8-7
Order Tree

Product Order Tree

- All Categories — Root
  - Accessories — Level 1 - Categories
    - Bag
    - Belt — Level 2 - Product under a category
      - Edward Logan, ordered 1 — Level 3 - Number of ordered quantity
      - Edward Logan, ordered 3
      - Fiorello LaGuardia, ordered 6
      - John Dulles, ordered 2
      - Riaz Ahmed, ordered 1
    - Wallet
  - Mens
  - Womens

Collapse All | Expand All

Here are the steps to create the tree view.

1. Create a new page.

2. Select the **Tree** option.

3. Complete the next couple of screens using the following table and click **Next**.

Property	Value
Page Number	19
Page Name	Product Order Tree
Page Mode	Normal
Region Template	Standard
Region Name	Product Order Tree
Breadcrumb	do not use breadcrumbs on page
Navigation Preference	Identify an existing navigation menu entry for this page
Existing Navigation Menu Entry	Reports

4. Accept the *Table/View Owner*, select **DEMO_PRODUCT_INFO** for *Table Name*, and click **Next**.

5. Click **Next** to accept default entries on the *Query* screen, as illustrated below. A tree is based on a query and returns data that can be represented in a hierarchy. A *start with .. connect by* clause will be used to generate the hierarchy for your tree. Use this page to identify the columns you want to use as the ID, the Parent ID, and text that should appear on the nodes. The *Start With* column will be used to specify the root of the hierarchical query and its value can be based on an existing item, static value, or SQL query returning a single value.

6. Click **Next** again to skip the *Where Clause*.

7. In the final screen, put checks on **Collapse All** and **Expand All** to include these buttons on the page. Set *Tooltip* to **Static Assignment (value equals Tooltip Source attribute)** and enter **View Details** in *Tooltip Source*. The text "View Details" appears when you move over a tree node. Click **Next**.

8. Click **Create** to finish the wizard.

9. In the Page Designer, click the **Product Order Tree** node under *Content Body*.

10. Replace the existing **SQL Query** statement with the one shown below, which comprises links. After replacing the query save the page and run it from the *Reports* menu.

```
with data as
(
select 'R' as link_type,
       null as parent,
       'All Categories' as id,
       'All Categories' as name,
       null as sub_id
from demo_product_info
union
select distinct('C') as link_type, 'All Categories' as parent, category as id,
       category as name, null as sub_id
from demo_product_info
union
select 'P' as link_type,
       category parent,
       to_char(product_id) id,
       product_name as name,
       product_id as sub_id
from demo_product_info
union
select 'O' as link_type,
       to_char(product_id) as parent,
       null as id,
       (select c.cust_first_name || ' ' || c.cust_last_name
        from demo_customers c,  demo_orders o
        where c.customer_id = o.customer_id and
              o.order_id = oi.order_id ) || ', ordered '|| to_char(oi.quantity) as name,
       order_id as sub_id
from demo_order_items oi
)
select case
       when connect_by_isleaf = 1 then 0
       when level = 1 then 1
       else -1
       end as status, level, name as title, null as icon, id as value, 'View' as tooltip,
       case
       when link_type = 'R'
```

```
                then apex_util.prepare_url('f?p='||:APP_ID||':3:'||:APP_SESSION||'::NO:RIR')
           when link_type = 'C'
                then apex_util.prepare_url('f?p='||:APP_ID||':3:'||:APP_SESSION||
                                    '::NO:CIR:IR_CATEGORY:' || name)
           when link_type = 'P'
                then apex_util.prepare_url('f?p='||:APP_ID||':6:'||:APP_SESSION||
                                    '::NO::P6_PRODUCT_ID:' || sub_id)
           when link_type = 'O'
                then apex_util.prepare_url('f?p='||:APP_ID||':29:'||:APP_SESSION||
                                    '::NO::P29_ORDER_ID:' || sub_id)
           else null
           end as link
      from data
      start with parent is null
      connect by prior id = parent
      order siblings by name
```

This custom query is used to form the tree using the following syntax:

```
SELECT status, level, name, icon, id, tooltip, link
FROM ...
WHERE ...
START WITH...
CONNECT BY PRIOR id = pid
ORDER SIBLINGS BY ...
```

Line #	Tree Query Code
1	WITH data AS (
2	select 'R' as link_type, null as parent, 'All Categories' as id, 'All Categories' as name, null as sub_id from demo_product_info
3	UNION
4	select distinct('C') as link_type, 'All Categories' as parent, category as id, category as name, null as sub_id from demo_product_info
5	UNION
6	select 'P' as link_type, category parent, to_char(product_id) id, product_name as name, product_id as sub_id from demo_product_info
7	UNION
8	select 'O' as link_type, to_char(product_id) as parent, null as id, (select c.cust_first_name || ' ' || c.cust_last_name from demo_customers c, demo_orders o where c.customer_id = o.customer_id and o.order_id = oi.order_id) || ', ordered '|| to_char(oi.quantity) as name, order_id as sub_id from demo_order_items oi
	)

The *WITH query_name AS* clause lets you assign a name to a subquery block. This statement creates the query name "data" with multiple SELECT statements containing UNION set operators. UNION is used to combine the result from multiple SELECT statements into a single result set, as illustrated in Figure 8-8.

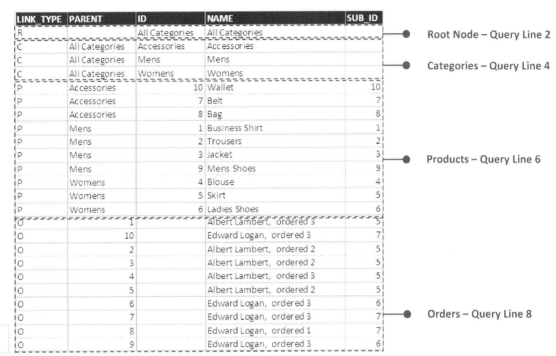

LINK_TYPE	PARENT	ID	NAME	SUB_ID	
R		All Categories	All Categories		● Root Node – Query Line 2
C	All Categories	Accessories	Accessories		
C	All Categories	Mens	Mens		
C	All Categories	Womens	Womens		● Categories – Query Line 4
P	Accessories	10	Wallet	10	
P	Accessories	7	Belt	7	
P	Accessories	8	Bag	8	
P	Mens	1	Business Shirt	1	
P	Mens	2	Trousers	2	
P	Mens	3	Jacket	3	● Products – Query Line 6
P	Mens	9	Mens Shoes	9	
P	Womens	4	Blouse	4	
P	Womens	5	Skirt	5	
P	Womens	6	Ladies Shoes	6	
O	1		Albert Lambert, ordered 3	5	
O	10		Edward Logan, ordered 3	7	
O	2		Albert Lambert, ordered 2	5	
O	3		Albert Lambert, ordered 2	5	
O	4		Albert Lambert, ordered 3	5	
O	5		Albert Lambert, ordered 2	5	
O	6		Edward Logan, ordered 3	6	
O	7		Edward Logan, ordered 3	7	● Orders – Query Line 8
O	8		Edward Logan, ordered 1	7	
O	9		Edward Logan, ordered 3	6	

Figure 8-8

Line #	Tree Query Code
1	select case
2	when connect_by_isleaf = 1 then 0
3	when level = 1 then 1
4	else -1
5	end as status, level, name as title, null as icon, id as value, 'View' as tooltip,
6	case
7	when link_type = 'R'
8	then apex_util.prepare_url('f?p='||:APP_ID||':3:'||:APP_SESSION||'::NO:RIR')
9	when link_type = 'C'
10	then apex_util.prepare_url('f?p='||:APP_ID||':3:'||:APP_SESSION||'::NO:CIR:IR_CATEGORY:' || name)
11	when link_type = 'P'
12	then apex_util.prepare_url('f?p='||:APP_ID||':6:'||:APP_SESSION||'::NO::P6_PRODUCT_ID:'||sub_id)
13	when link_type = 'O'
14	then apex_util.prepare_url('f?p='||:APP_ID||':29:'||:APP_SESSION||'::NO::P29_ORDER_ID:' || sub_id)
15	else null
16	end as link
17	from data

The CASE statement within the SQL statement is used to evaluate the four link types (R=root, C=categories, P=products, and O=orders). It has the functionality of an IF-THEN-ELSE statement. Lines 8, 10, 12, and 14 make the node text a link. The R link type leads you to the main Products page (Page 3). The C link type also leads to Page 3, but applies a filter on category name. The P link type calls Product Details page (Page 6) to display details of the selected product. The final O link type displays details of the selected order on the Order Details page (Page 29).

The CONNECT_BY_ISLEAF pseudocolumn, in the first CASE statement, returns 1 if the current row is a leaf of the tree. Otherwise, it returns 0. This information indicates whether a given row can be further expanded to show more of the hierarchy.

If no condition is found to be true, then the CASE statement will return the null value defined in the ELSE clause on line 15.

Run all these reports from the *Graphical Reports* submenu under the *Reports* menu. When you click the *Graphical Reports* option, a page (Page 26) comes up with a list of reports from where you can give them a test-run.

Summary

Report is the most significant component of any application. It allows digging information from the data mine for making decisions. This chapter not only demonstrated the power of Oracle Application Express to graphically present the information but also exhibited how to drill-down to a deeper level to obtain detailed information using different types of charts, calendar, map, and tree. The chapter highlighted some mandatory properties related to charts and other features. There are many more and explaining each one of them is beyond the scope of this book. The best way to understand these properties is to make the Help tab active and experiment by changing the properties in various ways. The next chapter continues with this topic and reveals how to produce advance PDF reports in Oracle APEX.

Chapter 9

Produce Advance Reports

9.1 About Advanced Reporting

You have seen the use of interactive reporting feature in Oracle APEX to create professional looking onscreen reports. Interactive reports also have the ability to export reports to PDF, RTF, Microsoft Excel, and Comma Separated Values (CSV) formats. However, it is not possible to define a custom report layout in interactive reports. If you download PDF version of these reports to print a hard copy, what you get is a generic report in simple row-column format without any control breaks and conditional formatting. For serious printing, you have to define an external reporting server to present data in desired format. This chapter will teach you how to utilize Oracle BI Publisher to enjoy high level formatting.

Oracle Application Express provides the following three printing options:

Oracle REST Data Services - Select this option if you are using the Oracle REST Data Services (formerly called Application Express Listener) release 2.0 or later. It enables you to use the basic printing functionality, which includes creating report queries and printing report regions using the default templates provided in Application Express and using your own customized XSL-FO templates. The Oracle REST Data Services option does not require an external print server, instead the report data and style sheet are downloaded to the listener, rendered into PDF format by the listener and then sent to the client. The PDF documents in this setup are not returned back into the database, thus the print APIs are not supported when using the Oracle REST Data Services-based configuration.

External (Apache FOP) - Select this option if you are using Apache FOP on an external J2EE server. This one enables you to use the basic printing functionality, which includes creating report queries and printing report regions using the default templates provided in Application Express and using your own customized XSL-FO templates.

Oracle BI Publisher - This option requires a valid license of Oracle BI Publisher. With this option, you can take report query results and convert them from XML to RTF format using Oracle BI Publisher. Select this option to upload your own customized RTF or XSL-FO templates for printing reports within Application Express. You have to configure Oracle BI Publisher as your print server. Besides standard configuration, Oracle BI Publisher has Word Template Plug-in to create RTF based report layouts, which provides greater control over every aspect of your report and allows you to add complex control breaks, logos, charts, and pagination control. The following list contains some reports that can be created using this advance option:

- Tax and Government Forms
- Invoices
- Ledgers
- Financial Statements
- Bill of Lading, using tables and barcode fonts
- Operational Reports with re-grouping, conditional highlighting, summary

- calculations, and running totals
  - Management Reports having Chart with summary functions and table with detail records
  - Check Print, using conditional formatting and MICR fonts
  - Dunning Letters

To print these professional reports, you have to pay for a valid Oracle BI Publisher license that is worth the price considering the following advantages:

- *Multiple Output Formats*: In addition to PDF, the other supported output formats include DOC, XLS, and HTML.
- *Included in Export/Import*: Being part of the application, RTF based layout are exported and imported along with the application.
- *Robust Report Layout*: Add complex breaks, pagination control, logos, header-footer, charts, and print data on pre-printed forms.
- *Report Scheduling*: This unique feature enables you to set up a schedule and deliver the report to the desired destinations including e-mail, fax, and so on.

To explore the features provided by this robust reporting server, you can download and install the limited license version to use the program only for the development purpose. Once again, this book protects you from all the hassle of downloading, installing and configuring BI Publisher Server in your environment, because in the online development environment you can enjoy this utility for free. The following list presents the steps you will perform to produce advance reports for Oracle APEX.

Steps to Produce Advance Reports
- Install BI Publisher Desktop
- Create report query in Oracle APEX
- Create report layout in Microsoft Word (I created my templates in Word 2003)
- Upload report layout to Oracle APEX
- Add links to run the report

9.2 Download and Install BI Publisher Desktop

In this chapter, you will take hard copies of reports in Portable Document Format (PDF). You will use Microsoft Word to create templates for these reports. For this purpose, you need Oracle BIPublisher Desktop to prepare the report templates. During BIPublisher Desktop installation, you might be asked to install Java Runtime Edition (JRE) and Dot Net Framework–in my scenario I executed *jre-6u11-windows-i586-p-s.exe* and *NetFx20SP1_x86.exe* files.

BI Publisher Desktop is a client-side tool to aid in the building and testing of layout templates. This consists of a plug-in to Microsoft Word for building RTF templates. You can downloaded this small piece of software from:
http://www.oracle.com/technetwork/middleware/bi-publisher/downloads/index.html

After the download, install the software on your PC using the .exe file. Once the installation completes, you'll see the BI Publisher plug-in as a menu item in Microsoft Word. In newer versions it is placed under the main Add-Ins menu.

9.3 Create Monthly Order Review Report

In Chapter 7 section 7.3.3, you created an onscreen alternative report named *Monthly Review* to see details of monthly orders. In the following exercise, you will create a PDF version of that report.

9.3.1 Create Report Query

You can print a report by defining a report query in Shared Component. A report query is a SQL statement that identifies the data to be extracted. You can associate a report query with a report layout and download it as a formatted document. If no report layout is selected, a generic layout is used. To make these reports available to end users, you integrate these reports with an application. For example, you can associate a report query with a button, list item, branch, or other navigational component that enables you to use URLs as targets. Selecting that item then initiates the printing process.

1. Go to **Shared Components** interface.

2. Click **Report Queries** in the *Reports* section.

3. Click the **Create** button to create a new report query.

4. Type **Monthly_Review** in the *Report Query Name* field, set *Output Format* to **PDF**, set *View File As* to **Attachment**, and then click **Next**. Enter the report query name as is or else you will encounter the error "*Error occurred while painting error page: ORA-01403: no data found ORA-22275: invalid LOB locator specified*" when you print this report.

5. Enter the following statement in *SQL Query* text area and click **Next**:
```
select o.order_id,
       to_char(o.order_timestamp,'Month yyyy') order_month,
       o.order_timestamp order_date,
       c.cust_last_name || ', ' || c.cust_first_name customer_name,
       c.cust_state,
       o.user_name sales_rep,
       (select count(*) from demo_order_items  oi
         where oi.order_id = o.order_id) order_items,
       o.order_total
from demo_orders o, demo_customers c
where o.customer_id = c.customer_id
```

6. Select **XML Data** for *Data Source for Report Layout*, to export your report definition as an XML file. The XML file contains column definitions and the data (fetched using the SELECT statement) to populate the report. Click the **Download** button. A file named **monthly_review.xml** will be saved to your disk. Double-click this file to see its contents.

7. Back in Oracle APEX, click the **Create Report Query** button.

8. On the *Confirm* screen, click the **Create** button to complete the wizard.

9.3.2 Create Report Template in Microsoft Word

The later versions of Microsoft Word produced errors while designing and testing report templates, so I created my templates in Microsoft Word 2003. If you fall into a situation like this, skip to section 9.3.8 and use the template provided in the book code.

1. In **Microsoft Word**, click **Oracle BI Publisher** (or *BI Publisher*) in the main menu to make its ribbon visible.

2. From the *Data* ribbon, select **Load XML Data** (or *Sample XML*) to load a data file. Select the **monthly_review.xml** file created in the previous section. The message *Data Loaded Successfully* will be is displayed.

3. Select **Table Wizard** from the *Insert* ribbon. Select **Table** for *Report Format* and click **Next**.

4. Click **Next** to accept **DOCUMENT/ROWSET/ROW** for *Data Set*.

5. Add all fields to the report by moving them to the right pane using the double arrow button and click **Next**.

6. Select **Order Month** in the first drop down list under *Group By* and click **Next**. This will group the report on the *Order Month* column.

7. Select **Order Date** in the first *Sort By* list and select **Order ID** in the first *Then By* list to sort the report first on the *Order Date* column and then on the *Order ID* column. Click **Next**.

8. On the label form screen, enter **State** for *Cust State* to give this column a meaningful name. Click **Finish** to complete the process. An output similar to Figure 9-1 will be displayed.

Figure 9-1
Raw Report Template
Created in Microsoft
Word

group ROW by ORDER_MONTH

ORDER_MONTH

Order Id	Order Date	Customer Name	State	Sales Rep	Order Items	Order Total
F ORDER_I D	ORDER_DA TE	CUSTOMER_NA ME	CUST_STA TE	SALES_R EP	ORDER_ITE MS	ORDER_TOT AL E

end ROW by ORDER_MONTH

9. Press **Ctrl+S** (or click the **Save** icon) to save the template. Enter **monthly_review** in the *File name* box, select **Rich Text Format** for its type, and click **Save**.

10. In the *Preview* ribbon, click the **PDF** option. The output as show in Figure 9-2 will be displayed. Note that you can format and preview this report offline if you have some data in the XML file.

11. **Close the PDF** and switch back to Microsoft Word.

December 2016

Order Id	Order Date	Customer Name	State	Sales Rep	Order Items	Order Total
6	05-DEC-16 09.14.58.0 00000 AM	Logan, Edward	MA	DEMO	4	1515
7	10-DEC-16 09.14.58.0 00000 AM	Logan, Edward	MA	DEMO	7	905
8	18-DEC-16 09.14.58.0 00000 AM	OHare, Frank	IL	DEMO	4	1060
9	24-DEC-16 09.14.58.0 00000 AM	Hartsfield, William	GA	DEMO	3	2355
10	27-DEC-16 09.14.58.0 00000 AM	Bradley, Eugene	CT	DEMO	3	870

Figure 9-2
Raw Report Template
Output

November 2016

Order Id	Order Date	Customer Name	State	Sales Rep	Order Items	Order Total
2	07-NOV-16 09.14.58.0 00000 AM	Dulles, John	VA	DEMO	10	2350
3	18-NOV-16 09.14.58.0 00000 AM	Hartsfield, William	GA	DEMO	5	1640
4	20-NOV-16 09.14.58.0 00000 AM	LaGuardia, Fiorello	NY	DEMO	5	1090
5	30-NOV-16 09.14.58.0 00000 AM	Lambert, Albert	MO	DEMO	5	950

9.3.3 Format Report

1. Place the cursor before the **ORDER_MONTH** field and type **Order Month:** in front of it to act as a label. You can use Microsoft Word's standard tools to change font, color, and size of the text. Also, drag field's width to a desired size.

2. Click the **ORDER_TOTAL** field and right-align it. Double-click it to call its properties. Select **Number** for its *Type* and **#,##0.00** for *Format*. Click **OK**.

3. Insert a blank line above **group ROW by Order_Month** text to add a title for this report. Type **ABC CORPORATION** and press **Enter** to add another line. Type **Monthly Orders Review Report** on the new line. You can also add a logo, page number, and other options using Microsoft Word's standard tools.

9.3.4 Conditional Formatting

In these steps, you will change font and background color of orders for which the amount is less than or equal to 900, as you did in the onscreen report version in Chapter 7.

1. Select the **Order Total** field by clicking its name (not the heading) in the column.

2. Select **Conditional Format** from the *Insert* ribbon.

3. Perform the following steps on the *Properties* tab:
   a. Select the **ORDER_TOTAL** column for *Data* field.
   b. Select **Number** in the adjacent list.
   c. Put a check on **Apply to Entire Table Row** to apply the condition to the whole report.
   d. Select **Less than or equal to** in the *Data* field.
   e. Enter **900** in the box next to the *Data* field.
   f. Click the **Format button**.
   g. Put a check on the **Background Color** option.
   h. Click the **Select** button to choose different *Font* and *Background* colors.
   i. Click **OK**.

4. Preview your work and see the application of conditional formatting to all the rows with Order Total less than or equal to 900.

Use the same procedure and change font and background color for orders greater than 2000. Select *Greater than* for the condition and enter 2000 in the value. This time, do not check the *Apply to Entire Table Row* option to highlight specific cells only. After performing these steps, save your work and preview the report.

9.3.5 Summary Calculation

In this section you will add a summary to reveal average orders for the month.

1. Place your cursor on the blank line before the text **end ROW by ORDER_MONTH**.

2. Click the **Field** option in the *Insert* ribbon.

3. In the *Field* dialog box, click the **Order Total** field, select **average** for *Calculation*, select **On Grouping**, and click the **Insert** button. A summary field, *average ORDER_TOTAL* will be added to the report. Close the dialog box.

4. Type **Monthly Average:** before the field to act as field's label. Double-click the calculated field, set the *Type* property to **Number**, and the *Format* property to **#,##0.00**. Align the whole expression to the right under the *Order Total* field.

9.3.6 Add a Summary Chart

1. Insert a blank row above **group ROW by ORDER_MONTH**.

2. Select **Chart** from the *Insert* ribbon.

3. From the *Data* tree, drag the **ORDER_TOTAL** field to the *Values* box, set *Aggregation* to **Sum**, drag **ORDER_MONTH** to *Labels*, put a check on **Group Data**, select **Bar Graph - Horizontal** for *Type*, and **April** in *Style*. The completed screen should look like Figure 9-3. Click **OK** to close the dialog box.

4. Right-click the newly added chart in Microsoft Word and select **Insert Caption**. Type **Monthly Orders Review** in *Caption*.

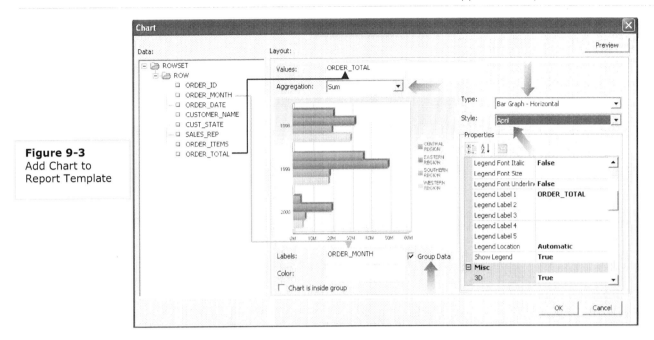

Figure 9-3
Add Chart to
Report Template

1. In Microsoft Word, click the line just after the text **end ROW by ORDER_MONTH**.

2. Select **Pivot Table** from the *Insert* ribbon.

3. Drag **CUST_STATE, CUSTOMER_NAME, ORDER_MONTH,** and **ORDER_TOTAL** fields to the layout section, as shown in Figure 9-4. Drag the CUST_STATE and CUSTOMER_NAME fields and drop them in the left layout pane one after the other. Click the **Preview** button to see the output within the dialog box. Click the **OK** button to dismiss the Pivot Table dialog box. Format the table using Microsoft Word's toolbar so that it matches the output shown in Figure 9-6. Browse the report in PDF. **Save the template** and close Microsoft Word.

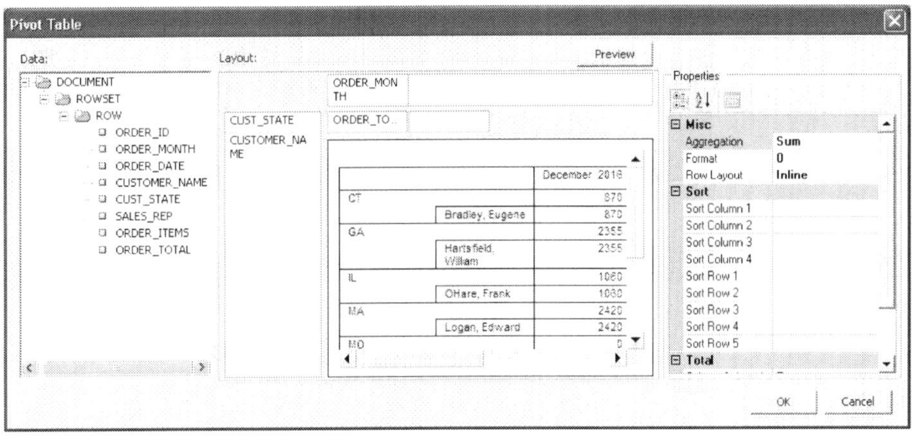

Figure 9-4
Pivot Table
Settings

9.3.8 Upload Report Template to Oracle APEX

Report Layouts are used in conjunction with report queries to render data in a printer-friendly format, such as PDF. A report layout has been designed using Oracle BI Publisher's plug-in for Microsoft Word and will now be uploaded to Oracle APEX as an RTF file type.

1. In the **Shared Components** interface, click **Report Layouts** under the *Reports* section.

2. Click the **Create** button.

3. Select the option **Named Columns (RTF)** and click **Next**. A named column report layout is a query-specific report layout designed to work with a defined list of columns in the query result set. This type of layout is used for custom-designed layouts when precise control of the positioning of page items and query columns is required. This layout is uploaded as an RTF file.

4. In *Layout Name* enter **monthly_review**, click the **Choose File** button, and select the Microsoft Word template file **monthly_meview.rtf**, which was created in the previous section.

5. Click the **Create Layout** button.

6. Move back to **Shared Components**.

7. Click the **Report Queries** link under the *Reports* section.

8. Click the **Monthly_Review** icon.

9. In *Report Query Attributes* section, change *Report Layout* from *Use Generic Report Layout* to **monthly_review** to apply this layout to the report query.

10. Write down or copy the URL appearing in the *Print URL* box, which should be – *f?p=&APP_ID.:0:&SESSION.:PRINT_REPORT=Monthly_Review.*
    Report queries can be integrated with an application by using this URL as the target for buttons, navigation list entries, list items, or any other type of link. You will use this link in the next section to run the report.

11. Click **Apply Changes**.

You have created the Report Layout in Oracle APEX by uploading the Microsoft Word template and linked it to your Report Query. In the next section, you will create a link to run this report.

In this section, you will configure *Monthly Review Report* menu entry in the main navigation menu to run this report.

1. Switch back to the **Shared Components** interface.

2. Click the **Lists** link under the *Navigation* section and then click **Desktop Navigation Menu**.

3. Click the **Monthly Review Report** entry.

4. Set the *Target Type* property to **URL** and enter or paste the URL **f?p=&APP_ID.:0:&SESSION.:PRINT_REPORT=Monthly_Review** in the *URL Target* box.

5. Save your work by click the **Apply Changes** button.

6. Run the application. Expand **Advance Reports** under the **Report** menu and click **Monthly Review Report**. The report will be downloaded to your PC. Open the report with Adobe Acrobat Reader, which should look something like Figure 9-5 and Figure 9-6. I formatted the layout using standard Microsoft Word tools, including header-footer, tables, page number, font, and so on.

7. The same report has a link on Page 26, which is associated with a list. Go to **Shared Components** and call **Reports List** (in the *Lists* option under *Navigation*). Modify the *Monthly Review Report* entry by setting *Target Type* property to **Page in this Application**, *Page* property to **0**, and *Request* property to **PRINT_REPORT=Monthly_Review**. This is an alternate method to send the same print request used in step 4. Save these setting and run the report through this link in the main *Reports* page (Page 26).

Congratulations! You have successfully created a professional looking report (Figure 9-5) that not only matches the onscreen report of Chapter 7, but also adds more value to it by incorporating a pivot table, to display the same data from a different perspective. Add a new order in the application and see its reflection in the report.

ABC CORPORATION
35-A/3, ABC House, Raymond Street off Mansfield Street,
Chicago-IL, 6350, USA.

Orders Monthly Review Report

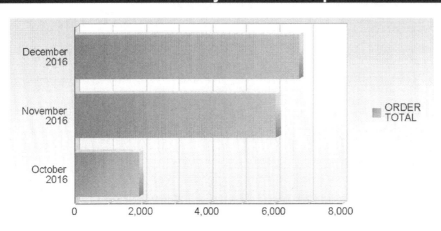

Figure 1: Monthly Order Chart

Order Month: December 2016

Order#	Order Date	Customer	State	Sales Rep	Order Items	Order Total
10	27-DEC-2016 09:14AM	Bradley, Eugene	CT	DEMO	3	870.00
6	05-DEC-2016 09:14AM	Logan, Edward	MA	DEMO	4	1,515.00
7	10-DEC-2016 09:14AM	Logan, Edward	MA	DEMO	7	905.00
8	18-DEC-2016 09:14AM	OHare, Frank	IL	DEMO	4	1,060.00
9	24-DEC-2016 09:14AM	Hartsfield, William	GA	DEMO	3	2,355.00
					Average Order:	1,341.00

Order Month: November 2016

Order#	Order Date	Customer	State	Sales Rep	Order Items	Order Total
2	07-NOV-2016 09:14AM	Dulles, John	VA	DEMO	10	2,350.00
3	18-NOV-2016 09:14AM	Hartsfield, William	GA	DEMO	5	1,640.00
4	20-NOV-2016 09:14AM	LaGuardia, Fiorello	NY	DEMO	5	1,090.00
5	30-NOV-2016 09:14AM	Lambert, Albert	MO	DEMO	5	950.00
					Average Order:	1,507.50

Order Month: October 2016

Order#	Order Date	Customer	State	Sales Rep	Order Items	Order Total
1	24-OCT-2016 09:14AM	Bradley, Eugene	CT	DEMO	4	1,910.00
					Average Order:	1,910.00

Figure 9-5 – Monthly Order Review Report

ABC CORPORATION
35-A/3, ABC House, Raymond Street off Mansfield Street,
Chicago-IL, 6350, USA.

Table 1: Revenue By States

State	Customer	December 2016	November 2016	October 2016	Total
CT		870.00	0.00	1,910.00	2,780.00
	Bradley, Eugene	870.00	0.00	1,910.00	2,780.00
GA		2,355.00	1,640.00	0.00	3,995.00
	Hartsfield, William	2,355.00	1,640.00	0.00	3,995.00
IL		1,060.00	0.00	0.00	1,060.00
	OHare, Frank	1,060.00	0.00	0.00	1,060.00
MA		2,420.00	0.00	0.00	2,420.00
	Logan, Edward	2,420.00	0.00	0.00	2,420.00
MO		0.00	950.00	0.00	950.00
	Lambert, Albert	0.00	950.00	0.00	950.00
NY		0.00	1,090.00	0.00	1,090.00
	LaGuardia, Fiorello	0.00	1,090.00	0.00	1,090.00
VA		0.00	2,350.00	0.00	2,350.00
	Dulles, John	0.00	2,350.00	0.00	2,350.00
TOTAL		**6,705.00**	**6,030.00**	**1,910.00**	**14,645.00**

2 | P a g e   0 3 / 0 1 / 2 0 1 7   5 : 1 7 : 0 1   A M

Figure 9-6 – Pivot Table Report

9.4 Create a Commercial Invoice

In this exercise, you will generate commercial invoices for the placed Orders. You will use the same techniques used in the previous section. This time, you will create a parameters form to print specific orders by passing parameter values to the underlying report query.

9.4.1 Create A List of Values

Create the following LOV from scratch in the Shared Components interface. You will utilize it in the next section to print only those orders entered by the user selected from this list.

Property	Value
Name	Users
Type	Dynamic
Query	SELECT DISTINCT user_name d, user_name r FROM demo_orders

9.4.2 Create Report Parameters Page

1. Create a **Blank Page** using the following parameters. The page will receive parameters to print specific invoices.

Property	Value
Page Number	50
Name	Invoice Parameters
Page Mode	Normal
Breadcrumb	don't use breadcrumbs on page
Navigation Preference	Identify an existing navigation menu entry for this page
Existing Navigation Menu Entry	Reports

2. On the *Rendering* tab, create a region under *Content Body*. Enter **Invoice Report** for the region's *Title*.

3. Add two *Page Items* under the *Invoice Report* region and set the following properties. Using these items you can print a single order or a range of orders.

Tip: After creating the first item, right-click its name in the *Rendering* tree, and select **Duplicate** from the context menu. This action will make a duplicate of the first item. Select the duplicate item, and set the values mentioned in the table's second column.

Property	Value	Value
Name	P50_INVOICEFROM	P50_INVOICETO
Type	Text Field	Text Field
Label	From Invoice Number:	To Invoice Number:
Template	Required	Required
Value Required	Yes	Yes
Type (*Default*)	Static Value	Static Value
Static Value	1	9999999999

4. Add a **Select List** under the two text field items and set the following properties. The select list will show the IDs of all users from which you can select one ID to print the orders entered by that particular user. The V('APP_USER') expression displays the ID of the logged-in user as a default value for this select list. For PL/SQL reference type, you use V('APP_USER') syntax of the built-in substitution string to assess the current user running the application.

Property	Value
Name	P50_USER
Type	Select List
Label	Entered by:
Type *(List of Values)*	Shared Components
List of Values	USERS
Type *(Default)*	PL/SQL Expression
PL/SQL Expression	V('APP_USER')

5. Right-click the *Invoice Report* region and select **Create Button**. Set the following properties for the new button. When you click this button, the page is submitted and an associated branch (created in section 9.5) forwards a print request to the print server.

Property	Value
Name	PRINT
Label	Print Invoice
Button Position	Next
Hot	Yes
Action	Submit Page

6. Save your work.

9.4.3 Create Query for the Invoice

1. Go to **Shared Components**.

2. Click **Report Queries** under the *Reports* Section.

3. Click the **Create** button to create a new report query.

4. Type **Invoice** in *Report Query Name*, set *Output Format* to **PDF**, *View File As* to **Attachment**, and click **Next**.

5. Enter the following statement in *SQL Query* text area and click **Next**. As you can see, the SQL query filters data using the three parameters passed to it from Page 50. You use bind variables (underlined in the WHERE clause) in SQL statements to reference parameter values.

```
Select o.order_id, o.Order_timestamp, o.user_name,
       c.cust_first_name || ' ' || c.cust_last_name as customer,
       c.cust_street_address1, c.cust_street_address2, c.cust_city,
       c.cust_state, c.cust_postal_code, oi.ORDER_ITEM_ID,
       pi.PRODUCT_NAME, oi.UNIT_PRICE, oi.QUANTITY,
       oi.Unit_Price * oi.Quantity as Amount
from   DEMO_ORDERS o, DEMO_ORDER_ITEMS oi,
       DEMO_PRODUCT_INFO pi, DEMO_CUSTOMERS c
where o.ORDER_id = oi.ORDER_id and pi.PRODUCT_ID = oi.PRODUCT_ID and
       o.customer_id = c.customer_id and
       o.ORDER_id BETWEEN :P50_INVOICEFROM and
       :P50_INVOICETO and o.user_name = :P50_USER
```

6. Select **XML Data** for *Data Source for Report Layout* to export your report definition as an XML file. Click the **Download** button. A file named **invoice.xml** will be saved to your disk.

7. Click the **Create Report Query** button followed by the **Create** button on the *Confirm* page. Unlike the previous XML file, this one doesn't contain any data due to the involvement of parameters. So, you cannot test the invoice report offline.

9.4.4 Create Invoice Template in Microsoft Word

Perform the following steps in Microsoft Word to create a template for the invoice report. For your convenience, I have provided both XML and RTF files with the book's code.

1. In Microsoft Word, select the **A4** size page and set the margins.

2. From the *Data* ribbon, select **Load XML Data | invoice.xml**, and then click **Open** to load the XML file you downloaded in the previous section.

3. From the *Insert* ribbon, choose **Table Wizard** to add a table. This table will be used to output order details. Set *Report Format* to **Table** and *Data Set* to **DOCUMENT/ROWSET/ROW**.

4. Move **Order Id, Product Name, Unit Price, Quantity,** and **Amount** columns to the right pane.

5. Select **Order Id** in *Group By* to group the report according to order numbers.

6. Do not select any field for *Sort By*.

7. Set **labels** (Product, Price, Quantity, and Amount) for the report columns.

8. Click **Finish**.

9.4.5 Template Formatting

Follow these steps to format the template:

1. Double-click the group field titled **group ROW by ORDER_ID**. On the *Properties* tab, set *Break* to **Page**. This will print each new invoice on a separate page.

2. From the **Insert** ribbon select **Field**. Select the **ORDER_ID** field and click the **Insert** button to add this field to the next row just after the group titled *group Row by ORDER_ID*. Similarly, add ORDER_TIMESTAMP, CUSTOMER, CUST_STREET_ADDRESS1, CUST_STREET_ADDRESS2, CUST_CITY, CUST_STATE, CUST_POSTAL_CODE, and USER_NAME on subsequent lines. I inserted a table to place these fields accordingly–see Figure 9-7.

3. Double-click the **AMOUNT** field. Set its *Type* to **Number** and *Format* to **#,##0.00**. Right-align the field using Microsoft Word's alignment option.

4. Add a **blank row** to the details table. Select **Field** from the *Insert* ribbon. In the *Field* dialog box, select **AMOUNT**. From **Calculation** list, select **sum**, put a **check** on '*On Grouping*', and click **Insert**. Put a label **Total** and then format and align the field, as shown in the template. This step will add a new row (just after the last transaction) to display the sum of the *Amount* column.

5. Save the report to your hard drive as **invoice** and select **Rich Text Format (RTF)** as its *type*.

6. Close Microsoft Word.

9.4.6 Upload Template to Oracle APEX

1. Call the **Shared Components** interface and click **Report Layouts** under *Reports*.

2. Click the **Create** button.

3. Select the option **Named Columns (RTF)** and click **Next**.

4. In *Layout Name* enter **invoice**, click the **Choose File** button, select the template file **invoice.rtf**, and then click the **Create Layout** button.

5. Move back to **Shared Components**.

6. Under the *Reports* section, click the **Report Queries** link.

7. Click the **Invoice** icon.

8. In *Report Query Attributes* section, change *Report Layout* from *Use Generic Report Layout* to **invoice** to apply this layout.

9. Click **Apply Changes**.

9.5 Create Branch

Call Page 50 to create the following branch. This branch is being added to send a print request when the *Print Invoice* button is clicked. On the *Processing* tab, right-click the *After Submit* node and select **Create Branch**. Set the following properties for the new branch. Note that the letter I in the word Invoice (in the *Request* attribute) should be in caps and the request value (PRINT_REPORT=Invoice) should not contain any leading or trailing space.

Property	Value
Name	Run Invoice Report
Point	After Submit
Type *(Behavior)*	Page or URL (Redirect)
Target Type	Type = Page in this Application
Page	0
Request *(under Advance)*	PRINT_REPORT=Invoice
When Button Pressed	PRINT

Test Your Work

From the main navigation menu, select **Customer Invoice** under the *Advance Reports* menu. This will bring up the parameters form page (Page 50). For the time being, accept all the default values in the form, including the default user, and hit the *Print Invoice* button. Open the report with Adobe Acrobat Reader, which should resemble the one show in Figure 9-7. Also, try to get this report using different parameters to test your work.

NOTE:

You may get the following error when you try to open the PDF: *Acrobat could not open 'invoice.pdf' because it is either not a supported file type or because the file has been damaged (for example, it was sent as an email attachment and wasn't correctly decoded)*. This error message is displayed when there is no data for the given criteria. To cope with this problem, you can add a validation to check for the existence of data prior to calling the report. The error also emerges when Oracle APEX is not configured to use BI Publisher as its print server. If Oracle APEX is configured with APEX Listener using XSL-FO server, you don't see the Named Columns (RTF) option when you access the Report Layout interface.

ABC CORPORATION
35-A/3, ABC House,
Raymond Street Off
Mansfield Street, NJ 07901
Phone #(908) 316-5599
info@abccorp.com

COMMERCIAL INVOICE

Customer:
John Dulles
45020 Aviation Drive

Sterling
VA 20166

Order Number	2
Order Date	07-NOV-2016 09:14AM
Sales Rep.	DEMO

Product Name	Unit Price	Quantity	Amount
Business Shirt	50	3	150.00
Trousers	80	3	240.00
Jacket	150	3	450.00
Blouse	60	3	180.00
Skirt	80	3	240.00
Ladies Shoes	120	2	240.00
Belt	30	1	30.00
Bag	125	4	500.00
Mens Shoes	110	2	220.00
Wallet	50	2	100.00
TOTAL			**2,350.00**

Make all checks payable to ABC Corporation
THANK YOU FOR YOUR BUSINESS!

Figure 9-7 – Commercial Invoice

Chapter 10

Develop a Mobile Version for Smartphones

10.1 About Mobile Development

In the last few years there has been an eruption in the market for smartphones and mobile devices demand. As the sales are touching new heights every day, smartphone vendors are trying hard to provide the excellent product with latest technology. Things that used to be done traditionally by people on their laptops are now being done increasingly on mobile devices. Feeling the heat, application development companies are under pressure to quickly deliver web applications for smartphone and mobile platforms. For this, they need tools and frameworks to roll out new mobile enabled applications and adapt existing applications to mobile devices. The good news is that just like traditional web applications, mobile web applications are also developed using the same core technologies - HTML, CSS, and JavaScript.

With mobile web usage increasing every year, there is a huge demand in the market for applications supported on smartphones and tablets. To help develop new applications and extend existing web applications for mobile use, the Oracle APEX development team has enhanced the product with mobile development features. Probably the most significant new feature incorporated in Oracle APEX is the ability to build applications specifically aimed at mobile devices. Now you can easily build applications for modern smartphones and tablets, such as the iPhone, iPad, Android, and BlackBerry using Oracle APEX. The jQuery Mobile framework is integrated to render an application for the vast majority of mobile devices. Besides, a new mobile-specific theme is incorporated to support touch input and gestures such as swipe, tap, and orientation change. Another theme takes care of responsive design, to automatically adjust the interface according to different screen dimensions, which aids in using the same interface on desktop, tablet, and smartphone devices.

Types of Mobile Applications

Mobile Applications are split into two broad categories:

Web-Based: The application you'll be creating in this chapter is known as a web-based application or simply a mobile web application. These types of applications are accessed using browsers in mobile devices. In this chapter, you'll declaratively build a mobile web application. Oracle APEX allows you to rapidly build applications that can be accessed on the desktop, a mobile device, or both. The mobile development interface uses a collection of templates based on the jQuery Mobile framework. This framework is designed to seamlessly run and correctly deliver mobile web application on various mobile devices with different operating systems. For you, as a developer, the good news is that you develop such applications with the tools you're already familiar with. To build a mobile application, you use the same App Builder, the same SQL and PL/SQL code, and with similar methods you applied while developing the desktop version. Because of a single codebase, a mobile web application can be accessed from any mobile device, irrespective of operating system. The process of accessing such applications is very simple. All that is needed is to have the correct URL that you put into the mobile browser, and respective ID with password. The application code is not stored on the device but is delivered by the application server. This way, you can easily handle application updates. You only need to update the application on the server, allowing potentially thousands of users to enjoy the latest version. The second advantage to this approach is that you are not required to send updates to every client (as required in native applications), which ensures that the accessed application is current with all provided features. Here are some pros and cons to web-based applications:

Pros:

- Updates are uploaded only to the application server and become instantly available for all platforms and devices.
- Same application code for all browser-enabled mobile devices.
- Use of same application building procedures and core web technologies.
- Doesn't need app store approval.

Cons:

- To access these applications you need a reasonable Internet connection.
- Slower than native applications because these applications are based on interpreted code rather than compiled code.
- Not available in the app stores.
- Cannot interact with device hardware such as camera, microphone, compass, and so on.

Native (On-Device): These applications are on the other side and are built for a specific mobile operating system, such as Windows Mobile, Android, or iOS. Native mobile applications are written for a specific target operating system in its own supported language. For instance, to develop an application for a Windows device, you'll use C# (C Sharp), for iOS devices it is Objective-C, and for Android, you need to be a master of Java. This means your app is tied to a specific platform and won't run on another. Native applications are downloaded and stored locally on the device. Because of this capability, these applications are considered better performers. Additionally, these applications have the biggest advantage of being able to interact with different device hardware (camera, compass, accelerometer, and more). Using a local data store (SQLite), these applications can even work when disconnected from the Internet. As a developer you have to handle version discrepancies because updates of these applications are downloaded manually. Let's see what pros and cons this category has:

Pros:

- Being native, it performs better than its counterpart.
- Offline availability.
- Complete access to device's hardware.
- Can be added to and searched in an app store.

Cons:

- Expensive to develop.
- Single platform support. Need to build a separate app for a different OS, which means additional time and cost.
- To get space on the device's app store, your app is required to undergo an approval process.

10.2 Create Interface for Mobile Application

Oracle APEX allows you to create two types of interfaces: Desktop and Mobile. Each page in an application is associated with one user interface. If a user logs into the application with a mobile device, the pages created with mobile interface will be rendered. If a desktop is used, the desktop user interface is delivered. You created and used the desktop interface in previous chapters. Here, you'll use Mobile interface for your mobile application.

1. Click the **Edit Application Properties** button in the main Sales Web Application interface.
   Edit Application Properties

2. Click the **User Interface** tab.
   User Interface

3. Click the **Add User Interface** button.
   Add User Interface >

4. On the User Interface screen, set the properties as follows and click **Next**.

Property	Value
Type	Mobile
Display Name	Mobile (Specifies a display name for the user interface, which is shown in wizards)
Auto Detect	Yes
Home URL	f?p=&APP_ID.:HOME_JQM_SMARTPHONE:&SESSION. (Specifies the home page of the application for the current user interface)
Login URL	f?p=&APP_ID.:LOGIN_JQM_SMARTPHONE:&SESSION. (Points toward the login page of the application for the current user interface)

5. On the *Identify Theme* page, select **Standard Themes** for *Theme Type*, and select **Mobile (Theme 51)** as the mobile application theme. Click **Next**.

6. On the final screen, click **Create** to create the mobile interface.

> **NOTE:**
> In chapter 3 section 3.3.1, you created a navigation bar entry to access the mobile application and entered 30 for the mobile home page ID. To point to the correct mobile home page, you have to replace that ID with the one created here.

Recall that when you initially created the desktop application, the application wizard created two pages for you: Home and Login. The mobile interface too, creates two default pages: Home (Page 30 in my scenario) and Login (Page 1001). In addition to these pages, the wizard creates a third one: Global Page - Mobile (Page 0). The Global Page of your application functions as a master page. You can add a separate Global Page for each user interface. The Application Express engine renders all components you add to a Global Page on every page within your application.

Run the Login Page 1001 that will look like Figure 10-1.

Figure 10-1
Mobile Log in
Page

Application Menu and Log Out buttons appearing on the Log In Screen

Enter the credentials you've been using so far and hit the **Login** button. A blank mobile home page will appear resembling the one illustrated in Figure 10-2.

Figure 10-2
Mobile Home
Page

Click the **Logout** link. You'll land on to the desktop login page, which is not correct. Call definitions of the Global Page. Select the **Logout** button in the *Region Buttons* section. Scroll down to **Behavior** section. Set *Action* to **Redirect to Page in this Application**. Click the **Target** link and enter **1001** for *Page* property. Save these settings to inform Oracle APEX where to land when the *Logout* button is clicked. Call and run the mobile Home page again. Enter your credentials to login and click the Logout button. This time, you'll see the correct login page, which is Page 1001.

Let's move on to fine tune the auto-generated pages by changing some properties, starting with the Global Page.

10.3 Modify the Global Page - Page 0

10.3.1 Modify Region - Header

1. Click the **Global Page** to call its definitions.

2. Click the **Header** region in the *Regions* section.

3. In *Pages* property (under *Server-side Condition*), enter **1001**. The region is created with a default condition–*Current Page Is NOT in comma delimited list.*

By supplementing the condition with the mobile login page number, you suppressed this region from appearing on the login page. See Figure 10-1 where the two buttons under this region (Menu and Logout) appear on the login page.

4. Just like the desktop version, the mobile version is created with a navigation menu that appears in a special panel on the left side. You can access the menu using the Menu button (see Figure 10-2). The Global Page contains a default dynamic action named *open panel*, which is responsible for showing the menu panel. By default, the *Button* property of this dynamic action is set to *LOGOUT*, which prevents the menu from appearing. Click the **Dynamic Actions** tab. Expand the **Click** node and click the **open panel** dynamic action. In the Properties pane, change the *Button* attribute from *LOGOUT* to **MENU** to open the panel when this button is clicked.

5. Apply the change and test your work. This time, the login screen should not display the two buttons.

10.3.2 Create List - Footer Controls

This static list carries two options (*Full Site* and *Logout*) and will be displayed at the bottom in the *Footer Controls* region. The first option will take you to the Home page of the desktop version, while the second one will log you out of the mobile application and will show the mobile login page. Go to **Shared Components**. In the *Navigation* section, click the **Lists** link and then click the **Create** button to create a new list from scratch. Enter **Footer Controls** for *Name* and select **Static** as *Type*. Fill in the *Static Values*, as shown below:

	List Entry Label		Target Page ID or custom URL	
1	Full Site		1	∧
2	Logout		1001	∧

10.3.3 Create Region - Footer Controls

The list you created in the previous section will be displayed in this region. Call the Global Page again. Create a new region by right-clicking the *Header* region node and selecting **Create Region**. Select the new region and modify it using the following table:

Property	Value
Title	Footer Controls
Type	List
List *(Source)*	Footer Controls
Template	Footer Toolbar (Fixed)
Custom Attributes	style="text-align:center" *(to centralize the list carrying the two buttons)*
Type *(Server-side Condition)*	Current page is not in comma delimited list
Pages	1001 *(prevents it from appearing on the mobile login page)*
List Templates *(under Attributes)*	Button Control Group

10.3.4 Create Region - Mobile Styles

Right-click the **Footer Controls** region and select **Create Region**. Enter **Mobile Styles** for its *Title*, and set *Type* to **Static Content**. Enter the following style rules in the *Text* property under *Source*. Note that these rules were created and described earlier in the desktop version to style the *Select Items* page (Page 12), and were defined in the inline page attribute. Here, you added it to the global page to test another approach to style Select Items page (Page 217) of the mobile version. Since the classes defined in these rules are referenced only by Page 217, other pages in the application are not affected. See section 10.11.1.

```
<style>
    div.CustomerInfo strong{font:bold 12px/16px Arial,sans-
    serif;display:block;width:120px;}
    div.CustomerInfo p{display:block;margin:0; font: normal 12px/16px Arial, sans-serif;}
    div.Products{clear:both;margin:16px 0 0;padding:0 8px 0 0;}
    div.Products table{border:1px solid #CCC;border-bottom:none;}
    div.Products table th{background-color:#DDD;color:#000;font:bold 12px/16px
    Arial,sans-serif;padding:4px 10px;text-align:right;border-bottom:1px solid #CCC;}
    div.Products table td{border-bottom:1px solid #CCC;font:normal 12px/16px Arial,sans-
    serif;padding:4px 10px;text-align:right;}
    div.Products table td a{color:#000;}
    div.Products .left{text-align:left;}
    div.CartItem{padding:8px 8px 0 8px;font:normal 11px/14px Arial,sans-serif;}
    div.CartItem a{color:#000;}
    div.CartItem span{display:block;text-align:right;padding:8px 0 0;}
    div.CartItem span.subtotal{font-weight:bold;}
    div.CartTotal{border-top:1px solid #FFF;margin-top:8px;padding:8px;border-top:1px
    dotted #AAA;}
    div.CartTotal span{display:block;text-align:right;font:normal 11px/14px Arial,sans-
    serif;padding:0 0 4px 0;}
    div.CartTotal p{padding:0;margin:0;font:normal 11px/14px Arial,sans-
    serif;position:relative;}
    div.CartTotal p.CartTotal{font:bold 12px/14px Arial,sans-serif;padding:8px 0 0 0;}
    div.CartTotal p.CartTotal span{font:bold 12px/14px Arial,sans-serif;padding:8px 0 0 0;}
    div.CartTotal p span{padding:0;position:absolute;right:0;top:0;}
</style>
```

10.4 Modify the Mobile Home Page

10.4.1 Modify the Page properties

1. Call the mobile **Home** page.

2. Set the *Name* of this page to **Mobile Home Page**. Make sure the *Page Alias* displays HOME_JQM_SMARTPHONE. An alias is a nick name. You can enter an alphanumeric alias for a page. It is used to reference a page instead of a page number. For example, if you were working on page 1 of application 100, you could create an alias called "home", which could then be accessed from other pages using a URL like this: *f?p=100:home*.

3. Enter **Sales Web Application** in *Title* and save the amendments.

10.4.2 Modify Mobile Navigation Menu

Go to **Shared Components** and click **Navigation Menu** under the *Navigation* section. Click **Mobile Navigation Menu**. It's a default menu created for the mobile application and carries just one entry: Home. Using the **Create Entry** button, add the following four entries to this menu:

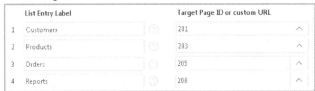

	List Entry Label		Target Page ID or custom URL	
1	Customers		201	∧
2	Products		203	∧
3	Orders		205	∧
4	Reports		208	∧

10.4.3 Mobile Reports List

Create another list named *Mobile Reports* for the mobile application. Oracle APEX provides a utility that lets you make a copy of an existing component. Here are the steps to create the new list by making a copy of *Reports List* you created in Chapter 3.

1. In Shared Components, click the **Lists** link under *Navigation*.

2. Click the **Copy** button.

3. In the first wizard step, select **List in this application** and move on.

4. In *Copy List*, select **Reports List**. Enter **Mobile Reports** for *New List Name* and click the **Copy** button.

5. On the *Lists* page, click **Mobile Reports** you just copied. In the mobile version we will create four reports, as shown in the following table. Note that maps, trees, and PDF are not supported on this platform. Click each link individually and set the *Page* attribute in the *Target* section as follows. Delete all other report options.

List Entry	Page
Customer Orders	209
Sales by Category and Product	210
Order Calendar	211

Test Your Work

The three default mobile pages created by Oracle APEX wizard are ready for a test-run. You might have noticed that we didn't work on the mobile login page 1001 (we didn't work on the desktop login page either). Application Express is smart enough to create these pages with basic functionalities, suffice to cope with our needs. Access the mobile application from the Mobile navigation bar entry. Click the **Menu** button, which should open a panel carrying the mobile navigation menu. Except for the Home entry, the remaining four entries will display error messages if click them, because the target pages set for these menu options are not available at the moment. Click the **Full Site** button at the bottom to call the Home page of the desktop version. Get back to the mobile version and test the *Logout* button.

10.5 Create Customers Page - Page 201

1. As usual, click the **Create Page** button to create the first mobile application page yourself.

2. Note that for *User Interface* you now have two options: *Desktop* and *Mobile*. Select the **Mobile** option for the *User Interface*, and click the **Report** icon to move ahead.

   Note: You must select the *Mobile* user interface option for all pages you create in this chapter.

3. On the next screen, select the **Reflow Report** option. In this exercise, you will create a responsive report for mobile applications using the Reflow Report feature. Reflow Report wraps each column or changes to displaying multiple lines on very small screens. When there is not enough space available to display the report horizontally, the report works by collapsing the table columns into a stacked presentation that looks like blocks of label and data pairs for each row–see Figure 10-3.

4. Type **201** for *Page Number* and **Customers** for *Page Name*. Leave *Page Mode* to **Normal** and move on by clicking **Next**.

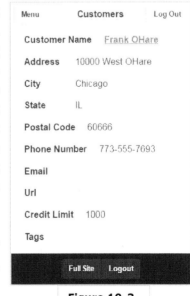

Figure 10-3

253

5. Set *Navigation Preference* to **Identify an existing navigation menu entry for this page** and select **Customers** for *Existing Navigation Menu Entry*. Click **Next**.

6. For *Source Type*, select **SQL Query** and enter the following query in *Region Source*:

    **select customer_id, cust_first_name||' '||cust_last_name customer_name, cust_street_address1, cust_city, cust_state, cust_postal_code, cust_email, phone_number1, url, credit_limit, tags
    from DEMO_CUSTOMERS**

7. Click **Create** to finish the wizard.

8. In the Page Designer, expand the **Columns** node. Set suitable headings for all the columns and arrange them according to Figure 10-3.

9. Click the **CUSTOMER_ID** column and set its *Show* property to **No**. This specifies to hide the column at run time. Even if hidden, columns can always be referenced using substitution syntax, &COLUMN_NAME..

10. Click the **CUSTOMER_NAME** column to set the following properties. The values set for these properties will transform the customer name column into a link. When clicked, it calls a form page where you can browse and manipulate customer information. For Link Text, click the adjacent Quick Pick button and select CUSTOMER_NAME from the list. The selected value will be displayed as a substitution variable.

Property	Value
Type	Link
Target Type	Type = Page in this application Page = 202 Name = P202_CUSTOMER_ID Value = &CUSTOMER_ID. Clear Cache = 202
Link Text	&CUSTOMER_NAME.

11. Click the **CREDIT_LIMIT** column and set its *Alignment* and *Column Alignment* properties to **Start**. These two settings will left-align the column's heading and its value.

> **NOTE:** Mobile pages created in Oracle APEX do not support constructs such as interactive reports, tabular forms, and master-detail pages.

254

10.5.1 Add Button - Create

Right-click the *Customers* region and select **Create Button**. Set the following properties for this button, which is added to create a new customer's record.

Property	Value
Button Name	CREATE
Label	Create
Button Position	Bottom of Region
Hot	Yes
Action	Redirect to Page in this Application
Target	Type = Page in this application Page = 202 Clear Cache = 202

Save and test the page, which should look like Figure 10-3. Note that the target page will be created in the next section.

10.6 Create Maintain Customer Page - Page 202

The page created in this section is depicted in Figure 10-4. It will allow you to add, modify, and delete a customer's record.

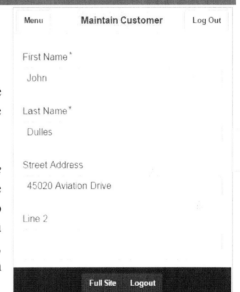

Figure 10-4

1. Create another mobile page and this time select the **Form** option followed by the **Form on a Table** option.

2. Set the following properties on the *Page Attributes* screen and click **Next**. The last two attributes will take you back to the *Customers* report page when you submit this page (after adding, modifying, or deleting a record) or when you click the *Cancel* button.

Property	Value
Page Number	202
Page Name	Maintain Customer
Page Mode	Normal
Branch Here on Submit	201
Cancel and Go To Page	201

3. Set *Navigation Preference* to **Identify an existing navigation menu entry for this page** and select **Customers** for *Existing Navigation Menu Entry*. Click **Next**.

4. Accept the default *Table/View Owner* on the *Source* screen. For *Table/View Name*, select the **DEMO_CUSTOMERS** table. After ensuring all the table columns are selected (that is, they all appear in the right pane), click **Next** to proceed.

5. For *Primary Key Type*, select the **Managed by Database (ROWID)** option. You've been using the second option (*Select Primary Key Column*) in the desktop application exercises to select a primary key for the selected table. This time, you're using the alternate method. The ROWID is a pseudo column in a table and it is used to identify rows to update and delete. This option is usually selected for tables with multiple primary key columns (more than two). Click the **Create** button to finish the wizard.

10.6.1 Modify Items

Modify properties of the page items, as shown in the following table:

ITEM	ATTRIBUTE:VALUE	ATTRIBUTE:VALUE	ATTRIBUTE:VALUE
P202_CUSTOMER_ID	Type : Hidden	-	-
P202_CUST_FIRST_NAME	Label : First Name	-	-
P202_CUST_LAST_NAME	Label : Last Name	-	-
P202_CUST_STREET_ADDRESS1	Label : Street Address	-	-
P202_CUST_STREET_ADDRESS2	Label : Line 2	-	-
P202_CUST_CITY	Label : City	-	-
P202_CUST_POSTAL_CODE	Label : Postal Code	Template : Required	Value Required : Yes
P202_CUST_EMAIL	Label : Email	-	-
P202_ PHONE_NUMBER1	Label : Phone Number	-	-
P202_ PHONE_NUMBER2	Label : Alternate Number	-	-
P202_URL	Label : URL	-	-
P202_CREDIT_LIMIT	Label : Credit Limit	Template : Required	Value Required : Yes
P202_TAGS	Type : Text Field	-	-

Click the **P202_CUST_STATE** item to modify the following properties. These setting will display the State field as a select list carrying a list of states. Save you work after making the adjustments.

Property	Value
Type	Select List
Label	State
Template	Required
Value Required	Yes
Type (*under List of Values*)	Shared Components
List of Values	STATES

From the mobile menu, select **Customers**. Click any customer's record to see how the page looks like. Click the **Cancel** button to move back to the *Customers* report page. Click the **Create** button, located at the bottom of the *Customers* page. A new form will be presented with two buttons: *Cancel* and *Create*. Create a new customer record and click the **Create** button to store it in the DEMO_CUSTOMERS table. Call the new record and save it after modifying some information. Finally, delete this record. Using the instructions provided in the desktop version, add two validations to check customers' credit limits and prevent the deletion of customers who have already placed orders.

1. Create a new page by clicking the **Create Page** button.

2. Select **Mobile** for the *User Interface* and click the **Report** icon to move ahead.

3. On the second wizard screen, select the **List View** option that creates a responsive report for mobile applications. The report works by collapsing the table columns into a stacked presentation that looks like blocks of label and data pairs for each row. This switch occurs when there is not enough space available to display the report horizontally.

4. Type **203** for *Page Number* and **Products** for *Page Name*. Leave *Page Mode* to **Normal** and move on by clicking **Next**.

5. Set *Navigation Preference* to **Identify an existing navigation menu entry for this page**, select **Products** for *Existing Navigation Menu Entry*, and click **Next**.

6. On the *Source* wizard screen, select **SQL Query** as *Source Type*, and enter the following SQL statement in *Region Source*.

```
select a.ROWID as "PK_ROWID", a.*
from "#OWNER#"."DEMO_PRODUCT_INFO" a
order by a.product_name
```

7. Set properties on the *Settings* screen as illustrated in the following figure and click the **Create** button.

When you click the option *Show Image*, some more relevant properties appear on your screen. The same behavior applies to the *Enable Search* option. The first option is checked because we need to display images of products, while the second option is checked to add search functionality. If lists are embedded in a page with other types of content, the *Inset List* option packages the list into a block that sits inside the content area with a bit of margin and rounded corners. The selected *Text Column*, PRODUCT_NAME, will appear next to the image at runtime. The *Image Type* attribute specifies what kind of image is displayed and where it is read from. The displayed image can be an icon with a size of 16x16 or a thumbnail with a size of 80x80. The source for the image can be a database BLOB column or a URL to a static file. After setting the *Image Type* attribute, you're required to provide the *Image BLOB Column*, which in our case is PRODUCT_IMAGE. The *Image Primary Key* attribute specifies the primary key or a unique database column that is used to lookup the image. The value for this attribute (ROWID) is selected by the wizard. In the Customers module we set link target through the Property Editor, here we entered a link **(f?p=&APP_ID.:204:&APP_SESSION.::&DEBUG.:RP,204:P204_ROWID:&PK_ROWID.)** manually that you can verify by accessing the *Link Target* property under the region's attributes node. The *Search Type* attribute defines how a search will be performed. The selected option, *Server: Like & Ignore Case*, will use Oracle's LIKE operator (LIKE %UPPER([search value])%) to query the result.

After creating the page, click the **Attributes** node under the *Products* region. Set *Search Column* to **PRODUCT_DESCRIPTION** and enter **Search Product Description** in the *Search Box Place holder* property. The *Search Column* specifies an alternative database column used for the search. The text added to the *Search Box Placeholder* will appear in the search box at runtime to inform users what to put in the search box.

10.7.1 Add Button - Create

Right-click the *Products* region and select **Create Button**. Set the following properties for this button, which is being added to create a new product.

Property	Value
Name	CREATE
Label	Create
Button Position	Bottom of Region
Hot	Yes
Action	Redirect to Page in this Application
Target	Type = Page in this application Page = 204 Clear Cache = 204

Save the page and run the application. From the mobile menu, click the **Products** option. You'll see the main *Products* page. Enter **shoes** in the search box and hit enter. Two shoe products (Ladies Shoes and Men Shoes) should appear. Enter **low heel** in the search box. The page will be refreshed with one record, displaying Ladies Shoes. This is because the words *low heel* exist only in this product's description. Type **lower**

258

lace in the search box. This time, *Men Shoes* will be displayed. Click the *Clear text* (cross) icon in the search box. All the products will re-appear.

Make this page more meaningful by performing the following steps. The *Advanced Formatting* option enables you to style your list even further. The first option, *List Attributes*, is used to style the list by overriding the standard list or divider theme. The *List Entry Attributes* can be set to pick an icon other than the standard right arrow. The mandatory option, *Text Formatting*, gives you the opportunity to show more in the list than just the product name. In this example, you wrap product name and description in a HTML <h3> heading element. You can add more stuff to the list with the help of *Supplemental Information*. The *Supplemental Information* appears on the right side of the list item to present product price.

1. Click the region's **Attributes** node.

2. In the Property pane, put a check on **Advanced Formatting** to make the corresponding formatting properties visible.

3. In *List Attributes*, type: **data-divider-theme="b"**. The theme for list dividers can be set by adding the data-divider-theme to the list and specifying a swatch letter. We set swatch "b" on the dividers.

4. Enter **data-icon="plus"** in *List Entry Attributes* to replace the default right arrow icon with a plus icon.

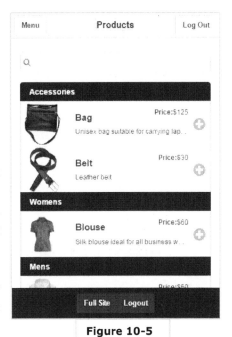

Figure 10-5

5. In *Text Formatting*, type:
   <h3>&PRODUCT_NAME.</h3><p>&PRODUCT_DESCRIPTION.</p>

6. In *Supplemental Information*, type
   Price:$&LIST_PRICE. (including the terminating period).

7. Enter **&CATEGORY.** In the *List Divider Formatting* property to show the category of each product. Save the changes and run the page to see an output similar to Figure 10-5.

10.8 Create Maintain Product Page - Page 204

1. Create another mobile page and select the **Form** option followed by the **Form on a Table** option.

2. Set the following attributes on the *Page Attributes* screen and click **Next**.

Property	Value
Page Number	204
Page Name	Maintain Product
Page Mode	Normal
Branch Here on Submit	203
Cancel and Go To Page	203

3. Set *Navigation Preference* to **Identify an existing navigation menu entry for this page**, select **Products** for *Existing Navigation Menu Entry*, and click **Next**.

4. Accept the default *Table/View Owner* on the *Source* screen. For *Table/View Name*, select the **DEMO_PRODUCT_INFO** table. Select all table columns except MIMETYPE, FILENAME, IMAGE_LAST_UPDATE, and PRODUCT_IMAGE. Click these columns in the right page and use the left arrow key icon in the shuttle to push them back to the left pane. Click **Next** to proceed after removing these columns.

5. Once again, select the **Managed by Database (ROWID)** option for *Primary Key Type* and click **Create** to finish the wizard.

10.8.1 Modify Items

Modify properties of the page items as shown in the following table:

ITEM	ATTRIBUTE:VALUE	ATTRIBUTE:VALUE	ATTRIBUTE:VALUE
P204_PRODUCT_ID	Type : Hidden	-	-
P204_PRODUCT_NAME	Label : Product	Template : Required	Value Required : Yes
P204_LIST_PRICE	Label : List Price	Template : Required	Value Required : Yes
P204_TAGS	Type : Text Field	-	-

Click the **P204_CATEGORY** item. Modify the following properties of this item to display the three categories in a select list.

Property	Value
Type	Select List
Label	Category
Template	Required
Value Required	Yes
Type (*under List of Values*)	Shared Components
List of Values	CATEGORIES

Next, click the **P204_PRODUCT_AVAIL** item to modify the following properties. Recall that in Chapter 6 we attached the *Y or N* LOV to the *Product Available* item in the desktop application. This time, we are using the *Switch* built-in alternate.

Property	Value
Type	Switch
Label	Product Available
Template	Required
Value Required	Yes

10.8.2 Create Item

Right-click the *Items* folder under the *Maintain Product* region, and select **Create Page Item**. Set the following attributes for this hidden item, which is being created to store the row ID of a product on Page 204. Note that the row ID is forwarded to this item by the *Link Target* set in Section 10.7 step 7.

Property	Value
Name	P204_ROWID
Type	Hidden
Value Protected	Yes
Type (*under Source*)	Database Column
Database Column	ROWID

10.8.3 Modify Process

On the *Rendering* tab, open *Pre-Rendering | After Header | Processes*, and click the **Fetch Row from DEMO_PRODUCT_INFO** process. As you already know, this process is responsible to fetch a row from the corresponding table. This process is being modified because the wizard set its *Primary Key Column* and *Primary Key Item* to *PRODUCT_ID* and *P204_PRODUCT_ID*, respectively. If you keep these values and click a product on Page 203, you won't see details of the selected record, because you mapped ROWID parameters in the *Link Target* in Section 10.7 step 7. Set the following properties with the correct values to fetch and display product details.

Property	Value
Primary Key Column	ROWID
Primary Key Item	P204_ROWID

Test Your Work

Save your work and run the module from the *Products* link in the main mobile menu. On the *Products* page, click any product to see an output similar to Figure 10-6. Try to create a new product, modify it, and then delete it.

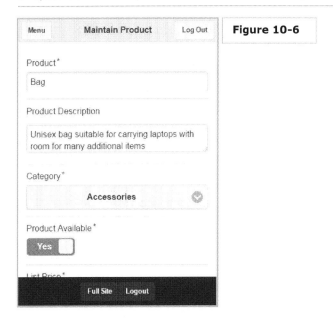

Figure 10-6

10.9 Create Orders Page 205

For desktop version you used the *Master Detail Form* option to simultaneously create *Orders* (Page 4) and *Order Details* (Page 29) pages. Since Master-Detail option is not available for mobile platform, you will use an Oracle APEX feature called *Column Toggle Report* instead. By setting a region to the *Column Toggle Report* type, you build reports that display all data on any mobile device. *Column Toggle* enables you to specify the most important columns and those that will be hidden as necessary on smaller screens.

1. Click the **Create Page** button. Set *User Interface* to **Mobile**. Select **Report** on the initial screen followed by the **Column Toggle Report** option.

2. Enter **205** for *Page Number* and **Orders** for *Page Name*. Keeping the default *Page Mode* to **Normal**, click **Next**.

3. Set *Navigation Preference* to **Identify an existing navigation menu entry for this page**, select **Orders** for *Existing Navigation Menu Entry*, and click **Next** to proceed.

4. After selecting **SQL Query** as the *Source Type* for this page, enter the following SQL statement in *Region Source* and click the **Create** button.

```
select o.rowid,
       o.order_id,
       to_date(to_char(o.order_timestamp,'mm yyyy'), 'mm yyyy') order_month,
       o.order_timestamp order_date,
       o.user_name sales_rep,
       o.order_total,
       c.cust_last_name || ', ' || c.cust_first_name customer_name,
       (select count(*) from demo_order_items oi
        where oi.order_id = o.order_id) order_items,
       o.tags tags
from  demo_orders o, demo_customers c
where o.customer_id = c.customer_id
order by order_timestamp desc
```

10.9.1 Add Button - Create

Right-click the *Orders* region and select **Create Button**. The button will be used to create a new order. Set the following properties for this button:

Property	Value
Name	CREATE
Label	Create
Button Position	Create
Hot	Yes
Action	Redirect to Page in this Application
Target	Type = Page in this application Page = 216 Clear Cache = 216

Save and run the page. Initially, the page will display all the columns defined in the SQL query. Click the **Columns** button. In the ensuing columns list, remove checks from all columns, except **Order Id**, **Order Month**, and **Customer Name** to show these three columns in the main report, which should resemble Figure 10-7.

Figure 10-7

In the desktop version we created a wizard to record customer orders. Here too, you'll adopt the same process to enter a new order sequentially. In the desktop module, the first page that appeared after clicking the *Enter New Order* button was Page 11, where you allowed users to select an existing customer or to create a new one. To save some time, you'll copy that page from the desktop version for the mobile module. Let's see how it is done.

1. Call the **Identify Customer** page (Page 11) in the Page Designer.

2. Click the **Create** menu button to your right in the toolbar and select **Page as Copy**. Recall that you used this technique earlier to create Page 11 from Page 7 in the desktop version. Here, you are using it for the mobile user interface.

3. Select the option **Page in this application** and click **Next**.

4. On *Page to Copy* screen, set the following properties. Note that this time we are using the *Mobile* option for the *User Interface*.

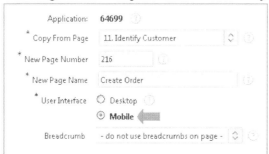

5. Set *Navigation Preference* to **Identify an existing navigation menu entry for this page**, select **Orders** for *Existing Navigation Menu Entry*, and click **Next** to proceed.

6. Accepting the default values on the *New Names* screen, click **Copy** to create the page.

If you run the page at this stage (using the *Create* button on Page 205), you'll see an error message: *Application 64699 Dialog page 216 cannot be rendered successfully.* This is because the *Page Mode* attribute of the new page is set to *Modal Dialog*. Set it to **Normal** to prevent the error. Even after making this amendment, you will encounter error dialogs if you run this page. To make this page suitable for mobile devices, execute the following sub-section.

10.10.1 Delete/Modify Regions

1. Delete the **Order Progress** region, because it is not supported under mobile platform.

2. Delete the **New Customer Details** region. You will create a new customer through Page 202 that will be called via the CREATE button – see the next section.

3. Modify the **Buttons** region. Its *Position* property will be displaying *REGION_POSITION_03 (Invalid)*. Change it to **Body3**.

10.10.2 Modify Buttons

1. Click the **Cancel** button to set the following properties. The name and functionality of this button is being modified to create a new customer via Page 202.

Property	Value
Button Name	CREATE
Label	Create New Customer
Button Position	Bottom of Region
Horizontal Alignment	Left
Button Template	Standard Button
Action	Redirect to Page in this Application
Target	Type = Page in this application Page = 205 Clear Cache = 205

2. Set the following properties for the **Next** button.

Property	Value
Button Position	Bottom of Region
Horizontal Alignment	Right
Button Template	Standard Button
Hot	Yes

10.10.3 Modify Items

1. Modify the Radio Group item **P216_CUSTOMER_OPTIONS** using the following properties:

Property	Value
Label	*Make it clear*
Template	Optional
Value Required	Yes
Display Extra Values	No

265

2. Modify **P216_CUSTOMER_ID** using the following properties to transform this item into a Select List.

Property	Value
Type	Select List
Template	Required
Value Required	Yes
Type (*LOV*)	SQL Query
SQL Query	select cust_last_name || ', ' || cust_first_name d, customer_id r from demo_customers order by cust_last_name
Display Extra Values	No
Display Null Values	Yes
Null Display Value	- Select Customer -

3. Set *Template* to **Required** for the following five items. You can use Ctrl+Click to select all these items and set the property at once.
   P216_CUST_FIRST_NAME, P216_CUST_LAST_NAME, P216_CUST_STATE, P216_CUST_POSTAL_CODE, P216_CREDIT_LIMIT

4. Set *Template* to **Optional** for:
   P216_CUST_STREET_ADDRESS1, P216_CUST_STREET_ADDRESS2, P216_CUST_CITY, P216_CUST_EMAIL, P216_URL, P216_TAGS

5. Modify **P216_PHONE_NUMBER1** and **P216_PHONE_NUMBER2** as follows:

Property	Value
Type	Text Field
Subtype	Phone Number
Template	Optional

6. Set *Start New Row* properties of all these items (mentioned in steps 3, 4, and 5) to **Yes** to place them vertically upon each other. **Tip**: Use Shift+Click or Ctrl+Click to select all these items and then set the property to *Yes*. This way, the value will be applied to all the selected items in one go.

10.10.4 Modify Branch

Modify the sole branch (*Go To Page 12*) on the *Processing* tab using the following properties:

Property	Value
Name	Go To Page 217
Target Type	Type = Page in this Application Page = 217 Clear Cache = 217
When Button Pressed	NEXT

Save and run the page using the mobile menu route. After clicking the **Create** button, you'll see the page illustrated in Figure 10-8. To enter an order for an existing customer, select the customer from the *Customer* list. To create a new customer, click the **Create New Customer** button.

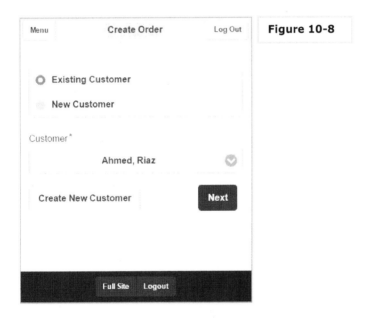

Figure 10-8

10.11 Create Select Order Items Page – Page 217

Using the same copy utility, you'll create this page as well to select order items. In the desktop version you created Page 12 for this purpose and that is the page you'll use as the source for your mobile application. The copied page will inherit all items and processes from the source.

1. Call the **Order Items** page (Page 12) in the Page Designer.

2. Once again, click the **Create** menu button in the toolbar and select **Page as Copy**.

3. Select the option **Page in this application** and click **Next**.

4. On *Page to Copy* screen, set properties according to the following screen shot. Don't forget to select the *Mobile* option for the *User Interface*. Click **Next** to proceed.

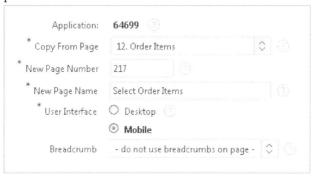

5. Set *Navigation Preference* to **Identify an existing navigation menu entry for this page**, select **Orders** for *Existing Navigation Menu Entry*, and click **Next** to proceed.

6. Accept the default values on the *New Names* screen and click **Copy** to create the page.

7. Once you are in the Page Designer, set *Page Mode* property to **Normal** for the new page (217).

10.11.1 Modify Regions

1. Click the **Select Items** (*PL/SQL Dynamic Content* type) region. Choose the -**Select**- placeholder for the *Parent Region* property to remove the parent region (*Order Progress*) reference. You removed this reference because in the next step you will delete the *Order Progress* region, which is the parent region to the *Select Items* region. Note that when you remove a parent region, any sub-regions are also removed from the page. Change the *Template* property of this region from *Plain (No Title)* to **Region (With Title)**. This will add a title (*Select Items*) at the top of this region at runtime.

2. Delete the **Order Progress** region.

3. Replace the *Select Items* region's *Source PL/SQL Code* with the following. Note that this code is similar to the desktop version (section 7.6.3) except for the items marked in bold that are modified to represent mobile version's page items.

```
declare
 l_customer_id varchar2(30) := :P216_CUSTOMER_ID;
begin
-- display customer information
sys.htp.p('<div class="CustomerInfo">');
if :P216_CUSTOMER_OPTIONS = 'EXISTING' then
 for x in (select * from demo_customers where customer_id = l_customer_id) loop
  sys.htp.p('<div class="CustomerInfo">');
  sys.htp.p('<strong>Customer:</strong>');
  sys.htp.p('<p>');
  sys.htp.p(sys.htf.escape_sc(x.cust_first_name)||' '||sys.htf.escape_sc(x.cust_last_name)||'<br/>');
  sys.htp.p(sys.htf.escape_sc(x.cust_street_address1) || '<br />');
  if x.cust_street_address2 is not null then
   sys.htp.p(sys.htf.escape_sc(x.cust_street_address2) || '<br />');
  end if;
  sys.htp.p(sys.htf.escape_sc(x.cust_city) || ', ' || sys.htf.escape_sc(x.cust_state) || ' ' ||
  sys.htf.escape_sc(x.cust_postal_code));
  sys.htp.p('</p>');
 end loop;
else
 sys.htp.p('<strong>Customer:</strong>');
 sys.htp.p('<p>');
 sys.htp.p(sys.htf.escape_sc(:P216_CUST_FIRST_NAME)||' '||sys.htf.escape_sc(:P216_CUST_LAST_NAME)
 || '<br />');
 sys.htp.p(sys.htf.escape_sc(:P216_CUST_STREET_ADDRESS1) || '<br />');
 if :P216_CUST_STREET_ADDRESS2 is not null then
  sys.htp.p(sys.htf.escape_sc(:P216_CUST_STREET_ADDRESS2) || '<br />');
 end if;
 sys.htp.p(sys.htf.escape_sc(:P216_CUST_CITY) || ', ' ||
 sys.htf.escape_sc(:P216_CUST_STATE) || ' ' ||
 sys.htf.escape_sc(:P216_CUST_POSTAL_CODE));
 sys.htp.p('</p>');
end if;
sys.htp.p('</div>');
-- display products
sys.htp.p('<div class="Products" >');
sys.htp.p('<table width="100%" cellspacing="0" cellpadding="0" border="0">
<thead>
<tr><th class="left">Product</th><th>Price</th><th></th></tr>
</thead>
<tbody>');
for c1 in (select product_id, product_name, list_price, 'Add to Cart' add_to_order
from demo_product_info
where product_avail = 'Y'
```

```
order by product_name) loop
sys.htp.p('<tr><td class="left">' ||
sys.htf.escape_sc(c1.product_name)||'</td><td>'||trim(to_char(c1.list_price,'999G999G990D00'))||
  '</td><td><a
          href="'||apex_util.prepare_url('f?p=&APP_ID.:217:'||:app_session
          ||':ADD:::P217_PRODUCT_ID:'||c1.product_id)||'"
          class="t-Button"><span>Add</span>
  </a></td></tr>');
end loop;
sys.htp.p('</tbody></table>');
sys.htp.p('</div>');
-- display current order
sys.htp.p('<div class="Products" >');
sys.htp.p('<table width="100%" cellspacing="0" cellpadding="0" border="0">
<thead>
<tr><th class="left">Current Order</th></tr>
</thead>
</table>
<table width="100%" cellspacing="0" cellpadding="0" border="0">
<tbody>');
declare
   c number := 0; t number := 0;
begin
-- loop over cart values
for c1 in (select c001 pid, c002 i, to_number(c003) p, count(c002) q, sum(c003) ep, 'Remove' remove
from apex_collections
where collection_name = 'ORDER'
group by c001, c002, c003
order by c002)
loop
sys.htp.p('<div class="CartItem"><a href="'||
apex_util.prepare_url('f?p=&APP_ID.:217:&SESSION.:REMOVE:::P217_PRODUCT_ID:'||sys.htf.escape_sc(c1.pid))|
|'"><img src="#IMAGE_PREFIX#delete.gif" alt="Remove from cart" title="Remove from cart" /></a>  
'||sys.htf.escape_sc(c1.i)||'
<span>'||trim(to_char(c1.p,'$999G999G999D00'))||'</span>
<span>Quantity: '||c1.q||'</span>
<span class="subtotal">Subtotal: '||trim(to_char(c1.ep,'$999G999G999D00'))||'</span>
</div>');
  c := c + 1;
  t := t + c1.ep;
end loop;
sys.htp.p('</tbody></table>');
if c > 0 then
   sys.htp.p('<div class="CartTotal">
```

```
<p>Items: <span>'||c||'</span></p>
    <p class="CartTotal">Total: <span>'||trim(to_char(t,'$999G999G999D00'))||'</span></p>
</div>');
else
    sys.htp.p('<p class="CartTotal">You have no items in your current order.</p>');
end if;
end;
sys.htp.p('</div>');
end;
```

10.11.2 Modify Buttons and Region

1. Modify the **Buttons** region by switching its *Position* property from *REGION_POSITION_03 (Invalid)* to **Body3**.

2. Click the **Cancel** button to set the following properties:

Property	Value
Button Position	Bottom of Region
Horizontal Alignment	Left
Button Template	Standard Button
Action	Redirect to Page in this Application
Page (*under Target*)	205

3. Click the **Previous** button to set the following properties:

Property	Value
Button Position	Bottom of Region
Horizontal Alignment	Left
Button Template	Standard Button
Icon CSS Classes	*Remove fa-chevron-left value*
Action	Redirect to Page in this Application
Page (*under Target*)	216

4. Set the following properties for the **Next** button:

Property	Value
Button Position	Bottom of Region
Horizontal Alignment	Right
Button Template	Standard Button
Hot	Yes

10.11.3 After Submit Process

Click the **Processing** tab, then click the **Place Order** process, and replace the existing *Source PL/SQL Code* with the following. This one is also the same PL/SQL procedure used in section 7.6.8 in the desktop module. Items marked in bold are modified in the code to reflect mobile page elements.

```
declare
  l_order_id   number;
  l_customer_id varchar2(30) := :P216_CUSTOMER_ID;
begin
  -- Create New Customer
  if :P216_CUSTOMER_OPTIONS = 'NEW' then
    insert into DEMO_CUSTOMERS (
      CUST_FIRST_NAME, CUST_LAST_NAME, CUST_STREET_ADDRESS1,
      CUST_STREET_ADDRESS2, CUST_CITY, CUST_STATE, CUST_POSTAL_CODE,
      CUST_EMAIL, PHONE_NUMBER1, PHONE_NUMBER2, URL, CREDIT_LIMIT, TAGS)
    values (
      :P216_CUST_FIRST_NAME, :P216_CUST_LAST_NAME, :P216_CUST_STREET_ADDRESS1,
      :P216_CUST_STREET_ADDRESS2, :P216_CUST_CITY, :P216_CUST_STATE,
      :P216_CUST_POSTAL_CODE, :P216_CUST_EMAIL, :P216_PHONE_NUMBER1,
      :P216_PHONE_NUMBER2, :P216_URL, :P216_CREDIT_LIMIT, :P216_TAGS)
    returning customer_id into l_customer_id;
    :P216_CUSTOMER_ID := l_customer_id;
  end if;
  -- Insert a row into the Order Header table
  insert into demo_orders(customer_id, order_total, order_timestamp, user_name)
  values(l_customer_id, null, systimestamp, upper(:APP_USER)) returning order_id into l_order_id;
  commit;
  -- Loop through the ORDER collection and insert rows into the Order Line Item table
  for x in (select c001, c003, sum(c004) c004 from apex_collections
        where collection_name = 'ORDER' group by c001, c003)
  loop
    insert into demo_order_items(order_item_id, order_id, product_id, unit_price, quantity)
    values (null, l_order_id, to_number(x.c001), to_number(x.c003),to_number(x.c004));
  end loop;
  commit;
  -- Set the item P218_ORDER_ID to the order that was just placed
  :P218_ORDER_ID := l_order_id;
  -- Truncate the collection after the order has been placed
  apex_collection.truncate_collection(p_collection_name => 'ORDER');
end;
```

272

10.11.4 Modify Branch

1. Modify the first branch (*Go To Page 14*) using the following properties:

Property	Value
Name	Go To Page 218
Target Type	Page in this Application
Page	218

2. Delete the other two branches – **Go To Page 4 / 11**.

Save your work. Call this page from the mobile menu route. The page should look like the following screen shot.

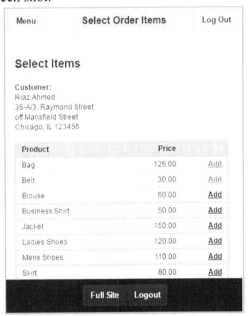

Figure 10-9

10.12 Create Order Summary Page 218

Once again, use the page copy utility to create the *Order Summary* page from Page 14 of the desktop application using the following screen shot. After creating the page, set its *Page Mode* attribute to **Normal**.

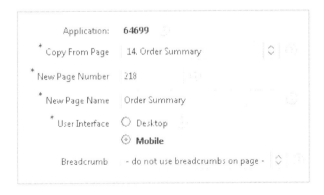

273

10.12.1 Modify Regions

1. Click the **Order Lines** region and change its *Template* property to **Region (With Title)**.

2. Delete the **Order Progress** region.

3. Modify the **Buttons** region by switching its *Position* property from *REGION_POSITION_03 (Invalid)* to **Body3**.

4. Expand the **Columns** node under the *Order Lines* region. Click the **EXTENDED_PRICE** column. Set its *Compute Sum* property (under *Advanced*) to **Yes**. This will add a *Report total* row to show the order total.

10.12.2 Modify Button

Click the **Back** button and set the following properties:

Property	Value
Button Position	Bottom of Region
Horizontal Alignment	Right
Button Template	Standard Button
Hot	Yes
Action	Redirect to Page in this Application
Page	205

Test Your Work

Run the module using the **Orders** option in the mobile menu. Click the **Create** button to enter a new order. Select an existing customer and click **Next**. Select some items using the **Add** link and click the **Place Order** button. The *Order Summary* page, as illustrated in Figure 10-10, should come up displaying a summary of the most recent order. Click the **Back To Orders** button to move back to the main orders listing where you'll see this order added to the list. Create an order using the *New Customer* option.

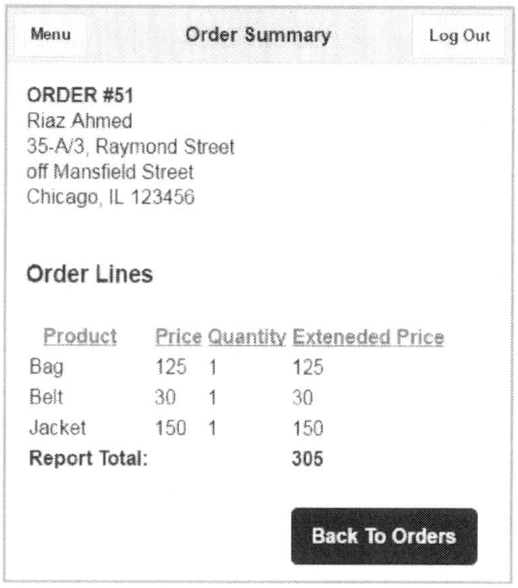

Figure 10-10

Menu   Order Summary   Log Out

ORDER #51
Riaz Ahmed
35-A/3, Raymond Street
off Mansfield Street
Chicago, IL 123456

Order Lines

Product	Price	Quantity	Extended Price
Bag	125	1	125
Belt	30	1	30
Jacket	150	1	150
Report Total:			305

Back To Orders

In the previous sections, you created interfaces to add a new order. What if you want to correct a mistake in an order or what will you do to get rid of an entire order? In this section, you will create two pages (Page 206 and 207) to perform orders modification and delete operations.

1. Create a new mobile page and select the **Form** option followed by the **Form on a Table** option.

2. Set the following properties on the *Page Attributes* screen and click **Next**.

Property	Value
Page Number	206
Page Name	Maintain Order
Page Mode	Normal
Branch Here on Submit	205
Cancel and Go To Page	205

3. Set *Navigation Preference* to **Identify an existing navigation menu entry for this page**, select **Orders** for *Existing Navigation Menu Entry*, and click **Next**.

4. Accept the default *Table/View Owner* on the *Source* screen. For *Table/View Name*, select the **DEMO_ORDERS** table. Select all table columns, and click **Next** to proceed.

5. Select the **Managed by Database (ROWID)** option for *Primary Key Type* and click **Create** to finish the wizard.

10.13.1 Modify Process, Region and Create Items

1. On the *Rendering* tab, expand *Pre-Rendering | After Header | Processes*, and click the **Fetch Row from DEMO_ORDERS** process. Set its *Primary Key Column* and *Primary Key Item* properties to **ROWID** and **P206_ROWID**, respectively. For an explanation of this step, see Section 10.8.3.

2. On the *Rendering* tab, click the **Maintain Order** region. Set its *Title* to **Order #&P206_ORDER_ID.** and *Template* to **Region (With Title Bar)**. By setting this title and template, you will be able to see the order number.

3. Right-click the *Items* folder under THE *Order #&P206_ORDER_ID* region and select **Create Page Item**. Set the following attributes for this hidden item, which is being created to store the row ID of an order on Page 206. Note that a row ID will be forwarded to this item by the *Link Target* set in Section 10.7 step 7. After creating this item, drag and drop it at the top in the *Items* folder.

Property	Value
Name	P206_ROWID
Type	Hidden
Value Protected	Yes
Type (*under Source*)	Database Column
Database Column	ROWID

4. Right-click the *P206_CUSTOMER_ID* item and select *Create Page Item*. This action will add a new item just after the selected item. Set the following properties for the new item, which is being added to display customer information as display-only text. Note that when you enter the following query, you may get an invalid query error message. Save the page by click the Save button to get rid of this message. If you keep the default *Yes* value for *Escape Special Characters* property, the customer information appears on a single line with <br/> tags. The *Save Session State* property is set to *No* to clear the value of this item from the session state when the page gets submitted.

Property	Value
Name	P206_CUSTOMER_INFO
Type	Display Only
Label	Customer
Save Session State	No
Type (*Source*)	SQL Query (return single value)
SQL Query	select apex_escape.html(cust_first_name) || ' ' || apex_escape.html(cust_last_name) || ':' || apex_escape.html(cust_street_address1) || decode(cust_street_address2, null, null, ' ' || apex_escape.html(cust_street_address2)) || ',' || apex_escape.html(cust_city) || ',' || apex_escape.html(cust_state) || ' ' || apex_escape.html(cust_postal_code) from demo_customers where customer_id = :P206_CUSTOMER_ID
Escape Special Characters	No

10.13.2 Modify Items

Edit the following items individually and set the corresponding properties shown under each item.

P206_ORDER_ID

Property	Value
Type	Hidden
Session State Protection	Unrestricted

P206_CUSTOMER_ID

Property	Value
Type	Hidden

P206_ORDER_TOTAL

Property	Value
Type	Display Only
Format Mask	$5,234.10

P206_ORDER_TIMESTAMP

Property	Value
Label	Order Date
Format Mask	YYYY-MM-DD

P206_USER_NAME

Property	Value
Type	Select List
Label	Sales Rep
Type (*List of Values*)	SQL Query
SQL Query	select distinct user_name d, user_name r from demo_orders union select upper(:APP_USER) d, upper(:APP_USER) r from dual order by 1
Display Extra Values	No
Display Null Value	No

P206_TAGS

Property	Value
Type	Text Field

10.13.3 Modify Buttons

Set the following properties for **Delete**, **Save**, and **Create** buttons.

Property	Value
Button Position	Bottom of Region
Horizontal Alignment	Left

10.13.4 Create Region – Order Items

This region is created to display, modify, delete, and add line item details.

1. Right-click the *Regions* node and select **Create Region**. Set the following properties for the new region. In the *Page Items to Submit* property you enter page or application items to be set into session state when the region is refreshed by a partial page refresh. For multiple items, separate each item name with a comma. You can manually type in the names or pick items from the list of available items. If you pick from the list and there is already text entered, then a comma is placed at the end of the existing text, followed by the item name returned from the list.

Property	Value
Title	Order Items
Type	List View

SQL Query	select oi.order_item_id, pi.product_name,
	        oi.unit_price, oi.quantity,
	        to_char((oi.unit_price * oi.quantity),
	        'FML999G999G999G999G990D00')
	        extended_price,
	        pi.product_id, pi.product_image product_image
	from DEMO_ORDER_ITEMS oi,
	        DEMO_PRODUCT_INFO pi
	where oi.ORDER_ID = :P206_ORDER_ID and
	        oi.product_id = pi.product_id

Page Items to Submit	P206_ORDER_ID
Template	Region (With Title Bar)

2. Click the **Attributes** node under the *Order Items* region and set the following attributes. You went through all these attributes in a previous section. The only one new to this scenario is the *Counter Column*, which specifies the database column containing the value to be displayed in a count bubble, as shown in Figure 10-11. In that figure price for each item is displayed in a count bubble.

Property	Value
Advanced Formatting	*Checked*
Show Image	*Checked*

Text Formatting	`<h3>&PRODUCT_NAME.</h3>`
	`<p>`
	`<strong>Unit Price:</strong>`
	`$&UNIT_PRICE. /`
	`<strong>Quantity:</strong>&QUANTITY.`
	`</p>`

Counter Column	EXTENDED_PRICE
Image Type	Image stored in BLOB
Image BLOB Column	PRODUCT_IMAGE
Image Primary Key Column 1	PRODUCT_ID
Link Target	Type = Page in this application Page = 207 Name = P207_ORDER_ITEM_ID Value = &ORDER_ITEM_ID. Clear Cache = 207

10.13.5 Create Button

Right-click the *Order Items* region and select **Create Button**. Set the following properties for the new button, which is being created to add more products to an existing order via a new page–Page 207.

Property	Value
Button Name	ADD_ITEM
Label	Add Item
Button Position	Bottom of Region
Horizontal Alignment	Left
Action	Redirect to Page in this Application
Target	Type = Page in this application Page = 207 Name = P207_ORDER_ID Value = &P206_ORDER_ID. Clear Cache = 207

10.13.6 Create Link

Page 206 is ready for a test-run. But before that, you have to create a link on Page 205. This link will call Page 206 to display an order.

1. Call **Page 205** in the Page Designer.

2. Expand the *Columns* folder and click the **ORDER_ID** column to set the following properties:

Property	Value
Type (*under Settings*)	Link
Target	Type = Page in this application Page = 206 Name = P206_ROWID Value = &ROWID. Clear Cache = 206
Link Text	&ORDER_ID.

Test Your Work

Once again, click the **Orders** option in the mobile menu. In the orders report page, click any order number link to bring up Page 206, as illustrated in Figure 10-11. Using this page, you can delete an order and can also modify Date, Sales Rep, and Tag values. Make some changes in these fields and click the **Apply Changes** button. Call this record again to see the modifications. You created this page on a single table (*DEMO_ORDERS*), so the wizard added processes to fetch and save data from and to that table only. You also manually added a List View region (*Order Items*) to display details of the selected order. For mobile version, you have to create a separate page to add or remove items to and from an existing order. Moreover, this page will also allow you to change a product and quantity. The next section guides you on this.

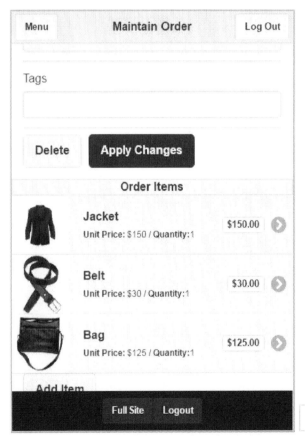

Figure 10-11

1. Create a new mobile page. On the initial wizard screen, select the **Form** option followed by the **Form on a Table** option.

2. Set the following attributes on the *Page Attributes* screen and click **Next**.

Property	Value
Page Number	207
Page Name	Maintain Order Items
Page Mode	Normal
Branch Here on Submit	206
Cancel and Go To Page	206

3. Set *Navigation Preference* to **Identify an existing navigation menu entry for this page**, select **Orders** for *Existing Navigation Menu Entry*, and click **Next**.

4. Accept the default *Table/View Owner* on the *Source* screen. For *Table/View Name*, select the **DEMO_ORDER_ITEMS** table. Ensure that all the table columns are selected. Click **Next** to proceed.

5. Fill in the *Form Attributes* screen as illustrated in the following figure and click the **Create** button to finish the wizard.

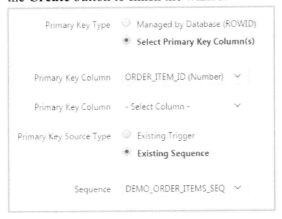

6. In the Page Designer, click the *Maintain Order Items* region and set its *Title* to **Order #&P207_ORDER_ID.**.

7. Set *Button Position* and *Horizontal Alignment* properties to **Bottom of Region** and **Left**, respectively, for all four buttons.

8. Set the *Type* property of the *P207_ORDER_ID* item to **Hidden**.

9. Modify the **P207_PRODUCT_ID** item using the following properties. In this step you're using a technique to eliminate inclusion of products to the list already on the order. A cascading LOV means that the current item's list of values should be refreshed if the value of another item on this page gets changed. It receives a

comma separated list of page items to trigger the refresh. You then use these page items in the WHERE clause of the SQL statement. Suppose you have page items for Car Make and Model. Model would identify Car Make as the *Cascading LOV Parent Item* so that whenever Car Make is changed, the LOV for Model would be refreshed. In the current scenario, the ORDER_ID item represents Car Make, while ORDER_ITEM_ID acts as Car Model, which gets refreshed with each order.

Property	Value
Type	Select List
Label	Product
Type (*List of Values*)	SQL Query

SQL Query	select product_name d, product_id r
	from demo_product_info pi
	where pi.product_avail = 'Y' and
	    pi.product_id not in
	      (select oi.product_id
	      from demo_order_items oi
	      where oi.order_id = **:P207_ORDER_ID** and
	        oi.order_item_id <>
	        nvl(**:P207_ORDER_ITEM_ID**,0))
	order by 1

Display Extra Values	No
Display Null Value	Yes
Null Display Value	- Select -
Cascading LOV Parent Item(s)	P207_ORDER_ID,P207_ORDER_ITEM_ID

10. Modify the **P207_QUANTITY** item as follows. It shows how to declare static display and return values (from 1 to 10, where each pair is separated by a comma), to receive ordered quantity. The technique shows how to apply minimum and maximum input limit.

Property	Value
Type	Select List
Type (*List of Values*)	Static Values
Static Values	STATIC2:1;1,2;2,3;3,4;4,5;5,6;6,7;7,8;8,9;9,10;10
Display Extra Values	No

11. If you run the page at this stage, you'll notice that after selecting a product the *Unit Price* field doesn't show anything. To automatically populate this field with the corresponding price, you need to create a dynamic action. Click the *Dynamic Actions* tab. Right-click the *Change* folder and select **Create Dynamic Action**. Click the *New* node and set the following properties. These settings inform Oracle APEX to fire the dynamic action when the user changes a product.

Property	Value
Name	Get List Price
Event	Change
Selection Type	Item(s)
Item(s)	P207_PRODUCT_ID

Now, click the **Show** node (under the *True* node) and set the following properties. The *Set Value* action is fired when you change a product to fetch the list price of the selected product (via the SQL Statement) and store it in a page item – P207_UNIT_PRICE.

Property	Value
Action	Set Value
Set Type	SQL Statement
SQL Statement	select list_price from demo_product_info where product_id = :P207_PRODUCT_ID
Items to Submit	P207_PRODUCT_ID
Selection Type	Item(s)
Item(s)	P207_UNIT_PRICE

That's it! Now you can delete or add items from and to orders. Click any order number on Page 205. On the *Maintain Order* page, click the **Add Item** button. Select a product from the *Product* list and a value from the *Quantity* list–the *Unit Price* field gets populated with the price of the selected product using the *Get List Price* dynamic action. Click the **Create** button to add the product. The product will appear on the order. In the *Maintain Order* page, click the newly added product. On the *Maintain Order Items* page, select a different product and quantity, and then click the **Apply Changes** button. The previous product will be replaced with the new one. Click the new product and then click the **Delete** button. The product will vanish from the order.

Display Reports on Smartphones

10.15 List of Reports Page – Page 208

This is the main reports navigation page for smartphone platform carrying a list of available reports. It is almost similar to the one you went through in the desktop version.

1. Create a **Blank Page** using the *Mobile User Interface* option.

2. Enter **208** for *Page Number*, **Reports** for *Name*, select **Normal** for *Page Mode*, and click **Next**.

3. On the *Navigation Menu* screen, set *Navigation Preference* to **Identify an existing navigation menu entry for this page**, and set *Existing Navigation Menu Entry* to **Reports**. Click **Next**.

4. Click **Finish** to end the wizard.

5. Create a region on this page and set the following properties for it. The region will carry the *Mobile Reports* list, created in section 10.4.3.

Property	Value
Title	Reports
Type	List
List	Mobile Reports

10.16 Customer Orders Report - Page 209

The reports you'll be creating in the following sections are the same you created earlier in Chapter 8. Starting with the Customer Orders Report. Let's see how graphical reports are created for smartphones.

1. Create another **Blank Page** using the *Mobile* Interface. Set its number to **209**, enter **Customer Orders** for its name, and select **Normal** for *Page Mode*. Select **Reports** for navigation menu entry.

2. Create a new region on this page and set the following properties:

Property	Value
Title	Customer Orders
Type	Chart

3. Click the **Attributes** folder under the *Customer Orders* chart region to set the following properties. *Bar* charts are useful for comparing values across categories or over time. The *Horizontal* value displays the data items of the chart horizontally. The *Yes* value set for the *Stack* property stacks the data items. We selected the *Bottom* position on the chart to show the legend. The *Hide and Show Behavior* is performed when you click a legend item. For example, deselecting a legend item will hide its associated data series on the chart. By selecting the *Rescale* value, the chart axes will rescale as the minimum and maximum values of the visible data increase or decrease. This is useful for series with largely varying values.

Property	Value
Type	Bar
Orientation	Horizontal
Stack	Yes
Height	300
Title (*Under Legend*)	Categories
Position (*Under Legend*)	Bottom
Hide and Show Behavior	Rescale

4. Click the **New** node under *Series* to set the following properties. We selected the *CATEGORY* column, which is used for defining multi-series dynamic query. The *CUSTOMER_NAME* column is used for defining the label(s) of the x-axis on the chart, while the SALES column is selected to be used for defining the value on this chart on the y-axis.

Property	Value
Name	Series 1
Source Type	SQL Query

SQL Query	select c.customer_id,
	    c.cust_last_name||', '||c.cust_first_name Customer_Name,
	    p.category, sum (oi.quantity * oi.unit_price) Sales
	from demo_customers c, demo_orders o, demo_order_items oi, demo_product_info p
	where c.customer_id = o.customer_id and
	    o.order_id = oi.order_id and oi.product_id = p.product_id
	group by c.rowid, c.customer_id, c.cust_last_name, c.cust_first_name, p.category
	order by c.cust_last_name

Series Name	CATEGORY
Label	CUSTOMER_NAME
Value	SALES
Type (Link)	Redirect to Page in this Application
Target Type	Type = Page in this Application Page = 202 Name = P202_CUSTOMER_ID Value = &CUSTOMER_ID. Clear Cache = 202

Save the page. Access the mobile application and click **Menu \| Reports**. The mobile reports page (Page 208) will come up displaying a list of reports. Click the **Customer Orders** option in the reports list to see an output similar to Figure 10-12.

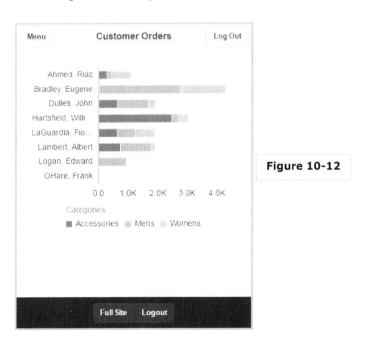

Figure 10-12

285

This report was also created earlier in the desktop version.

1. Create another **Blank Page** using the *Mobile* Interface. Set its number to **210** and enter **Sales by Category and Product** for its name. Select **Reports** for navigation menu entry.

2. Create a new region on this page and set the following properties:

Property	Value
Title	Sales by Category
Type	Chart
Template	Region (With Title Bar)

3. Click the **Attributes** folder under the *Sales by Category* chart region and set the following attributes:

Property	Value
Type	Pie
Position (*Legend*)	Bottom
Hide and Show Behavior	Rescale

4. Click the **New** node under *Series* and set the following properties.

Property	Value
Source Type	SQL Query

SQL Query	select p.category label,
	        sum(o.order_total) total_sales
	from demo_orders o,
	        demo_order_items oi,
	        demo_product_info p
	where o.order_id = oi.order_id and
	        oi.product_id = p.product_id
	group by category order by 2 desc

Label	LABEL
Value	TOTAL_SALES
Show (*Label*)	Yes
Position (*Label*)	Outside Slice

5. Create another region and set the following properties:

Property	Value
Title	Sales by Product
Type	Chart
Template	Region (With Title Bar)

6. Click the **Attributes** folder under the *Sales by Product* chart region and set the following properties:

Property	Value
Type	Bar
Orientation	Horizontal

7. Click the **New** node under *Series* and set the following properties.

Property	Value
Source Type	SQL Query
SQL Query	select p.rowid link, p.product_name||' [$'||p.list_price||']' product, SUM(oi.quantity * oi.unit_price) sales from demo_order_items oi, demo_product_info p where oi.product_id = p.product_id group by p.rowid, p.product_id, p.product_name, p.list_price order by sales desc
Label	PRODUCT
Value	SALES
Type (*Link*)	Redirect to Page in this Application
Target	Type = Page in this Application Page = 204 Name = P204_ROWID Value = &LINK. Clear Cache = 204

8. Click the **x** node under *Axes* and enter **Product** for *Title*. Then, click the **y** node, and type **Sales** for its *Title*.

9. Save your work and access this page from the second option in the *Reports* menu to see the output as illustrated in Figure 10-13.

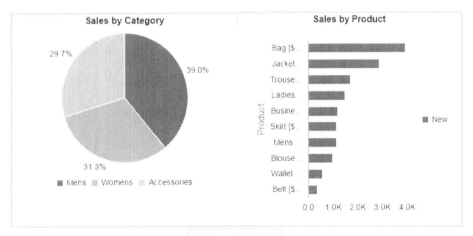

Figure 10-13

1. Create a new mobile page.

2. Click the **Calendar** icon .

3. Fill in the next couple of page according to the following table and click **Next**.

Property	Value
Page Number	211
Page Name	Order Calendar
Page Mode	Normal
Navigation Preference	Identify an existing menu entry...
Existing Navigation Menu Entry	Reports

4. On the *Source* screen, select the second option **SQL Query** and type the following query in the *Enter Region Source* box. Then, click **Next** to move on.

```
select order_id,
       (select cust_first_name||' '||cust_last_name from demo_customers c
        where c.customer_id = o.customer_id )
       ||' ['||to_char(order_total,'FML999G999G999G999G990D00')||']'
       customer, order_timestamp
from demo_orders o
```

5. Set the properties on the next screen as follows. The *Start Date Column* attribute specifies which column is used as the date to place an entry on the calendar, while the *Display Column* specifies the column to be displayed on the calendar.

Save and run the page. The small blue circles in the date columns indicate some orders. Clicking the circled date will show the order under the calendar.

That's it! You have successfully created the mobile version of your sales web application. In the remaining chapters of this book, you will set up a security module for your application.

Figure 10-14

288

Chapter 11

Define Application Segments for Security

The Application Segments module is a hierarchical representation of all the segments included in the application. Just like a site map created for web sites, it is a tree view of our application, which is being created to implement the application security. As illustrated in Figure 11-1, there are three main components in the application you would like to apply security to. These are: Menus (including main and submenus), Pages, and Items (such as buttons and select lists). The fourth one (App) is there just to identify the application. It is the root node, which is used to distinguish segments of multiple applications. After creating all the application segments here, you will use them in the next chapter to enforce application access rules. It's a flexible module and is designed in such a way to accommodate future application enhancements.

Figure 11-1
Application
Segments
Hierarchy

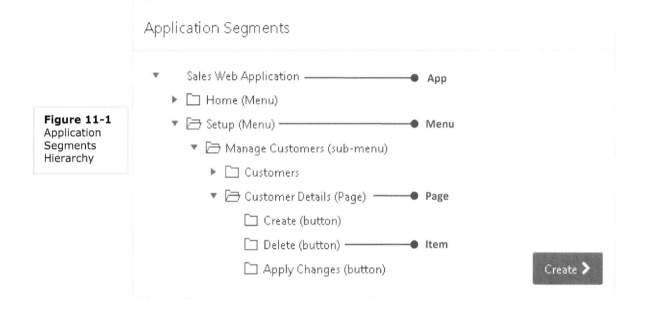

11.1 Create Database Objects

In this section, you will create three database objects (table, sequence, and trigger) to populate application segments' data. These objects will be created interactively in one go via a wizard. The table object (*APP_SEGMENTS*) will hold actual data, while the trigger object (*BI_APP_SEGMENTS*) will generate primary key values using a sequence object (*APP_SEGMENTS_SEQ*). Execute the following steps to create these objects.

1. Click **SQL Workshop | Object Browser**.

2. To your right in the *Object Browser*, click the **Create** menu and select **Table** from the available options to launch the *Create Table* wizard.

3. Enter **APP_SEGMENTS** for the *Table Name*. Fill in the column attributes as illustrated in the following figure and click **Next**. For further details on creating database tables, see *Chapter 7 Creating Tables* in my free e-book.

4. On the *Primary Key* screen, select the options as illustrated in the following figure. In this step, you choose how you would like the primary key to be populated and identify the column, which is to be used as the primary key. As usual, you have chosen to populate the primary key using a sequence object. But this time the wizard will create a sequence along with a trigger on the table that will populate the selected primary key column–SEGMENTID. After making you selections, click **Next** to proceed.

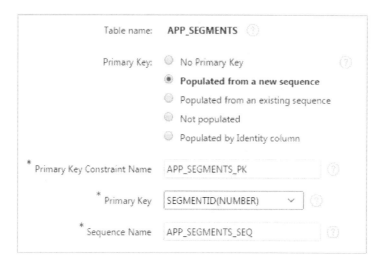

5. The table doesn't have a parental relation with any existing table, so leave the defaults on the *Foreign Key* screen and click **Next**.

6. You are not going to create any Check or Unique constraints either, so move on by clicking **Next**.

7. On the *Confirm* screen, click the **Create Table** button to end the wizard. You will be taken back to the *Object Browser* interface, where you will see the structure of the APP_SEGMENTS table. Take a moment to see the objects created by the wizard. In the upper-left corner of the Object Browser is a select list that contains the objects in the current schema. Click this list and select **Sequences**. You will see a sequence named APP_SEGMENTS_SEQ created by the wizard. Now, select **Triggers** from this list. You will see a trigger named BI_APP_SEGMENTS (BI stands for *Before Insert*). The trigger will fire before you insert a new segment record to generate the primary key value. Click this trigger and then click the **Code** tab to see the auto-generated code for the trigger, which uses the APP_SEGMENTS_SEQ to fill in the SEGMENTID primary key. With these backend objects in place, you are now ready to create the frontend interface for the module.

11.2 Create LOVs

Create two *static* LOVs from *scratch* using the following tables. The values included in these LOVs will be utilized in segment creation form to identify the type of segments and the roles performed by page items, respectively.

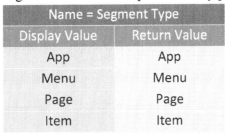

Name = Segment Type	
Display Value	Return Value
App	App
Menu	Menu
Page	Page
Item	Item

Name = Item Role	
Display Value	Return Value
Create	Create
Modify	Modify
Delete	Delete

11.3 Create Segments' Setup Pages

Execute the following steps to create two *Desktop* user interface pages for this setup. On the first wizard screen, select **Report**, and on the next screen select **Report with Form on Table**.

1. On the *Page Attributes* wizard screen, select **Interactive Report** for *Report Type* and set the remaining attributes for the two pages as illustrated in the following figure. Click **Next** to proceed.

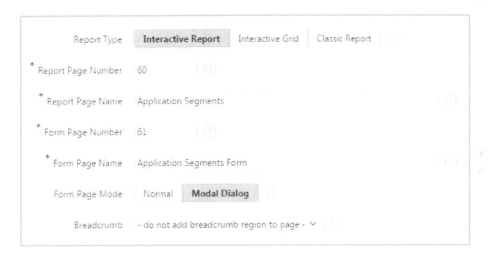

2. On the *Navigation Menu* screen, set *Navigation Preference* to **Identify an existing navigation menu entry for this page**, set *Existing Navigation Menu Entry* to **Administration**, and click **Next**.

3. Accept the default *Table/View Owner* on the *Source* screen. For *Table/View Name*, select the **APP_SEGMENTS** table. Select all columns from the table and click **Next** to proceed.

4. Fill in the *Form Page* screen as illustrated in the following figure and click the **Create** button to finish the wizard. Note that the Sequence (APP_SEGMENTS _SEQ) you picked up here was created in Section 11.1 by the *Create Table* wizard.

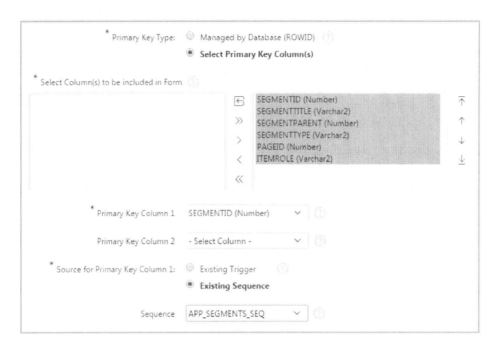

Amend the segment form (Page 61) items as follows. The P61_SEGMENTPARENT item is being transformed into a pop-up LOV. It will display title and type columns from the segments table to select a parent for a new entry. Note that *Item* is the last level in the segments hierarchy and doesn't have any child, so it is not going to act as a parent and is thus excluded from the LOV using a WHERE clause condition in the SQL Query. Do not forget to provide suitable **labels** to these items–see Figure 11-2. **Save** your work after incorporating all these amendments.

Action	Property	Value
Modify Items Title, Parent, & Type	Template	Required
	Value Required	Yes
Modify Item P61_SEGMENTPARENT	Type	Popup LOV
	LOV Type	SQL Query
	SQL Query	SELECT segmentTitle||' ('||segmentType||')' d, segmentID r FROM app_segments WHERE segmentType != 'Item' ORDER BY pageID,segmentID,segmentParent
	Default Type	Static Value
	Static Value	0
Modify Item P61_SEGMENTTYPE	Type	Select List
	LOV Type	Shared Component
	List Of Values	SEGMENT TYPE
Modify Item P61_PAGEID	Width	4
	Maximum Length	4
Modify Item P61_ITEMROLE	Type	Select List
	LOV Type	Shared Component
	List Of Values	ITEM ROLE

11.5 Add a Tree Region

Right now the report page (Page 60) contains an interactive report region to display all segments in a matrix report. In this section, you will change this appearance to display all the segments in a tree view, as illustrated in Figure 11-1. First, **delete** the interactive report region (**Report 1**) from page 60. Then, add a new region to Page 60 and set its *Type* to **Tree**. Set the properties listed in the following table and **save** your work. The SQL Query creates a tree, which specifies a hierarchical relationship by identifying the SEGMENTID and SEGMENTPARENT columns in the APP_SEGMENTS table. Recall that you used a similar query in Chapter 8 Section 8.8 to produce a Product Order Tree.

Property	Value
Title	Application Segments
Type	Tree
SQL Query	select case when connect_by_isleaf = 1 then 0 when level = 1 then 1 else -1 end as status, level, segmenttitle as title, NULL as icon, segmentid as value, 'View' as tooltip, apex_util.prepare_url('f?p='||:APP_ID||':61:'||:APP_SESSION|| '::NO::P61_SEGMENTID:'||segmentid) As link from app_segments start with segmentparent = 0 connect by prior segmentid = segmentparent order siblings by segmentid

11.6 Add Button

Add a button to the *Application Segments* region. It will be used to create a new application segment.

Property	Value
Button Name	CREATE
Label	Create
Region	Application Segments
Button Position	Copy
Button Template	Text with Icon
Hot	Yes
Icon CSS Classes	fa-chevron-right
Action	Redirect to Page in this Application
Page	61 (*in Link Builder*)
Clear Cache	61 (*in Link Builder*)

Save Page 60. After saving the page call Page 61 to add a couple of validations, as follows.

In Page 61, go to the *Processing* tab, right-click the **Validating** node, and select **Create Validation** from the context menu. Set the following properties for this new validation. Note that the first validation (*Check Segment*) will be effective after completing Chapter 12, because the table GROUPS_DETAIL used in the SELECT query will be created in that chapter. If you get an error for this table, comment out the SELECT statement (using double hyphen --) for the time being. This validation will prevent the deletion of application segments whose access privileges have been granted to a users group–see Chapter 12.

Property	Value
Name	Check Segment
Type	PL/SQL Function (returning Error Text)

PL/SQL Function	declare
	  Vutilized number := 0;
	  Verrortext varchar2(60);
	begin
	  select count(*) into Vutilized from **groups_detail**
	  where segmentId=:P61_SEGMENTID;
	  if Vutilized > 0 then
	    Verrortext := 'Cannot delete this segment because it is utilized';
	  end if;
	  return rtrim(Verrortext);
	end;

When Button Pressed	DELETE

Create another validation as follows. This one will prevent the deletion of an application segment with one or more child segments. For example, you cannot delete the Home menu entry if it has the Home page and Add button child entries.

Property	Value
Name	Check Child Segment
Type	PL/SQL Function (returning Error Text)

PL/SQL Function	declare
	  VchildExist number := 0;
	  Verrortext varchar2(60);
	begin
	  select count(*) into VchildExist from app_segments
	  where segmentParent=:P61_SEGMENTID;
	  if VchildExist > 0 then
	    Verrortext := 'Cannot delete, this segment it has child entries';
	  end if;
	  return rtrim(Verrortext);
	end;

When Button Pressed	DELETE

Everything is set. Test your work by calling the main *Application Segments* page from *Administration | Application Segments* menu. Click the **Create** button and enter the following values individually one after the other in the segments form. After clicking the *Create* button on the segments form, you are brought back to the main page to display the created segments in a hierarchical tree view. If you don't see these segments, click the browser's Reload button.

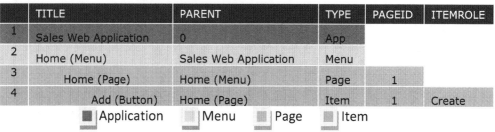

	TITLE	PARENT	TYPE	PAGEID	ITEMROLE
1	Sales Web Application	0	App		
2	Home (Menu)	Sales Web Application	Menu		
3	Home (Page)	Home (Menu)	Page	1	
4	Add (Button)	Home (Page)	Item	1	Create

■ Application ▢ Menu ▢ Page ▢ Item

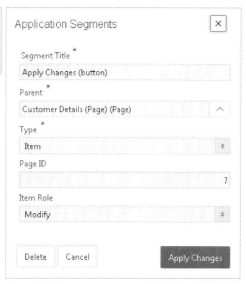

Figure 11-2
Application
Segments
Input Form

The first entry will create the application root, so no parent will be assigned to it. Recall that you assigned the default value (zero) for the parent item in section 11.4. The second main menu entry will come under the application root. The *Page* entry defined on serial number 3 will be placed under the Home Menu along with the corresponding page number. The last level of our application hierarchy belongs to page items (serial number 4). The Home page contains three buttons to add records, so the Add (Button) item is placed under page 1 to represent all three. When you mark the *Type* of an entry as *Item*, then you must also specify its role. Roles will be used in a subsequent chapter to implement application security. This list is a subset of a comprehensive list that covers all the application segments. You can find this list in **application_segments.xlsx** file in the book code's Chapter 11 folder. Open this file and add all application segments to complete this chapter. Note that it is not necessary to follow the defined sequence while creating new segments. You can add an entry to any level, any time. The important thing is to select the correct parent to place a new entry under it.

The preferred way to test this module is to feed each and every entry provided in the *application_segments.xlsx* file manually. However, if you are sick of the data entry work, then SQL Workshop's *Data Workshop* utility is your best resort that not only allows you to load data from Text, XML, and Spreadsheet files, but also provides you with an *Unload* option, using which you can export data from an Oracle schema. In this section, I'll guide you on how to load complete data from a spreadsheet file to the APP_SEGMENTS table. Here's how you can do this.

1. Open **SQL Workshop** | **SQL Commands**. Enter the following statement and click the **Run** button to execute it. Note that this statement is executed to delete all existing records you entered manually using the instructions mentioned in the previous section. Skip this step if the table doesn't have any record.

    DELETE FROM app_segments

2. To access the Data Load/Unload page, click **SQL Workshop** | **Utilities** | **Data Workshop**.

3. In the *Data Load* section, click **Spreadsheet Data**. Using this option you can copy and paste spreadsheet data directly into the Load Data Wizard.

4. On the *Target and Method* wizard screen, select **Existing table** for *Load To*, **Copy and paste** for *Load from*, and click **Next**.

5. On *Table Owner and Name* screen, accept the default *Table Owner*, and select **APP_SEGMENTS** table from the *Table Name* list. This is the table into which you'll load the data. Click **Next**.

6. Double click **load_application_segments.xlsx** file (located in BookCode/Chapter11 folder) to open in Microsoft Excel. Select all rows and columns from this spreadsheet carrying data (including column headings) and press **Ctrl+C** to copy this information to the clipboard. Do not select any empty rows, because selecting such rows may cause errors in the data load process. Switch back to Oracle APEX and press **Ctrl+V** to paste these records into the *Data* text area. Remove the comma appearing in the *Separator* box, which is there to handle comma separated values. Scroll within the screen to ensure the *First row contains column names* box is checked. Click **Next**.

7. On the final screen, the wizard parses the pasted data and matches the column names using the first row of the spreadsheet data with the column names of the APP_SEGMENTS table. If it fails to match column names, it leaves the mapping to you that you can easily perform using the drop-down lists provided at the top. Once you are satisfied with this matching, click the **Load Data** button to finish the process. After loading the data, you see the *Spreadsheet Repository* page, which displays the status of the imported

Spreadsheet data. The following figure shows that 41 rows were loaded into the table and zero errors occurred during this process. Navigate to the **Object Browser** interface, select the **APP_SEGMENTS** table, and click the **Data** tab to browse the loaded data.

8. Run the *Application Segments* page from *Administration | Application Segments* menu. You should see all segments' records. Expand **Home (Menu) | Home (Page)**, and click the **Add (Button)** entry. You will see that this button is properly associated with its page (*Home* in the *Parent* field), it is marked as a page item (*Type* field), shows the correct page ID, and has been assigned the *Create* role.

9. One last step. Click the **Create** button and try to add a new segment entry– you won't. When you try to save this new entry, you get *unique constraint (APP_SEGMENTS_PK) violated* error. This is because the sequence (APP_SEGMENTS_SEQ) generates a number for the SEGMENTID column that already exists in the table due to data loading. To get rid of this situation, the easiest way is to drop and re-create the sequence with the next available number. Execute the following two statements *individually* in *SQL Workshop | SQL Commands*. Because we have already loaded 41 records to the table, we are going to re-create the sequence starting from 42. After executing the following two statements, you can proceed with the module by adding new records.

DROP SEQUENCE app_segments_seq

CREATE SEQUENCE app_segments_seq START WITH 42 INCREMENT BY 1 CACHE 20

Summary

In this chapter, you laid the foundation of your application security that will be used to control application access in subsequent chapters. In the next chapter, you will set up user groups who will be granted application access privileges via the segments created in this chapter.

Chapter 12

Create Groups and Assign
Application Privileges

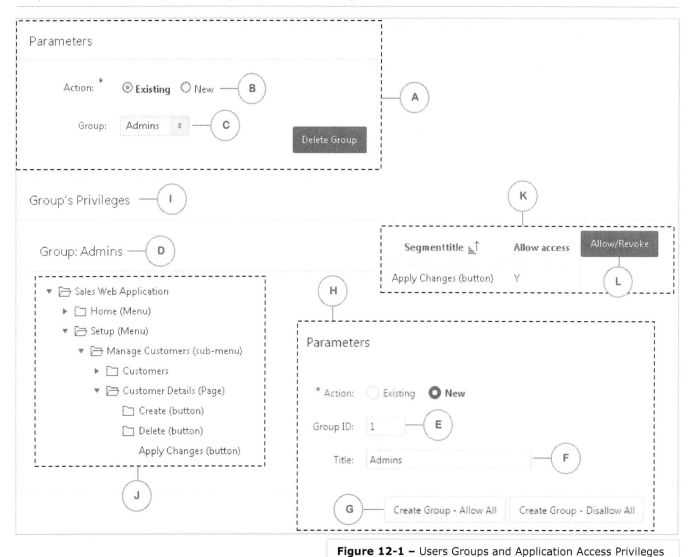

Figure 12-1 – Users Groups and Application Access Privileges

In the previous chapter, you laid the foundation of your application's security that will be imposed on menus, pages, and page items. In this chapter, you will establish a setup to create user groups, who will be assigned application rights. Allocating application rights to individual users is a tedious activity and it's not recommended as well. Instead, you create a few groups and assign application privileges to these groups. Users are created afterward and are associated with respective groups. This way, users inherit application rights from the group to which they belong. For example, to handle the security of an application being used by a staff of more than 100 employees, comprising managers and data entry clerks, you will create just two groups (Managers and Clerks) with different privileges. Any changes made to the privileges of these groups will be automatically inherited to all associated users.

In this setup you will be using two tables. The master table (GROUPS_MASTER) will hold IDs and titles of groups, while the details table (GROUPS_DETAIL) will contain all application privileges (specified in the segments setup) for each group. On this occasion, you are creating tables using SQL's CREATE TABLE command.

Go to **SQL Workshop | SQL Commands**, enter the following two statements individually, and click the **Run** button. The successful execution of these commands is indicated by the message *"Table Created"* in the *Results* tab. You can find these statements in the book code.

```
CREATE TABLE groups_master
(
groupID NUMBER(4), groupTitle VARCHAR2(25),
CONSTRAINT groups_pk PRIMARY KEY (groupID) ENABLE
)
```

```
CREATE TABLE groups_detail
(
groupID NUMBER(4) CONSTRAINT fk_Group_Details REFERENCES
groups_master(groupID), segmentID NUMBER CONSTRAINT fk_user_group
REFERENCES app_segments(segmentID), segmentParent NUMBER, segmentType
VARCHAR2(4), pageID NUMBER(4), itemRole VARCHAR2(10), allow_access
VARCHAR2(1)
)
```

12.2 Page & Parameters Region

Groups will be created using just one application page. This page will carry two main regions: *Parameters* and *Group's Privileges*. In the Parameters region, you indicate whether you are creating a new group or are willing to modify an existing one. Based on this selection, you'll be provided with the appropriate interface. For example, if you're trying to modify or delete an existing group, then you'll select the *Existing* option, followed by a group from the provided list, to show the privileges of the selected group in the second region. When you select the *New* option, the tree view will hide and a new interface will be presented to create a new group. This module is to be created using a blank page. So let's begin.

1. Create a **Blank Page** for *Desktop User Interface* and set the following properties for it:

Property	Value
Page Number	62
Name	User Groups
Page Mode	Normal
Breadcrumb	do not use breadcrumb...
Navigation Preference	Identify an existing navigation menu entry for this page
Existing Navigation Menu Entry	Administration

2. When you are in the Page Designer, create a region of *Static Content* type, and enter **Parameters** for its *Title*. Also, set *Column Span* attribute to **4** To make the region four columns wide. This region is marked as (A) in Figure 12-1.

3. Add a page item to the *Parameters* region and set the following properties. The item is marked as (B) in Figure 12-1 and its purpose will be discussed in the *Test Your Work* section at the end of this chapter.

Property	Value
Name	P62_EXISTINGNEW
Type	Radio Group
Label	Action:
Number of Columns	2
Page Action on Selection	Submit Page (*to show/hide Group's Privileges region*)
Template	Required
Type (*LOV*)	Static Values
Static Values	STATIC:New;NEW,Existing;EXISTING
Display Null Value	No
Type (*Default*)	Static Value
Static Value	EXISTING

4. Add another page item to the *Parameters* region with the following properties. It is added to display existing groups in a Select List and is marked as (C) in Figure 12-1.

Property	Value
Name	P62_GROUPID1
Type	Select List
Label	Group:
Page Action on Selection	**Submit Page** (*to refresh Selected Segment region*)
Type (*LOV*)	SQL Query
SQL Query	SELECT DISTINCT groupTitle d, groupID r FROM groups_master ORDER BY groupID
Type (*Server-side Condition*)	Item = Value
Item	P62_EXISTINGNEW
Value	EXISTING (*the list is displayed only when EXISTING option is on*)

5. Create a hidden page item as follows. The value held in this item will be used in section 12.8 to set group name as the title (D) for the Tree region created there. The *Used* property lets you select which value takes precedence, the value from session state or the item source value. In the current scenario, you opted to always replace the session state value with the value derived from the SQL Query. That way, the value of this page item is refreshed whenever you select a different group from the list created in step 4.

Property	Value
Name	P62_GROUPTITLE1
Type	Hidden
Type (*Source*)	SQL Query (return single value)
SQL Query	SELECT groupTitle FROM groups_master WHERE groupID=:P62_GROUPID1
Used (*Source*)	Always, replacing any existing value in session state

6. Add another item under the *Parameters* region and set the following properties. It will carry an auto-generated numeric ID (E) for a new group.

Property	Value
Name	P62_GROUPID2
Type	Text Field
Label	Group ID:
Width	4
Maximum Length	4
Type (*Source*)	SQL Query (return single value)
SQL Query	SELECT MAX(groupID)+1 FROM groups_master
Used (*Source*)	Always, replacing any existing value in session state
Type (*Default*)	Static Value
Static Value	1
Type (*Server-side Condition*)	Item = Value
Item	P62_EXISTINGNEW
Value	NEW (*the item is displayed only when NEW option is on*)

7. Add a last page item to the *Parameters* region and set the following properties. This one will receive titles (F) for *new* groups.

Property	Value
Name	P62_GROUPTITLE2
Type	Text Field
Label	Title:
Type (*Server-side Condition*)	Item = Value
Item	P62_EXISTINGNEW
Value	NEW

12.3 Buttons

Add the following two buttons. These buttons (G) appear on the new group creation form (H). Clicking the *Allow All* button will create a group with all the application access privileges, while the second one will create a group without any privilege. Of course, you can amend these privileges later on. Except for the name and label properties, the two buttons have similar attributes. After creating the first one, right-click its name under the *Region Buttons* folder in the *Rendering* tree and select **Duplicate** from the context menu. This action will make a copy of the first button. Select the copied button and change its name and label properties, as shown in the third column.

Property	Button 1	Button 2
Button Name	Allow	Disallow
Label	Create Group - Allow All	Create Group - Disallow All
Button Position	Create	Create
Action	Submit Page	Submit Page
Type (*Server-side Condition*)	Item = Value	Item = Value
Item	P62_EXISTINGNEW	P62_EXISTINGNEW
Value	NEW	NEW

12.4 New Group Process

Click the **Processing** tab and create a new process under the *After Submit* folder. This process is associated with the two buttons created in the previous section. The *Server-side Condition* says that if the request came from any of the two buttons, then execute the PL/SQL process to create the group with all or no privileges. The *When Button Pressed* property can handle request from just one button. To execute a process, which is requested by multiple buttons, you have to set the condition type to *Request is contained in Value* and then specify comma separated button names for the condition value.

Property	Value
Name	Create New Groups
Type	PL/SQL Code

PL/SQL Code	<pre>DECLARE
	VsegmentID number := 0;
	VsegmentParent Number;
	VsegmentType varchar2(4);
	vpageID number := 0;
	VitemRole varchar2(10);
	Vallow varchar2(1);
	VmasterRow number := 0;
	
	cursor segments_cur is
	select * from app_segments order by segmentID;
	
	segments_rec segments_cur%ROWTYPE;
	
	BEGIN
	  if :request='Allow' then
	    Vallow := 'Y';
	  else
	    Vallow := 'N';
	  end if;
	  for segments_rec in segments_cur loop
	    VsegmentID := segments_rec.segmentID;
	    VsegmentParent := segments_rec.segmentParent;
	    VsegmentType := segments_rec.segmentType;
	    VpageID := segments_rec.pageID;
	    VitemRole := segments_rec.itemRole;
	    if VmasterRow = 0 then
	      insert into groups_master values (:P62_GROUPID2,:P62_GROUPTITLE2);
	      commit;
	      VmasterRow := 1; -- A switch which indicates that the master row has been inserted
	    end if;
	    insert into groups_detail values
	(:P62_GROUPID2,VsegmentID,VsegmentParent,VsegmentType,VpageID,VitemRole,Vallow);
	      commit;
	  end loop;
	END;</pre>

Point	After Submit
Success Message	Group Created Successfully
Error Message	Could not create group
Type (*Server-side Condition*)	Request is contained in Value
Value	Allow,Disallow (*Case-sensitive, should match with the button names created above*)

12.5 Delete Group Button

This button is being added to delete an existing group. On submit, a process named *Delete Group* (created next) is executed. The button will be visible only when you select an *Existing* group.

Property	Value
Button Name	Delete
Label	Delete Group
Button Position	Create
Hot	Yes
Action	Submit Page
Type (*Server-side Condition*)	Item = Value
Item	P62_EXISTINGNEW
Value	EXISTING

12.6 Delete Group Process

Create a new process (under the *Processing* folder) to drop a group. To avoid deletion of a group with associated users and to present a custom error message, you can add a validation. I'm ignoring it on purpose to preserve some space. However, we'll define a constraint in the APP_USERS table (in the next chapter) on the groupID column to eliminate accidental deletion of groups. The following process will execute only when you select an existing group–that is, when there is some value in P62_GROUPID1 page item.

Property	Value
Name	Delete Groups
Type	PL/SQL Code
PL/SQL Code	DELETE FROM groups_detail WHERE groupID=:P62_GroupID1; DELETE FROM groups_master WHERE groupID=:P62_GroupID1;
Point	Processing
Success Message	Group Deleted Successfully
Error Message	Could not delete group
When Button Pressed	Delete
Type (*Server-side Condition*)	Item is NOT NULL and NOT zero
Item	P62_GROUPID1

12.7 Group Privileges Region

This is another *Static Content* region (I) created to carry the tree (J) and classic report (K) regions to display application access privileges of a selected group.

Property	Value
Title	Group's Privileges
Type	Static Content
Type (*Server-side Condition*)	Item = Value
Item	P62_EXISTINGNEW
Value	EXISTING

12.8 Tree Region

Add a sub-region to the *Group's Privileges* region to display application access rights of a selected group. The query used for this tree region is similar to the one used in the Segments setup (Chapter 11), except for the link column, which uses the inline JavaScript call - 'javascript:pageItemName('||apex_escape.js_literal(segmentid)||')' As link - to a function named *pageItemName*, defined underneath. The APEX_ESCAPE package provides functions for escaping special characters in strings to ensure the data is suitable for further processing. The JS_LITERAL function of the APEX_ESCAPE package escapes and optionally enquotes a JavaScript string.

The function (*pageItemName*) is called in the tree's query link. The calling procedure (in the query), passes a segment ID to the function's *selectedNode* parameter. The *$s*, which is a JavaScript function, sets the value of a hidden page item (P21_SELECTED_NODE) to the value received in the *selectedNode* parameter, which is then used to refresh another region (*Selected Segment - K*), to display the relevant segment along with its access privilege.

Property	Value
Title	Group: &P62_GROUPTITLE1.
Type	Tree
SQL Query	select case when connect_by_isleaf = 1 then 0 when level = 1 then 1 else -1 end as status, level, segmenttitle as title, NULL as icon, segmentid as value, 'View Right' as tooltip, 'javascript:pageItemName('||apex_escape.js_literal(segmentid)||')' As link from app_segments start with segmentparent = 0 connect by prior segmentid = segmentparent order siblings by segmentid
Parent Region	Group's Privileges
Select Node Page Item (*Attributes*)	P62_SELECTED_NODE (*to save the Tree state*)

Create a hidden item under the tree region. This item is created (and is referenced in the tree) to save the Tree state.

Property	Value
Name	P62_SELECTED_NODE
Type	Hidden
Value Protected	No
Region	Group: &P62_GROUPTITLE1.

Click the root node (**Page 62: User Groups**) and enter the following code:

Property	Value

Function and Global Variable Declaration	function pageItemName(selectedNode)
	{
	  $s('P62_SELECTED_NODE', selectedNode);
	}

12.9 Add a Classic Report Region

Add a sub-region under the *Group's Privileges* region. This is a Classic Report (K) to show the name of the selected segment along with its access privilege. A button will also be added to this region, which will be used to allow/revoke access rights. The report is presented using a query, which is based on the value of the P62_SELECTED_NODE hidden item.

Property	Value
Title	Selected Segment
Type	Classic Report

SQL Query	SELECT s.segmentTitle,g.allow_access
	FROM app_segments s, groups_detail g
	WHERE s.segmentID=:P62_SELECTED_NODE AND
	    s.segmentID=g.segmentID AND
	    g.groupID=:P62_GROUPID1

Page Items to Submit	P62_SELECTED_NODE
Parent Region	Group's Privileges
Start New Row	No
Type (*Server-side Condition*)	Item = Value
Item	P62_EXISTINGNEW
Value	EXISTING

12.10 Dynamic Action to Refresh Region

You also need to refresh the classic report region (*Selected Segment*) with the appropriate data when the user switches from one tree node to another. The following dynamic action serves this purpose. Create this dynamic action under the *Change* node.

Property	Value
Name	Refresh Region
Event	Change
Selection Type	Item(s)
Item(s)	P62_SELECTED_NODE
Action (*under Show node*)	Refresh
Selection Type	Region
Region	Selected Segment

12.11 Button To Allow/Revoke Segment Access Right

The button (L) will appear in the *Selected Segment* report region. When clicked, it will invoke the associated process (created next) to either allow or revoke access privilege to or from the selected group.

Property	Value
Name	ALLOW/REVOKE
Label	Allow/Revoke
Region	Selected Segment
Button Position	Next
Hot	Yes
Action	Submit Page

312

12.12 Process to Update Allow Access Column

Create a new process under the *Delete Groups* process using the following table. It is associated with the Allow/Revoke button. When you click a node in the segments tree, the corresponding segment appears in the right pane along with its access privilege. The Allow/Revoke button also displays to the right of this pane. When you click this button, the process defined below fires either to allow or revoke the access right.

Property	Value
Name	Update Allow_Access Column
Type	PL/SQL Code
| PL/SQL Code | ```
declare
  VrecordExist number := 0;
  Vallow varchar2(1);
  Vsegmenttype varchar2(4);
  Vpageid number;
  Vitemrole varchar2(10);
begin
  select count(*) into VrecordExist from groups_detail
  where groupID=:P62_GROUPID1 and
        segmentID=:P62_SELECTED_NODE;
  if VrecordExist = 1 then
    select allow_access into Vallow from groups_detail
    where groupID=:P62_GROUPID1 and
          segmentID=:P62_SELECTED_NODE;
    if Vallow='Y' then
      Vallow := 'N';
    else
      Vallow := 'Y';
    end if;
    update groups_detail set allow_access=Vallow
    where groupID=:P62_GROUPID1 and
          segmentID=:P62_SELECTED_NODE;
    commit;
  else
    select segmenttype,pageid,itemrole
    into Vsegmenttype,Vpageid,Vitemrole
    from app_segments
    where segmentID=:P62_SELECTED_NODE;
    insert into groups_detail values
    (:P62_GROUPID1,:P62_SELECTED_NODE,null,
     Vsegmenttype, VpageID,Vitemrole,'N');
    commit;
  end if;
end;
``` |
| When Button Pressed | ALLOW/REVOKE |

313
```

Test Your Work

Execute the following steps to test your work:

1. Click **User Groups** in the main navigation menu.

2. Click the **New** option in the *Parameters* region.

3. Accepting **1** as the *Group ID*, enter a title for the new group – I entered **Admins** for my group.

4. Click the button **Create Group – Allow All**. This action will create the specified group with all application rights.

5. Click the **Existing** option, and select the **Admins** group (you just created) from the select list. Click different tree nodes and watch changes in the right pane. Select any application segment and click the **Allow/Revoke** button to note the immediate reflection. Note that sometimes when you click a segment node you do not see anything in the *Selected Segment* region. This happens when you forget to select a group from the select list.

6. Add two more groups and grant them different access rights. Name the first one as **Managers** and the other one as **Clerks**.

Summary

You've successfully set up the application access privileges, but these privileges are not yet implemented. This is because the application is in the development phase and only after its completion will you be in a position to completely deploy the security module, which will be done in Chapter 14. In the next chapter, you will create application users who will be assigned the groups and consequently the privileges you set up in this chapter.

Chapter 13

Create Users and Assign Groups

After creating groups, you add application users and associate them to relevant groups. While creating a new user, you input the ID of that user in a text field. However, when you call up an existing user's record for modification, the ID is displayed as read-only text. Besides assigning an administrative group to a user, you also specify whether the user is an administrator. This is because we have a column (Admin) in the users table, which explicitly assigns administrative rights to those users marked as administrators, irrespective of the group to which they belong. This explicit marking is necessary in some cases to quickly assess whether a user is an administrator. You'll see an instance of this case in section 13.6.

13.1 Create Users Table

You went through a couple of techniques in the previous two chapters to create new database objects. In this section, you will use *SQL Scripts* to create a table named APP_USERS. Note that you used SQL Scripts in Chapter 5 to evaluate the new Master Detail Detail feature. A SQL script is a set of SQL commands saved as a file in the *SQL Scripts* interface. This file can carry one or more SQL statements or PL/SQL blocks. You can use SQL scripts to create, edit, view, run, and delete database objects. Here's how you can use this utility to create new objects.

1. From the *SQL Workshop* menu at the top of your screen, select **SQL Scripts**.

2. On the *SQL Scripts* page, click the **Upload** button to upload a script from your local file system into *SQL Scripts*. In the *Upload Script* dialog box, click the **Choose File** button, and select **Users Table.txt** file from Chapter 13 folder in the book code. Enter **Users Table Script** for the *Script Name* and click the **Upload** button. The *SQL Scripts* page, which is an interactive report, will show the script you just uploaded.

3. Click the **Run** button (A) in the interactive report to execute the script.

4. The *Run Script* page appears. It displays the script name, when it was created and by whom, when it was last updated and by whom, the number of statements it contains, and its size in bytes. Click **Run Now** to submit the script for execution. The *Manage Script Results* page appears listing script results. To view script results, click the **View Results** icon in the far right column. The *Results* page appears, which displays the script name and status (Complete, Canceled, Executing, or Submitted) and lists the statements executed. Go to the **Object Browser** interface and select **APP_USERS** from the *Tables* list to view the definitions of this table.

Click the **Create Page** button. Select **Desktop** for *User Interface* and click the **Form** option followed by the **Report with Form on Table** option. This is the same option you selected in Chapter 11.

1. Fill in the *Page Attributes* wizard screen as follows and then click **Next** to proceed.

Property	Value
Report Type	Interactive Report
Report Page Number	63
Report Page Name	Application Users
From Page Number	64
Form Page Name	User Form
Form Page Mode	Modal Dialog
Breadcrumb	don't use breadcrumbs...

2. On the *Navigation Menu* screen, set *Navigation Preference* to **Identify an existing navigation menu entry for this page**, and set *Existing Navigation Menu Entry* to **Administration**. Click **Next**.

3. On the *Data Source* page, accept the default schema appearing in *Table/View Owner* and select **APP_USERS** for *Table/View Name*. Select all columns from the table and click **Next**. These columns will appear on the report page.

4. For *Primary Key Type*, select **Managed by Database (ROWID)**. In the *Select Column(s) to be included in Form* section leave three columns *USERID*, *GROUPID*, and *ADMIN* in the right pane and move the **Password** column to the left pane to exclude this column from appearing on the form page. click **Create** to complete the process.

After creation, modify both pages to set the following properties. The default query in the *Region Source* is replaced with a custom join query to also display groups' titles. Set *Width* and *Height* of Page 64 to **400** and **300**, respectively.

Action	Property	Value
Report Page (63) Modify Region Report 1	Title	Application Users
	SQL Query	select "U"."ROWID", "U"."USERID", "G"."GROUPTITLE", "U"."PASSWORD", "U"."ADMIN" from "APP_USERS" "U", "GROUPS_MASTER" "G" where "U"."GROUPID"="G"."GROUPID"
Form Page (64) Modify Region Form on APP_USERS	Title	Application User: &P64_USERID.

13.3 Create/Modify Items

Add and amend the following items on Page 64. The first *Display Only* item (P64_USERID2) is added (between two existing items: User ID and Group ID) to show the ID of the selected user as a read-only text. The value of the *Label* property is enclosed in HTML <b> tags to present the label in bold typeface. The *Sequence* property specifies the arrangement for this component and determines the order of evaluation. The value (25) set for this property places it between the USERID and GROUPID items. Alternatively, you can place an item between two existing items by right-clicking the item under which you want to place the new one, and selecting *Create Page Item* from the context menu. The *Server-side Condition* set for this item will display it only when you call a record of an existing user for modification. An opposite condition is set for the item P64_USERID to make that item visible only for new records.

Action	Property	Value
Add Item	Name	P64_USERID2
	Type	Display Only
	Label	<b>User ID:</b>
	Sequence	25
	Source Type	Database Column
	Database Column	USERID
	Type (*Server-side Condition*)	Item Is NOT NULL
	Item	P64_USERID

Action	Property	Value
Modify Item	Name	P64_USERID
	Type	Text Field
	Label	<b>User ID:</b>
	Value Placeholder	Enter in UPPER CASE
	Source Type	Database Column
	Database Column	USERID
	Type (*Server-side Condition*)	Item is NULL
	Item	P64_USERID

Action	Property	Value
Modify Item	Name	P64_GROUPID
	Type	Select List
	Label	<b>Group:</b>
	Template	Required
	Value Required	Yes
	LOV Type	SQL Query
	SQL Query	SELECT groupTitle d, groupID r FROM groups_master

318

Action	Property	Value
Modify Item	Item Name	P64_ADMIN
	Type	Radio Group
	Label	Administrator:
	No. of Columns	2
	List of Value Type	Static Values
	Static Values	STATIC:Yes;Y,No;N
	Display Null Value	No
	Default Type	Static Value
	Static Value	N

Test Your Work

1. Access Page 63 from **Administration | Users** in the main navigation menu.

2. Click the **Create** button.

3. Enter **SUPER** in *UserID*, select **Admins** from the *Group* list, select **Yes** for *Administrator*, and click **Create**. Note that the password column for this new user will be blank at this stage. You will create a setup to set users' passwords in the next section. Click the edit link (presented as a Pencil icon) to modify this user and take a look at the user ID, which should be displayed as a read-only text.

Figure 13-1
Application
Users Report
and Input
Form

4. Create two more users belonging to different groups and take some time to play with these pages.

13.4 Reset Password

A user who wants to access this application can do so only with a valid ID and password. So far, you have created some user accounts and assigned them relevant IDs and groups. In this exercise, you will create a setup to set initial passwords for those users, which they can alter later on using the same setup. Note that this segment will be invoked from the *Setup* menu. The *Reset Password* interface is self-explanatory. First, you select a user ID and then provide a new password for it followed by a confirmation added to match the actual password. As just mentioned, the same interface will be used to set initial passwords and to reset passwords for the application users in the future. Usually, the initial password allocation task is performed by the application administrator.

13.5 Add Custom Functions

The users you created in the previous section reside in the database table (APP_USERS) without passwords, so none of them can access the application at the moment. You'll create the password interface by adding a new page to the application, but first you have to add two custom functions (CUSTOM_AUTH and CUSTOM_HASH) to your database. After receiving login information, the Oracle

APEX engine evaluates and executes the current authentication scheme–to be configured at the end of this chapter. The scheme makes a call to the CUSTOM_AUTH function. In conjunction with the CUSTOM_HASH function, the CUSTOM_AUTH function authenticates users using their credentials stored in the APP_USERS table. The two functions are added to the database to implement custom authentication mechanism. The CUSTOM_HASH function is a subordinate function to the CUSTOM_AUTH function and is called from the parent function to obfuscate user password using hash algorithm. Besides assisting the custom authentication scheme, it is used to obfuscate new/updated passwords.

CUSTOM_HASH Function

```
create or replace function custom_hash (p_username in varchar2, p_password in varchar2)
return varchar2 is
  l_password varchar2(4000);
  l_salt varchar2(4000) := 'XV1MH24EC1IHDCQHSS6XQ6QTJSANT3';
begin
l_password := utl_raw.cast_to_raw(dbms_obfuscation_toolkit.md5
  (input_string => p_password || substr(l_salt,10,13) || p_username || substr(l_salt, 4,10)));
return l_password;
end;
```

The Custom_Hash function should be wrapped, as the hash algorithm is exposed here. See *Protecting Your Code with Oracle's Wrap Utility* later in this section.

CUSTOM_AUTH Function

```
create or replace function custom_auth (p_username in VARCHAR2, p_password in VARCHAR2)
return BOOLEAN is
 l_password varchar2(4000);
 l_stored_password varchar2(4000);
 l_count number;
begin
 -- First, check to see if the user exists in the APP_USERS table
 select count(*) into l_count from app_users where userid = p_username;
 if l_count > 0 then
  -- Fetch the stored hashed password
  select password into l_stored_password
  from app_users where userid = p_username;
  -- Apply the custom hash function to the password
  l_password := custom_hash(p_username, p_password);
  -- Compare passwords to see if they are the same and return either TRUE or FALSE
  if l_password = l_stored_password then
   return true;
  else
   return false;
  end if;
 else
  -- User doesn't exist in the APP_USERS table, so
  return false;
 end if;
end;
```

The Custom_Auth function receives username and password on line 1 as parameters from the login form and compares this information with the values stored in the APP_USERS table after applying the Custom_Hash function. If the provided information matches with the table values, the user is authenticated and is allowed to access the application.

Follow the instructions mentioned below to add the two database functions using *SQL Scripts* utility.

1. Select **SQL Scripts** from the *SQL Workshop* menu.

2. On the *SQL Scripts* page, click the **Upload** button. In the *Upload Script* dialog box, click the **Choose File** button, and select **Custom_Hash.sql** file from Chapter 13 folder in the book code. Enter **Custom Hash Function** for the *Script Name* and click the **Upload** button.

3. Click the **Run** button in the *SQL Scripts* page's interactive report to execute the *Custom Hash Function* script.

4. Click **Run Now** on the *Run Script* page to submit the script for execution.

5. Repeat steps 2-4 to add the Custom_Auth function using **Custom_Auth.sql** file.

6. For verification, call the **Object Browser** interface and locate the two functions in the *Functions* category.

Protecting Your Code with Oracle's Wrap Utility

Note that the instructions provided here are applicable to your local Oracle APEX environment, where you can access Oracle's BIN folder to run the Wrap utility.

As you can see, the hash algorithm (defined in l_salt variable) is exposed in the CUSTOM_HASH function and is visible to any person who is granted function access privileges. To protect this value, and the function as well, you have to wrap it using Oracle's Wrap utility.

Run the following from the operating system prompt. Note that the file (custom_hash.sql) should first be copied to the specified *bin* folder or else you will have to provide the complete path.

CD C:\oraclexe\app\oracle\product\11.2.0\server\bin

wrap iname=custom_hash.sql

The wrap utility should end with the following output. Note the final line of this output, which creates a .plb file.

PL/SQL Wrapper: Release 11.2.0.2.0 on Sat January 7 12:46:49 2017

Copyright (c) 1993, 2009, Oracle. All rights reserved.

Processing custom_hash.sql to custom_hash.plb

If you view the contents of the custom_hash.plb text file, the first line reads *CREATE or REPLACE FUNCTION custom_hash wrapped* and the rest of the file contents is hidden.

Now connect to your Oracle APEX schema in SQL*Plus and run the custom_hash.plb file as follows:

SQL> conn riaz1969/************

SQL> @c:\oraclexe\app\oracle\product\11.2.0\server\bin\custom_hash.plb

You will see the message *"Function created."*

The function looks something like Figure 13-2 if you access it from *SQL Workshop*.

Figure 13-2
Wrapped
Custom Hash
Function

DBMS_CRYPTO Package

Note that the DBMS_OBFUSCATION_TOOLKIT package (used in the CUSTOM_HASH function) has been deprecated in favor of DBMS_CRYPTO, which is now used to encrypt and decrypt data and provides support for various industry-standard encryption and hashing algorithms, including the Advanced Encryption Standard (AES) encryption algorithm. AES has been approved as a new standard to replace the Data Encryption Standard (DES). Oracle Database installs the DBMS_CRYPTO package in the SYS schema. To use this package, users must be granted access to it.

13.6 Create Page and Add Components

Create this interface using a blank page and then set the properties mentioned in the following table. The page will be called by the *Reset Password* option listed in the *Setup* menu. The *SQL query* defined for the *Server-side Condition Type* uses a WHERE clause (admin='Y') to quickly assess administrators, who are allowed to change password of any user. This is the case I mentioned at the beginning of this chapter for the incorporation of *Admin* column in the APP_USERS table. The Select List will display a list of all users (using the LOV SQL Query) and the specified condition will make it visible only to administrators. Normal users will see their own respective IDs through the *Display Only* item (P65_USERID2).

Action	Property	Value
Add a Blank Page	Page Number	65
	Page Name	Reset Password
	Page Mode	Normal
	Breadcrumb	don't use breadcrumbs...
	Navigation Preference	Identify an existing navigation menu entry for this page
	Menu Entry	Setup
Add Region	Title	Reset Password
	Type	Static Content
	Template	Standard
Add Page Item	Name	P65_USERID
	Type	Select List
	Label	\User ID:\
	Region	Reset Password
	LOV Type	SQL Query
	SQL Query	SELECT userid d, userid r FROM app_users
	Type (*Server-side Condition*)	Rows Returned
	SQL Query	SELECT 1 FROM app_users WHERE upper(userid) = upper(:APP_USER) AND admin = 'Y'

Add the items listed on the next page. The *Display Only* item (P65_USERID2) will show the ID of the current non-admin user using a substitution string (&APP_USER.). The *Save Session State* property is set to *YES* to store the current item value in the session state when the page gets submitted. If you don't set this value, you'll encounter an error message "*No user selected for the reset password process*", because there will be no value in the session state. We also used an opposite WHERE clause for *Server-side Condition* query, as compared to the previous one, to display non-admin IDs. Next, you added two password items. The first one is used to enter a new password, whereas the other one is added for its confirmation. The Password item is an HTML password form element. As the end user enters text, a black dot is displayed for that character instead of the actual character entered. The button (RESET_PW) submits the page. When set to *Yes*, the *Execute Validation* property executes all validations defined for the page as well as the built-in validations (such as required, valid number, or valid date). If set to *No*, none of the defined validations nor the built-in validations are executed. If you want a specific validation to execute independent of this setting, modify the validation and set the validation attribute *Always Execute* to *Yes*.

Action	Property	Value
Add Page Item	Name	P65_USERID2
	Type	Display Only
	Label	User ID:
	Save Session State	Yes
	Region	Reset Password
	Type (*Default*)	Static Value
	Static Value	&APP_USER.
	Type (*Server-side Condition*)	Rows Returned
	SQL Query	SELECT 1 FROM app_users WHERE upper(userid) = upper(:APP_USER) AND admin != 'Y'
Add Page Item	Name	P65_PASSWORD1
	Type	Password
	Label	New Password:
	Submit When Enter Pressed	No
	Region	Reset Password
	Template	Required
	Value Required	Yes
Add Page Item	Name	P65_PASSWORD2
	Type	Password
	Label	Confirm Password:
	Submit When Enter Pressed	No
	Region	Reset Password
	Template	Required
	Value Required	Yes
Add Button	Name	RESET_PW
	Label	Reset Password
	Region	Reset Password
	Button Position	Next
	Hot	Yes
	Action	Submit Page
	Execute Validation	Yes

13.7 Add Validations – Check User ID and Match Passwords

Click the **Processing** tab and create the following two validations under the *Validating* folder. The first validation checks for the existence of user ID, while the second one matches the two passwords.

Property	Value
Name	Check User ID
Type	PL/SQL Function (returning Error Text)

PL/SQL Function Body Returning Error Text	declare
	  Verrortext varchar2(100);
	begin
	  if :P65_USERID is null and :P65_USERID2 is null THEN
	    Verrortext := 'No user selected for the reset
	            password process';
	  end if;
	  return rtrim(Verrortext);
	end;

When Button Pressed	RESET_PW

Property	Value
Name	Match Passwords
Type	PL/SQL Function Body (returning Boolean)

PL/SQL Function Body Returning Boolean	begin
	  if :P65_PASSWORD1 = :P65_PASSWORD2 then
	    return true;
	  else
	    return false;
	  end if;
	end;

Error Message	Passwords do not match
When Button Pressed	RESET_PW

326

On the *Processing* tab, right-click the **After Submit** folder to create the following process, which stores the new password in the database table for the selected user.

Property	Value
Name	Update Password
Type	PL/SQL Code

PL/SQL Code	begin
	if :P65_USERID is not null then
	  update app_users set password = custom_hash(:P65_USERID,
	   :P65_PASSWORD1) where upper(userID) = upper(:P65_USERID);
	else
	  update app_users set password = custom_hash(:P65_USERID2,
	   :P65_PASSWORD1) where upper(userID) = upper(:P65_USERID2);
	end if;
	commit;
	end;

Point	After Submit
Success Message	Password changed successfully
Error Message	Could not change password
When Button Pressed	RESET_PW

If you run the page at this stage, you won't see the users select list. This is because of the condition set for the Select List item (P65_USERID), which shows the list only when the currently logged-in user is an administrator of the application. Since your account doesn't even exist in the APP_USERS table, the list doesn't appear as well. To make the list visible, create an admin account for yourself with the same ID you currently possess (which is usually your e-mail address in the online environment), from the *Users* option in the main menu. After creating your account, invoke the *Password* page (Figure 13-3) to test your work by setting passwords for all the application users. Verify addition of passwords to the table by accessing the table either from the *Object Browser* utility in *SQL Workshop* or from the *Users* menu – see Figure 13-4.

Figure 13-3
Reset
Password Page

Figure 13-4
Users Report
Showing
Encrypted
Passwords

13.9 Change Authentication Scheme

At this stage you can set and browse users' passwords, but you cannot use these passwords to login. This is because of the currently implemented authentication scheme, which was set to *Application Express Accounts* scheme when you initially created the workspace in Chapter 2 section 2.9. To authenticate the users with their new IDs and passwords, you have to create a custom authentication scheme. Here are the steps to implement this scheme:

1. In Shared Components, click **Authentication Scheme** (under the *Security* section).

2. Click the **Create** button.

3. For *Create Scheme*, select the option **Based on the pre-configured scheme from the gallery** and click **Next**.

4. Enter **Custom Scheme** in the *Name* box and select **Custom** as the *Scheme Type*. On the same page, enter **CUSTOM_AUTH** for the *Authentication Function Name* attribute. This is the name of the function you created in section 13.5 to verify a user's credentials on the login page.

5. Click the **Create Authentication Scheme** button. The new scheme will appear on the *Authentication Schemes* page with a check mark–if you are viewing the page in *View Icons* mode. Now you can access the application using the credentials stored in the APP_USERS table. If you want to revert to the *Application Express Accounts* scheme, just click it in the *Authentication Schemes* page and then click the *Make Current Scheme* button in the *Create/Edit* page to reactivate the scheme.

Summary

The chapter taught you how to create custom authentication scheme to allow initial access to your application. First, you created an interface to add application users. Then, you added two database functions to obfuscate passwords and authenticate users. Next, you created a page where users could input and reset their passwords. Finally, you switched your application's authentication scheme from the default *Application Express Accounts* to the new *Custom Scheme*. In the next chapter, you will implement authorization schemes to further protect your application.

Chapter 14

Implement Application Security

Now that you have completely developed your application and have also specified application segments, groups, and users, you are at the point where you can create and implement authorization schemes. By defining authorization schemes, you control users' access to specific components of your application. It is an important security measure implemented to augment the application's authentication scheme. An authorization scheme can be specified for an entire application, page, or specific page components such as a region, button, or item. For instance, you can apply an authorization scheme to determine which menu options a user can see or whether he is allowed to create a new order (using the *Create* button). Initially, you will apply security to the main navigation menu items, followed by pages and buttons.

14.1 Apply Security to Main Menu

1. Go to *Shared Components | Navigation Menu* and select **Desktop Navigation Menu**.

2. Click the **Home** entry.

3. On *List Entry Create/Edit* page, click the **Conditions** tab, set *Condition Type* to **PL/SQL Function Body Returning a Boolean**, enter the following code in *Expression 1* text area, and apply the change.

```
1   declare
2     Vadmin varchar2(1);
3     Vallow varchar2(1);
4   begin
5     select admin into Vadmin from app_users where upper(userid)=upper(:APP_USER);
6     if Vadmin = 'N' then
7       select allow_access into Vallow from groups_detail
        where segmentType='Menu' and segmentID=
                    (select segmentID from app_segments where segmentTitle like
                        'Home%' and segmentType='Menu') and
                groupID=(select groupID from app_users where
                        upper(userid)=upper(:APP_USER));
8       if Vallow='Y' then
9         return true;
10      else
11        return false;
12      end if;
13    else
14      return true;
15    end if;
16  exception
17    when NO_DATA_FOUND then return false;
18  end;
```

The statement on line 5 evaluates whether the currently logged-in user is an administrator. If so, then the code on line 14 is executed to return a true value. Note that admin users are exempt from restrictions and possess full access privileges to all application segments. On the contrary, if the user is not an administrator, the code specified from line 7 through 12 is executed. This block is specified for non-admins. It checks whether the user is privileged to access the *Home* menu. Note that this code is specific to the *Home* menu entry. Call all menu entries and add this code with the same *Condition Type*. The only thing you need to replace is the '*Home%*' entry (on line 7) with the corresponding menu entry. For example, if you are entering this code for the *Setup* menu entry, then replace the LIKE operator's string with '*Setup%*'. You can refer to the Microsoft Excel file (*application_segments.xlsx*) located in Chapter 11 folder to see all application menu entries.

14.2 Apply Security on Application Pages

While conditions control the *rendering* and *processing* of specific page controls or components, authorization schemes control *user access* to pages and page components. After protecting the application main menu from unauthorized access by applying conditions, the next line of defense is to make application pages secure and this can be done by adding *Authorization Schemes*. Note that even after protecting a specific menu option, a restricted user can access the pages listed under that menu option. For example, if you revoke the *Home* menu option from a user, she still gets it when she logs into the application.

You can specify an authorization scheme for an entire application, page, or specific control such as a region, item, or button. For example, you can use an authorization scheme to selectively determine which pages, regions, or buttons a user sees.

An authorization scheme either succeeds or fails. Common authorization *Scheme Types* include *Exists*, *Not Exists SQL Queries*, and *PL/SQL Function Returning Boolean*. If a component or control level authorization scheme succeeds, the user can view the component or control. If it fails, the user cannot view the component or control. If an application or page-level authorization scheme fails, then the Oracle APEX engine displays an error message.

When you define an authorization scheme, you give it a unique name. Once defined, you can attach it to any component or control in your application. To attach an authorization scheme to a component or control in your application, simply select an authorization scheme from the *Authorization Scheme* property.

Here are the steps to apply security to the application pages using Authorization Schemes.

1. Go to *Shared Components* and click **Authorization Schemes** (under the *Security* section).

2. Click the **Create** button to launch the scheme wizard.

3. On the *Creation Method* screen, select **From Scratch** to create a new scheme from scratch and click **Next**.

4. On the *Details* wizard screen, enter the following values and click the **Create Authorization Scheme** button. The PL/SQL code defined underneath is similar to the one entered for menu items, except for the segment type, which in this case is the application *Page*. The value *Once per page view* selected for the *Validate authorization scheme* property evaluates once for each request that is processed. You can use the memorized result if the authorization scheme is referenced in more than one component on the page.

Property	Value
Name	Page Access
Scheme Type	PL/SQL Function Returning Boolean

PL/SQL Function Body	declare
	  Vadmin varchar2(1);
	  Vallow varchar2(1);
	begin
	  select admin into Vadmin from app_users
	  where upper(userid)=upper(:APP_USER);
	  if Vadmin = 'N' then
	    select allow_access into Vallow from groups_detail
	    where pageID=:APP_PAGE_ID and
	          segmentType='**Page**' and
	          groupID=(select groupID from app_users
	                    where upper(userid)=upper(:APP_USER));
	  if Vallow='Y' then
	    return true;
	  else
	    return false;
	  end if;
	  else
	    return true;
	  end if;
	exception
	  when NO_DATA_FOUND then return false;
	end;

Error Message	You are not authorized to view this page! Click <a href="f?p=&APP_ID.:999:&SESSION.">here</a> to continue
Validation	Once per page view

After creating the authorization scheme, call the *Home* page (*Sales Web Application - Page 1*) in the Page Designer and click the root node–**Page 1: Sales Web Application**. In the Property Editor, scroll down to the *Security* section and set the *Authorization Scheme* property to **Page Access**. Click the **Save** button. The *Home* page is now associated with the *Page Access* authorization scheme. User groups who are not granted access privilege to the *Home* page will encounter the defined error message. After clicking the link in the error message, they will be taken to another page in the application. I created a page with 999 ID for such purpose. However, you can land them on any existing page.

14.3 Apply Security on Page Items

This is the last level of our application security, where we will apply security to individual page components. Oracle APEX allows you to apply authorization scheme to every component you create on a page. For the sake of simplicity, we just incorporated page buttons in the *Segments* setup and this is the only item we will be experimenting with in this section to test page item security.

1. Create another **Authorization Scheme** from scratch and set the following properties for it:

Property	Value
Name	Create
Scheme Type	PL/SQL Function Returning Boolean

PL/SQL Function Body	declare
	  Vadmin varchar2(1);
	  Vallow varchar2(1);
	begin
	  select admin into Vadmin from app_users
	  where upper(userid)=upper(:APP_USER);
	  if Vadmin = 'N' then
	    select allow_access into Vallow from groups_detail
	      where pageID=:APP_PAGE_ID and
	           itemRole Like **'Create%'** and groupID=
	           (select groupID from app_users
	            where upper(userid)=upper(:APP_USER));
	    if Vallow='Y' then
	      return true;
	    else
	      return false;
	    end if;
	  else
	    return true;
	  end if;
	exception
	  when NO_DATA_FOUND then return false;
	end;

Error Message	You're not allowed to create content in the database
Validation	Once per page view

2. Create two more schemes (*Modify* and *Delete*) using the same PL/SQL code. Replace the string '*Create%*' specified for *itemRole* with '*Modify%*' and '*Delete%*', respectively. The *Copy* button on the Authorization Schemes report page helps you create a scheme instantly from an existing one. Click the **Copy** button to launch the *Copy Authorization Scheme* wizard. On the first wizard screen, select **Create** from the *Copy Authorization Scheme* list. This is the list you want to copy. Enter **Modify** for *New Authorization Scheme Name* and click the **Copy** button. You are taken back to the interactive report page. Click the **Modify** scheme link in the interactive report and change the *LIKE* operator's string from *'Create%'* to **'Modify%'**. Also, replace the word *create* with **modify** in the error message. Save these modifications by clicking the **Apply Changes** button. Repeat the copy process to create the **Delete** authorization scheme.

3. Once again, call the *Home* page, click the **ADD_ORDER** button, and set its *Authorization Scheme* property to **Create**. Save the change. This button will disappear for all those who are not granted the *Create* privilege. Repeat this step to apply Create, Modify, and Delete authorization schemes to all buttons on all application pages.

To test the application security you just created, you must have at least two groups with one user assigned to each group. I created *Admins* and *Clerks* groups with all application access privileges. Assigned *Admins* group to a user named *super*, and associated user *ahmed* with *Clerks*. The *super* user was also marked as *Administrator*, while this option was revoked from *ahmed*.

1. Log in to the application using **super** user's credentials.

2. From the *Administration* menu, select **User Groups**.

3. With the *Action* option set to *Existing*, select **Clerks** from the *Group* list. The page will refresh to show this group's privileges.

4. Click the **Home** menu entry. If you create a group with all access privileges, the *Selected Segment* section shows *'Y'* (stands for *Yes*) under *Allow Access* column. If you create a group without any privileges, you see *'N'*. If the column displays *'Y'*, click the **Allow/Revoke** button to revoke the menu option from the *Clerks* group.

5. Sign out and then log back in using *ahmed's* credentials. The *Home* menu option disappears, but you are landed to the *Home* page. This is because the user has the privilege to see this page.

6. Log in again as *super* user.

7. Access the *User Groups* page and select the **Clerks** group. Expand the *Home* menu in the segments tree and click the **Home** page node. Revoke this option from the group.

8. Log in to the application using *ahmed's* credentials. This time, you will see the error *You are not authorized to view this page! Click here to continue.* Click the word *here* to switch to an accessible page.

9. Grant access privileges for the *Home* menu and *Home* page back to *Clerks*. Then, revoke the *Add* button privilege (under the *Home* page in the segments tree) from this group to test the button authorization scheme. When you log in using *ahmed's* credentials, you will notice all the buttons on the *Home* page used to create records have disappeared.

Summary

An authorization scheme extends the security of your application's authentication scheme. In this chapter, you learned how to secure your application menus, pages, and page components from unauthorized access. This completes the development phase of our application. In the next chapter, you will be guided on how to move an Oracle APEX application from your development machine to a production environment.

Chapter 15

Deploy Oracle APEX Applications

15.1 About Application Deployment

Oracle APEX application deployment consists of two steps. Export the desired components to a script file and import the script file into your production environment. Having completed the development phase, you definitely want to run your application in a production environment. For this, you have to decide where and how the application will run. The following section provides you some deployment options to choose from.

No Deployment: The development environment becomes the production environment and nothing is moved to another computer. In this option users are provided with just the URL to access the application.

Application: You will use this option if the target computer is already running a production Oracle database with all underlying objects. You only need to export the application and import it into the target database.

Application and Table Structures: In this deployment option you have to create two scripts, one for your application and another for the database table structures using the *Generate DDL* utility in *SQL Workshop*.

Application and Database Objects with Data: In this option you deploy your application along with all database objects and utilize oracle's data pump utility to export data from the development environment to the production environment.

Individual Components: With the development phase going on, you can supplement your deployment plan by exporting only selected components.

For simplicity, we will deploy the application in the same workspace to understand the deployment concept. The same technique is applicable to the production environment.

15.2 Export Application

This section will demonstrate how to export an Oracle APEX application that you can import into a new or the same workspace.

1. Sign in to Oracle APEX and click the **App Builder** icon.

2. Click the **Edit** button under **Sales Web Application**.

3. Click the **Export/Import** icon, as show in Figure 15-1.

4. On the ensuing page, click the **Export** icon.

5. In the *Choose Application* section, set *Application* to **Sales Web Application**, *File Format* to **DOS**, *Export Supporting Object Definitions* to **No**, and click the **Export** button.

6. A file something like **f64699.sql** will be saved in the *Download* folder under *My Documents* or in another folder specified in your browser. Yours might be saved with a different name.

Figure 15-1
Import/Export Icon

ORACLE Application Express   App Builder ⌄   SQL Workshop   Team Development   Packaged Apps ⌄

Application 64699

Application 64699 - Sales Web Application

Run Application   Supporting Objects   Shared Components   Utilities   Export / Import

> **File Format** - Select how rows in the export file are formatted:
> - Choose UNIX to have the resulting file contain rows delimited by line feeds.
> - Choose DOS to have the resulting file contain rows delimited by carriage returns and line feeds.
>
> **Supporting Object Definitions** include all configuration options and scripts and enable an application export to include database object definitions, image definitions, and seed data SQL statements encapsulated in a single file. The *No* option is selected because you are importing the application in the same schema.

15.3 Export/Import Data

If you want to also export the data from your test environment into your production environment, then you have the option to utilize Oracle's export and import data pump utilities. Oracle Data Pump technology enables very high-speed movement of data and metadata from one database to another. It includes *expdp* and *impdp* utilities that enable the exporting and importing of data and metadata for a complete database or subsets of a database.

15.4 Import Application

In this exercise, you will import the exported application (f64699.sql) into the existing workspace you are connected to with a different ID.

1. Go to the App Builder interface and click the **Import** icon.

Import

2. On the *Import* screen, click the **Choose File** button and select the exported file (f64699.sql). For *File Type*, select **Database Application, Page or Component Export** and click **Next**.

3. After a while the message *The export file has been imported successfully* will appear. The status bar at the bottom of your screen will show progress during the upload process. Click **Next** to move on.

4. On the *Install* screen, select the default value for *Parsing Schema*. Set *Build Status* to **Run and Build Application**, *Install As Application* to **Auto Assign New Application ID**, and click the **Install Application** button. After a short while, the application will be installed with a new ID for you to give it a test-run.

15.5 Remove Developers Toolbar

The Developers Toolbar is used to access the application source. In this exercise, we are going to prevent users from modifying the application by suppressing the toolbar.

1. Call the new application you imported in the previous step.

2. Click **Shared Components**.

3. Click the **Globalization Attributes** link (under *Globalization*).

4. Click the **Definition** tab.

5. Scroll down to the *Availability* section, set *Build Status* to **Run Application Only**, and click **Apply Changes**.

6. Go to the App Builder interface and see that the new application doesn't have the Edit link. Click the **Run** button and provide your sign in credentials. Note that the Developer Toolbar has disappeared as well.

That's it. You have successfully deployed your application in the same workspace. You can apply the same procedure to deploy the application to another environment.

Conclusion

Oracle Application Express has come a long way from its simple beginning. With the addition of new features in every release it provides so much possibilities and promises for today and for the days to come. I hope this book has provided you with a solid foundation of Oracle Application Express and set a firm ground to develop robust application systems to fulfill the information requirements of your organization. The sky is the limit, you are limited by your imagination. Be creative, and put the power of Oracle APEX to your work. Good luck!

Index

Symbols
|| Concatenation operator 89
:= 174
-moz- Prefix 115,117
-webkit- Prefix 115,117
: URL argument separator, 72
12 columns layout, 4, 7, 68

A
Accept Page Process, 25
Access Control (page), 27
Action (Property), 29, 79, 80, 81, 82, 91, 119, 123, 145, 157, 158, 185, 191, 193, 205, 206, 207, 239, 249, 255, 258, 263, 265, 271, 274, 279, 283, 296, 307, 309, 312, 325
Actions Menu, 26, 90, 98, 119, 128, 135, 136, 137, 141, 142, 143, 144, 197
Adding multiple regions, 5
Advanced Formatting (Mobile App), 259
After Rows (section), 118
Alignment (Property), 148, 149, 195, 254
Allowed Row Operations Column (Property), 106
Alternative Report, 98, 136, 140
    create, 136
Anchor tag <a>, 178
Apache FOP, 226
APEX Collection, 11,157,180,198
APEX.CONFIRM Function, 123, 132
APEX_ESCAPE package, 310
APEX_ESCAPE.HTML, 58
APEX$ROW_STATUS, 196
APEX_UTIL.GET_BLOB_FILE_SRC Function, 115, 123
APEX_UTIL.PREPARE_URL Function, 115,169-170, 177-178, 182, 219, 222-223, 270, 296
APEX URL Syntax *see f?p*
App Builder, 24, 25, 29, 34, 38, 39, 41, 45, 49, 50, 51, 52, 56, 65, 67, 84, 85, 86, 88, 89, 107, 113, 129, 152, 161, 217, 218, 219, 246, 338, 339, 340
    defined, 29
APP_ID, 36-37,71-72
APP_IMAGES, 37, 61
APP_PAGE_ID, 37, 333, 334
APP_SESSION, 35, 36, 37, 222, 223, 258, 296
APP_USER, 37, 44, 57, 147, 187, 194, 239, 272, 277, 323, 324, 325, 330, 333, 334
Application, 24
    copy Application, 40
    create Application, 38
    Date/Time format, 51

Delete Application, 40
deploy, 18
Desktop, 24
Edit Application Properties, 40, 248
Export, 18,29, 338
images, 61
Import, 18, 29, 339
logo, 4
Mobile, 24
name, 4,39
Packaged, 29
Primary Language, 51
Run, 41
Translate, 51
Application Definition Attributes, 40,44
Application Express engine, 3, 25, 27, 34, 35, 37, 44, 45, 48, 58, 65, 249
Application Express Listener, 226
Application Processes, 44
Application Security, *see Security*
Application Server Single Sign-On Server, 45
Attaching LOV, 121
Authentication Scheme, 39, 328
    Application Express Accounts, 40, 45, 101, 328
    change, 328
    custom scheme, 17, 40, 45, 320, 328
Authorization Schemes, 44, 46, 332, 335
Automatic Row Processing, 97, 104, 121, 132, 148, 196
Automatically Refresh a Page, 99

B
Background Color (Property), 137, 138,231
Backup, 20
Badge List, 73
Before Rows section, 117
BEGIN, 166, 172, 173, 174-175, 308
Bind Variable, 28, 35, 37, 174, 175
Blank Page, 26, 107, 161, 189, 201, 202, 208, 211, 238, 283, 284, 286, 304, 323
Blank with Attributes (Property value), 154, 155, 166, 189
BLOB column, 112, 115, 121, 180, 258
BLOB Last Update Column (Property), 121
Body Height (Property), 67, 69, 74, 75, 76, 77
Branch Here on Submit (Property), 255, 260, 275, 281
Branches, 32, 133, 188
    create, 162, 242
Breadcrumbs, 48, 86, 87, 88, 201, 202, 304
Button
    create, 78, 255, 258, 263

defined, 28

make duplicate, 307

Button Name (Property), 79, 80, 81, 82, 205, 207

Button Position (Property), 78, 79, 80, 81, 82, 91, 119, 148, 157, 185, 191, 194, 205, 207, 239, 255, 258, 263, 265, 271, 274, 278, 279, 281, 296, 307, 309, 312, 325

Button Template (Property), 79, 80, 81, 82, 119, 123, 145, 157, 185, 193, 205, 265, 271, 274, 296

Buttons Container, 149, 184, 190, 195

C

calculations, 15, 24

calendar, 13, 25, 54, 215, 216, 217, 224, 288

create link, 216

Calendar, 27, 53, 54, 200, 215, 216, 217, 253, 288

create link, 217

Cancel and Go To Page (Property), 255, 260, 275, 281

Cards (List Template), 201

Cascading LOV Parent Item(s) (Property), 282

CASE statement, 224

Change (Dynamic Action Event), 312

Change item type and attach LOVs, 9

Chart, 4, 5, 11, 13, 20, 24, 27, 28, 66, 67-68, 74, 75, 82, 139, 141, 171, 200, 203, 206-207, 208, 209-210, 212, 213-214, 218, 224, 226-227, 232, 284, 286

3d Pie, 13

aggregate function, 141-142

animated effects, 207

Bar, 13, 67, 75, 203, 210, 213, 214, 232, 284, 287

Column, 13

Donut, 209

Line with Area, iv, 212

series, 68, 74, 152, 203, 204, 207, 208, 212, 219, 284, 285

Stacked Bar chart, 13

Chart View, 139, 141

Classic Report, 27, 69, 76, 190, 311

Clear Cache, 36, 70, 71, 76, 78, 79, 80, 81, 82, 91, 135, 145, 161, 192, 193, 204, 210, 216, 254, 255, 258, 263, 265, 267, 279, 280, 285, 287, 296

CLOB, 180

Color (Property), 75, 137, 138

Column (Property) , 5, 67, 69, 73, 74, 75, 76, 77, 78, 92, 97, 108, 137, 313, 318

hide, 102

Column Alignment (Property), 148, 195, 254

Column Span (Property), 67, 69, 75, 76, 77, 92, 304

Column Toggle Report, 262

Columns Per Row (Property), 117

Comma Separated Values (CSV), 226

Commercial Invoice, 15, 238

Comparison Operators, 73

Computations (Processing), 32

Condition (control rendering of page elements), 122

Conditional Formatting (Report), 231

CONNECT_BY_ISLEAF pseudocolumn, 224

Control Breaks, 226

Copy Page, *see Page*

Counter Column (Property), 278, 279

Create (Dynamic Action), *see Dynamic Actions*

Create Chart Series, 204

Create Link (Property), 217

Create links to drill-down, 5

Create menu (toolbar), 152, 264, 267, 291

Create Opposite Action (Dynamic Action), 158

Create Page, 25, 40, 50, 70, 85, 88, 101, 107, 113, 123, 129, 161, 215, 218, 253, 257, 262, 317, 318, 323

Create Page Item, 70, 123, 154, 156, 190, 261, 276, 318

Create Report Template in Microsoft Word, 229

CREATE SEQUENCE (SQL Statement), 300

Create Sub Region, 122, 155, 167

Create Table (interactively), 291

CREATE TABLE (SQL Command), 303

Create Validation, 95, 96, 159, 160, 297

CREATE_OR_TRUNCATE_COLLECTION, 181

Creating custom links, 7

CSS, 2, 3, 9, 11, 20, 24, 30, 39, 47, 49, 67, 79, 113, 115, 117, 118, 162, 163, 166, 167, 168, 169, 170, 171, 174, 175, 177, 193, 198, 201, 246, 251

Currency (Property), 204, 205, 209, 213, 214

Current Page Is NOT in comma delimited list, 249

Custom Attributes (Property), 251

Custom Authentication Scheme, 17, 40, 45, 320, 328

Custom Functions, 320

Customer Review report, 141

Customizing wizard-generated pages, 7

D

dashboard, 4, 42, 64

Dashboard (App Builder), 29

Data

conditional formatting, 15

grouping and sorting, 15

Data Load Definition, 50

Data Loading, 27, 299

Data Workshop, 299

Database Account Credentials, 45

Database Action (Property), 97, 132

Database Column (Property), 261, 276, 318

Database Objects, 41

create, 291

database-centric web applications, 20

DBMS_CRYPTO Package, 323
DBMS_LOB.GETLENGTH Function, 115,122
Debug, 34, 36
Declarative Development, 2
DECLARE, 166, 174, 180, 308
DECODE Function, 89, 115, 146, 203, 276
Default (value), 121
Defined by Dynamic Action (Action value), 205
Delete
   Application, 40
   Page, 31
   Page Component, 66
DELETE (SQL Statement), 299, 309
Desktop Applications, 24
Detail View (Section), 117
Developers Toolbar, 4, 24, 35, 41, 90, 92, 340
   remove, 340
Development Environment, 30
Dialog Template (Property), 145, 163, 189
Dim on Hover (Property), 208, 209
Display Column (Property), 216, 288
Display Extra Values, 95, 104, 120, 121, 147, 156, 194, 265-266, 277, 282
Display Null Value, 95, 104, 120, 121, 147, 149, 155, 156, 194, 277, 282, 319
Display Only (item), 146-147, 193, 276
Display value, 13, 58, 95, 105, 119, 123, 148, 266, 293, 318
DML, 7, 32, 41, 97, 104, 121, 132, 133, 148, 187, 196
DROP SEQUENCE (SQL Statement), 300
Dynamic Actions, 11, 17, 32, 33, 46, 205
   create, 97, 99, 158, 206-207, 282, 312
   openpanel, 250
   tab, 32
Dynamic List, 47
Dynamic LOV, 58-89

E

Edit Application Properties, 248
Editing Enabled (Property), 87, 102
ELSE clause, 224
e-mail, 144
END, 89, 166, 172, 173, 174, 308
End Date Column (Property), 216
Enforce data validation, 7
Entry Name (Property), 86
Escape special characters, 116, 123
Escape Special Characters, 146, 276
ESCAPE_SC Function, 168,172
Event (Dynamic Action), 158, 205, 206, 207, 283, 312

EXCEPTION, 166
Exclude Link Column, 116
Execute Validation (Property), 325
Export Application, 338
Export/Import Data, 339

F

f?p syntax, 34, 36, 71, 73, 115, 169, 170, 177, 178, 179, 182, 219, 222, 223, 234, 235, 248, 252, 258, 270, 296, 333
Feedback, 27, 30, 46, 48
Fetch Row from (table) process, 97, 131, 157, 261, 275
Filename Column (Property), 121
Fire on Initialization (Property), 158, 206, 207
Fire When Event Result is (Property), 158
For Each Row (section), 118
FOR LOOP Statement, 173
Form *see Page*
Form Editable Interactive Grid, 26
Form on a Table, 26, 255, 260, 275, 281
Form Pagination process, 131
Format Mask (Property), 70, 77, 78, 135, 147, 149, 195, 277
Format Type (Property), 205, 209, 213
Function and Global Variable Declaration (Property), 97, 153, 311

G

Generate DDL utility, 338
Global Page, 27, 249, 250
Globalization Attributes, 51, 340
Group By View, 140, 142
Group Related Data, 11

H

Height (Property), 120, 145, 153, 163, 193, 203, 209, 210, 212, 214, 284
Help icon, 147
Hidden (value to hide page component), 70, 73, 77, 78, 90, 108, 109, 116, 147, 148, 184, 190, 256, 260, 261, 276, 277, 281, 305, 311
Hide and Show Behavior (Property), 203, 208, 209, 212, 284, 286
Hiding report columns, 9
High (Property), 210
Home Page, 23, 27, 64, 65, 252
Hot (Property), 91, 119, 145, 157, 185, 191, 193, 239, 255, 258, 263, 265, 271, 274, 296, 309, 312, 325
htf Package, 172

HTML, 2, 9, 11, 20, 24, 25, 30, 35, 37, 39, 47, 49, 50, 58, 65, 66, 67, 97, 115, 116, 117, 118, 129, 162, 163, 167, 171, 172, 173, 175, 176, 177, 178, 182, 189, 198, 227, 246, 259, 318, 324
htmldb_delete_message, 97, 132, 153
htp Package, 172
HTTP, 34, 45, 50
HTTP Header Variable, 45

I

Icon, 31, 38, 40, 51, 52, 54, 65, 74, 76, 79, 85, 87, 98, 115, 116, 117, 134, 140, 147, 221, 223, 234, 242, 258, 319
Icon CSS Classes (Property), 79, 80, 81, 82, 119, 123, 145, 157, 185, 205, 271, 296
Icon View, 40, 116, 117
Identification Type (Property), 121
IF (condition), 184
IF-THEN-ELSE statement, 224
Image Attributes (Property), 117
Image BLOB Column (Property), 258, 279
Image handling, 9
Image Primary Key Column (Property), 279
Image Source Column (Property), 117
Image Type (Property), 258, 279
Image/Class, 52, 53, 54, 57
Images, 61
Import Application, 339
Inline (CSS Property), 163
Install Packaged App, 101
Interactive Grid, 6, 7, 26, 28, 82, 84, 85, 87, 97, 99, 100, 101, 103, 104, 106, 107, 108, 109, 110, 116, 129, 131, 132, 133, 134, 148, 149, 150, 192, 195, 196
    aggregate, 100
    change column type, 104
    control break, 100
    delete row, 150
    editing data, 103
    freeze column, 100
    grouping columns, 101
    hide column, 100, 106
    master detail detail detail, 107
    protecting rows, 106
    Row Actions menu, 150
    save data, 133
    scroll paging, 107
Interactive Report, 9, 26, 28, 69, 71-73, 89, 99, 113-115, 118-119, 124, 128, 134-136, 140, 144, 162, 197-198, 226, 293, 296, 316-317, 321, 335
    aggregate functions, 11
    alternative report, 136
    compute, 144

control break, 137
download, 144
filter, 144
flashback, 144
group by view, 11
help, 144
hide column, 116, 135
highlight, 137
modify, 136
primary report, 136
private report, 98
public report, 140
reset, 144
rows per page, 144
save, 119, 136, 140
select column, 144
sort, 144
subscription, 144
Internet, 2, 50, 64, 247
intranet, 2
IRGTE, 72
Item
    change type, 94
    create, 70, 123, 154, 156, 190, 261, 276, 318
    defined, 28
    duplicate, 238
    positioning on a page, 67-68, 92
    suppressed from being rendered, 155
Item = Value, 159, 160
Item is NOT NULL, 131, 134, 159, 160, 318
Item is NOT NULL and NOT zero, 309
Item is NULL, 318
Item Name, 36, 73
Item Value, 36, 73
Item(s) (Dynamic Action), 158, 283, 312
Items to Submit (Property), 283

J

JavaScript, 2, 20, 24, 30, 32, 39, 46, 47, 49, 61, 66, 173, 206, 207, 246, 310
jQuery Mobile, 3, 27, 246

L

Label (Property), 67, 68, 74, 75, 79, 80, 81, 82, 91, 92, 119, 121, 123, 139, 145, 146, 147, 155, 156, 157, 185, 191, 193, 194, 203, 204, 205, 207, 209, 210, 213, 214, 238, 239, 256, 260, 261, 263, 265, 276, 277, 279, 282, 285, 286, 287, 296, 304, 305, 306, 307, 309, 312, 318, 319, 323, 325
Label Column Span (Property), 92, 155
Label Display, 154

LDAP Directory Verification, 45

Legend Position (Property), 203, 212, 284

Link Builder, 67, 68, 70, 76, 78, 90, 91, 296

Link Column (Property), 116, 117

Link Target (Property), 258

Link Text (Property), 70, 71, 76, 77, 78, 116, 135, 254, 280

List (Property), 154, 251

List Attributes (Property), 259

List Divider Formatting(Property), 259

List Entry Current for Condition, 55

List Entry Current for Pages Type, 55, 56

List Entry Label, 52, 53, 54, 57

List of Values, 46, 57
  create, 238, 293

List of Values (Property), 46, 51, 57, 58, 59, 60, 95, 104, 105, 120, 121, 147, 149, 155, 193, 194, 195, 239, 256, 260

List Template(Property), 154, 189

List View, 257

Lists, 20, 23, 24, 26, 27, 33, 35, 36, 44, 46, 47, 49, 50, 51, 52, 53, 54, 55, 56, 57, 58, 60, 62, 69, 70, 73, 74, 77, 78, 80, 81, 82, 84, 86, 90, 94, 95, 98, 114, 119, 169, 177, 178, 181, 224, 234, 251, 269, 270
  copy from another, 252

Login Page, 27, 40, 249

LOGIN_URL, 37

logos, 226

LOGOUT_URL, 37, 57

Low (Property), 210

M

Making and marking page items as mandatory, 9

Managed by Database (ROWID), 256, 260, 275, 317

Map, 13, 24, 27, 53, 54, 200, 217, 218, 219, 252

Map Region Column (Property), 219

Marking mandatory fields, 7

Master Column (Property), 108, 109

Master/Detail forms, 11

Maximum Row to Process (Property), 77, 78

Maximum Width (Property), 120, 145, 193, 203, 210

Messages tab, 66

Microsoft Excel, 50, 51, 226, 299, 331

Microsoft Word, 15, 50, 51, 226, 227, 228, 229, 230, 231, 232, 233, 234, 235, 241, 242
  create template, 15, 229

MIME Type Column (Property), 121

Mobile (Theme 51), 248

Mobile Applications, 3, 16, 25, 246
  create interface, 248

reports, 283

types, 246

Mobile Navigation Bar Entry, 56

Mobile Navigation Menu, 252

Modal Dialog, 86, 88, 114, 145, 193, 264, 317
  set dimensions, 145

Modal Page, 7

Multipurpose Internet Mail Extension (MIME), 113

N

Name (Property), 39, 52, 54, 55, 57, 58, 59, 60, 65, 70, 71, 76, 78, 80, 87, 88, 92, 96, 98, 99, 100, 101, 107, 116, 123, 124, 128, 135, 145, 146, 155, 156, 157, 158, 159, 160, 161, 177, 184, 188, 190, 201, 202, 203, 204, 205, 206, 207, 208, 209, 210, 211, 215, 216, 217, 238, 239, 240, 242, 250, 252, 253, 254, 256, 257, 261, 262, 263, 267, 272, 275, 276, 279, 280, 283, 285, 287, 297, 304, 305, 306, 307, 308, 309, 311, 312, 313, 316, 318, 319, 323, 325, 326, 327, 328, 333, 334

Navigation Bar, 4, 48, 56

Navigation Menu, 4, 48, 52, 88, 235, 252

New Column (Property), 92

NEW OR EXISTING CUSTOMER LOV, 60

NO (URL flag), 72

No Pagination (Show All Rows), 73

No Parent List Item, 52, 53, 57

Null Display Value, 95, 266, 282

Number of Columns (Property), 121, 154, 155, 304

O

Object Browser, 30, 41, 101, 107, 130, 291, 292, 300, 316, 321, 327

On Data Change (Property), 203

Optional (Property Value), 265, 266

Oracle BI Publisher, 226, 227, 229, 234
  download and install, 227

Oracle Data Pump, 339

Oracle database, 2, 3, 20, 21, 25, 51, 144, 171, 338

Oracle JET Charts, iv, 4, 66

Oracle REST Data Services, 226

Oracle's Wrap Utility, 320, 322

Order Wizard List, 55

Orientation (Property), 67, 203, 284, 287

P

Packaged Apps, 29-30, 100

Page, 25
  copy, 11, 152, 264, 267
  create, 40

delete, 31

elements positioning, 67-68, 92

form, 26, 88, 113, 129, 148, 255, 260, 262, 275, 281, 317

lock/unlock, 31-32

master detail form, 129

redirect, 28

refresh, 99

Save and Run, 31, 69, 73, 77-78, 82, 104, 116, 119, 136, 195

submits, 28

Page Action on Selection (Property), 304, 305

Page as copy, 152, 264, 267

Page Designer, 4, 25, 31, 32, 33, 41, 44, 62, 65, 67, 70, 85, 87, 89, 90, 92, 99, 102, 104, 106, 107, 108, 120, 152, 153, 157, 193, 195, 208, 216, 219, 221, 254, 264, 267, 268, 279, 281, 304, 333

Component View, 33

defined, 31

Help, 33

Messages, 33

Page Search, 33

tree pane, 32

Page in this application, 53, 54, 57, 67, 70-71, 76, 78, 79-82, 91, 81, 135, 145, 152, 161, 188, 191, 193, 204, 210, 216, 217, 235, 242, 249, 254- 255, 258, 263, 264, 265, 267, 271, 272, 274, 279, 280, 285, 287, 296

Page Items to Submit (Property), 278, 311

Page Mode (Property), 86, 88, 101, 107, 145, 193, 201, 202, 208, 211, 215, 218, 220, 238, 253, 255, 257, 260, 262, 264, 268, 273, 275, 281, 283, 284, 288, 304, 323

Page Name (Property), 86, 88

Page or URL (Redirect), 188

Page Search, 33

Pagination, 70, 72, 73, 77, 78, 103, 107

Pagination Type (Property), 77, 78

Parent Entry (Property), 86, 101, 114

Parent List Entry, 52, 53, 57

Parent Region (Property), 122, 156, 268, 310, 311

Pattern (Property), 213

PDF, 50, 51, 224, 226, 227, 228, 230, 233, 234, 240, 252

PHP, 2

Pie Chart, 74

Pivot Table, 15, 233

Pivot View, 143

PL/SQL, 2, 3, 20, 27, 30, 31, 37, 47, 69, 95, 162, 166, 167, 171, 172, 174, 175, 180, 187, 189, 196, 198, 239, 246, 268, 271, 297, 313, 316, 326, 332, 333, 334

PL/SQL Code, 157, 190, 308, 309, 313

PL/SQL Dynamic Content, 167, 190, 268

PL/SQL Expression, 70, 95, 96, 149, 195, 239

PL/SQL Function (returning Error Text), 297, 326

PL/SQL Function Body, 47, 96, 122, 123

PL/SQL Function Body (Returning Boolean), 96, 326, 330, 333, 334

Plug-ins, 24, 27, 46, 47

Point (Property), 242, 308, 309

Pre-Rendering Process, 131

Primary Key, 88, 90, 108, 109, 114, 131, 256, 258, 260, 261, 275, 292, 317

Primary Key Column (Property), 261

Primary Key Type (Property), 88

Primary Report, 9, 98, 136

PRINT_REPORT, 235, 242

PrinterFriendly, 36

Private Report, 98

Process

create, 309, 313, 327

Process Row of (table), 97, 132, 149, 156, 195-196

Processes

defined, 32

Processing tab, 32

Products With Price (LOV), 195

PRODUCTS WITH PRICE LOV, 58

programming language, 2, 166

Property Editor, 33

Public Report, 98, 140

Q

Query Only (Property), 148, 149, 195

R

Rapid Application Development (RAD) tool, 2

Redirect to Page in this Application, 68, 285, 287

Reflow Report, 253

Refresh (Dynamic Action), 312

Region

create, 66, 208

defined, 27

delete and re-create, 134

hide/show, 158

positioning, 67-68

Region (Property), 79, 80, 81, 82

Region (With Title Bar), 275, 278, 286

Region (With Title), 268, 273

Region Display Selector, 210, 212

Region Source (Property), 67, 68, 74, 75, 203, 204, 210, 216, 254, 257, 262, 288, 317

Regular Expression (Property), 160

Rendering tab, 32

Replacing wizard-generated links with customized links, 9

Report, 9, 11, 15, 20, 26, 28, 29, 51, 53, 54, 72, 76, 77, 85, 90, 98, 101, 119, 131, 136, 140, 200, 202, 208, 210, 215, 217, 224, 227, 228, 229, 231, 234, 235, 238, 239, 253, 257, 262, 284, 293, 311, 317
    Column Toggle, 262
    create parameterized report, 15
    create template, 229
    Interactive Report, 26
    mobile, 284, 286
    parameters, 238
    run a PDF report, 235
    upload template to APEX, 234, 242
Report Layout, 51, 234, 240, 242
Report Query, 15, 29, 50, 228, 234, 240, 242
Report Type (Property), 114
Report View, 40, 112, 124, 136, 141
Report with Form on Table, 26, 113, 293, 317
Representational State Transfer (REST), 50
REQUEST, 28, 35, 72, 178
Request (Property), 242
Request is contained in Value, 308
Required (Property Value), 92, 94, 120, 155, 156, 238, 256, 260, 261, 266, 295, 304, 318, 325
Rescale (Property Value), 203, 208, 209, 212, 284, 286
RESTful Services, 30
Return Value, 58, 105, 195, 293
RIR (Reset Interactive Report), 70, 71, 72, 80, 219, 222, 223
Row Actions menu, 150
ROWID, 261, 275
Rows Returned, 123, 323, 325
RP (Report Pagination), 72
RTF (Rich Text Format), 15, 50, 51, 226, 227, 234, 241, 242
Runtime Environment, 30

S

Save and Run (Page), 31, 69, 73, 77-78, 82, 104, 116, 119, 136, 195
Save Interactive Grid Data Process, 132, 133, 149
Save Session State(Property), 146, 276, 324, 325
Scheme Type (Property), 333, 334
Scripting Language, 2
Search Column (Property), 258
Search Type (Property), 258
Security, 17
    apply to application pages, 332
    apply to main menu, 330
    apply to page items, 334

Select List (Item), 21, 28, 66, 94, 105, 120, 147, 148, 149, 193, 194, 195, 239, 256, 260, 266, 277, 282, 295, 305, 318, 323, 327
Select Node Page Item (Property), 310
Selection Type (Property), 99, 158, 205, 206, 207, 283, 312
Sequence (Database Object), 6, 41, 84, 88, 114, 149, 292, 294
Sequence (Property), 132, 159, 160, 318
Series (Chart)
    create, 286
Series Name (Property), 213, 214
Server: Like & Ignore Case, 258
Server-side Condition (Property), 122, 123, 131, 134, 155, 159, 160, 186, 187, 249, 251, 305, 306, 307, 308, 309, 310, 311, 318, 323, 324, 325
Session, 34
Session State Protection (Property), 277
Sessionid (in URL), 72
Set dimensions of a modal page, 9
Set Type (Property), 283
Set Value (Action value), 283
Shape (Property), 213
Shared Components, 33, 44
Shortcuts (Shared Component), 47
Show (Property), 13, 25, 52, 73, 74, 75, 77, 78, 103, 105, 107, 117, 158, 176, 209, 210, 212, 213, 214, 254, 312
Show Group Name (Property), 214
Show Image (Property), 258, 279
Show Page (Process), 25
Show Time(Property), 216
Shuttle (Item), 105
Sign Out, 4, 56, 57
Simple Object Access Protocol (SOAP), 50
Single Page Master Detail Form, 26
Smartphones, 3, 25, 16, 246, 283
Source Type (Property), 87, 286
Spreadsheet Data (load), 299
Spreadsheet Repository, 299
SQL, 2, 3, 11, 20, 24, 26, 27, 28, 29, 30, 31, 32, 34, 37, 44, 45, 46, 47, 50, 57, 58, 59, 66, 67, 69, 70, 73, 74, 75, 76, 77, 82, 84, 86, 88, 89, 96, 97, 102, 104, 105, 106, 108, 109, 112, 114, 115, 116, 123, 135, 146, 147, 148, 156, 157, 164, 166, 168, 169, 궷170, 171, 173, 174, 175, 178, 180, 181, 190, 193, 194, 196, 198, 203, 209, 213, 214, 216, 217, 219, 220, 221, 224, 228, 238, 240, 246, 254, 257, 262, 263, 266, 276, 277, 278, 282, 283, 285, 286, 287, 288, 295, 296, 303, 305, 306, 310, 311, 317, 318, 322, 323, 325, 332
SQL Commands, 30, 86, 216, 299, 300, 303

SQL DELETE action, 132

SQL INSERT action, 132

SQL Query (return single value), 305, 306

SQL Scripts, 30, 107, 316, 321

SQL UPDATE action, 132

SQL Workshop, 30, 41, 101, 107, 130, 291, 299, 300, 303, 316, 321, 322, 327, 338

SQL*Plus, 322

Stack (Property), 203, 214, 284

Start Date Column, 216, 288

Start New Row (Property), 67, 69, 74, 75, 76, 77, 92, 266, 311

Start With (Property), 220

Static Application Files, 49, 61

Static Content, 28, 66, 67, 122, 131, 145, 154, 155, 251, 304, 310, 323

Static ID (Property), 206

Static List, 47, 55

Static Value (Property), 121, 154, 155, 238, 295, 306

Step (Property), 213

Storage Type (Property), 121

Submit When Enter Pressed (Property), 325

Substitution String, 35, 36, 37, 44, 48, 57, 61, 65, 70, 72, 73, 76, 78, 90, 118, 159, 196, 239, 324
built-in, 37

Supplemental Information (Property), 259

Switch (Item), 261

Switch (Property), 73, 105, 121

T

Table (database object), 41

Table/View Name (Property), 87, 114

Table/View Owner (Property), 87, 114

Tablets, 3, 16, 246

Tabular Form, 129

Target (Property), 34, 52, 53, 54, 55, 57, 67, 68, 70, 76, 78, 79, 80, 81, 82, 90, 91, 116, 119, 123, 132, 135, 145, 161, 188, 191, 193, 204, 210, 216, 217, 235, 242, 249, 252, 254, 255, 258, 263, 265, 267, 271, 272, 276, 279, 280, 285, 287, 299

Target Page ID, 54

Target Type, 52, 53, 54, 55, 57, 145, 217, 235, 272, 285

Team Development, 30

Template (Property), 24, 39, 51, 67, 68, 69, 73, 74, 75, 76, 77, 89, 94, 120, 123, 146, 149, 153, 154, 155, 156, 166, 167, 189, 193, 201, 212, 226, 238, 251, 256, 260, 261, 265, 266, 268, 273, 275, 278, 286, 295, 304, 318, 323, 325

Template Builder, 51

Template Options (Cards), 201

Template Options (Property), 24, 39, 67, 68, 69, 73, 74, 75, 76, 77

Text Column (Property), 258

Text Formatting, 259

Text Formatting (Property), 259, 279

Text Links, 4

Text with Icon, 157, 193, 296

Theme Style, 24, 39, 49

ThemeRoller, 3, 24, 39, 49

Themes and Templates, 49

Time Axis Type (Property), 212

Title (Property), 65, 67, 69, 74, 75, 76, 77, 108, 109, 120, 122, 135, 148, 154, 155, 156, 166, 189, 190, 201, 203, 204, 205, 208, 209, 212, 213, 218, 238, 251, 252, 275, 278, 281, 284, 286, 287, 296, 304, 306, 310, 311, 317, 323

Tooltip, 220

Translate Application, 51

Tree, 13, 17, 25, 27, 31-33, 53-54, 135, 200, 219, 220, 221-224, 238, 290, 296, 298, 304-305, 307, 310- 311, 312, 313, 314, 336

Trigger (Database Object), 41, 292

Two Page Master Detail, 26, 129

Type (Property), 23, 36, 41, 54, 55, 58, 59, 60, 61, 66, 67, 68, 69, 70, 72, 73, 74, 75, 76, 77, 78, 79, 80, 81, 82, 90, 91, 94, 95, 96, 97, 98, 102, 104, 105, 106, 107, 108, 109, 116, 120, 121, 122, 123, 124, 134, 135, 146, 147, 148, 149, 154, 155, 156, 157, 158, 159, 160, 161, 166, 184, 188, 189, 190, 193, 194, 201, 202, 203, 204, 208, 209, 210, 212, 213, 214, 238, 239, 241, 242, 248, 250, 251, 253, 254, 255, 256, 258, 260, 261, 262, 263, 265, 266, 267, 276, 277, 278, 279, 280, 281, 282, 284, 285, 286, 287, 295, 296, 297, 304, 305, 306, 307, 308, 309, 310, 311, 313, 317, 318, 319, 323, 325, 326, 327

U

Universal Theme, 24, 39, 48, 49, 52

UPDATE, 41

Upload Script, 107, 316, 321

URL in Oracle APEX. *See f?p*

URL Target, 57, 235

User Interface, 39, 48, 61, 248, 253, 257, 262, 264, 268, 283, 304, 317

Utilities (SQL Workshop), 30

V

Validation
add, 326
defined, 32

Validation (Property), 333-334

Value (Property), 52, 58, 65, 67, 68, 69, 70, 71, 74, 75, 76,
77, 78, 79, 80, 81, 82, 86, 87, 88, 91, 92, 94, 96, 116,
120, 121, 122, 123, 135, 145, 146, 148, 155, 157, 158,
159, 160, 161, 184, 185, 190, 203, 204, 209, 210, 213,
214, 216, 238, 254, 256, 260, 261, 277, 279, 280, 285,
286, 287, 305, 306, 307, 308, 309, 310, 311
Value Placeholder (Property), 95
Value Protected, 147, 276
Value Required (Property), 120, 156, 160, 238, 256, 260,
261, 265, 266, 295, 318, 325
View Reports, 119

W

Web Applications, 2, 5, 20, 28, 29, 44, 157, 246
Web Browsers, 2, 20, 30, 113, 172
Web Input Form, 7
Web Service, 24, 50
Websheet, 24, 25, 29
When Button Pressed (Property), 96, 124, 133, 161, 187,
188, 242, 267, 297, 307, 309, 313, 326, 327
Wizard Body, 145, 153, 154
Wizard Modal Dialog, 145, 153, 163, 189, 193
Wizard Progress, 153, 154, 166, 189
Workspace, 22
home page, 23
images, 61
request a free one, 23
Utilities, 29

X

x-axis (Charts), 203, 204, 210, 213, 285
XML, 15, 50, 180, 217, 226, 229, 230, 240, 241, 299
XSL-FO, 51, 226
XSS (Cross Site Scripting), 58, 116, 173

Y

y-axis (Charts), 204, 213, 214, 285

Printed in Great Britain
by Amazon